P9-CAT-081

## Praise for *The United States of Fear*

"Tom Engelhardt, as always, focuses his laser-like intelligence on a core problem that the media avoid: Obama's stunning embrace of Bush's secret government by surveillance, torture, and sanctioned assassination. A stunning polemic."
—Mike Davis, author of *In Praise of Barbarians* and *Planet of Slums*

## Praise for *The American Way of War*

"A tour de force."
—Jeremy Scahill, author of *Blackwater*

"There are a lot of ways to describe Tom Engelhardt's astonishing service to this country's conscience and imagination: you could portray him as our generation's Orwell, standing aside from all conventional framings to see afresh our dilemmas and blind spots, as the diligent little boy sending in regular dispatches on the nakedness of the emperor and his empire, as a Bodhisattva dedicated to saving all beings through compassion and awareness, but analogies don't really describe the mix of clear and sometimes hilarious writing, deep insight, superb information, empathy, and outrage that has been the core of Tom's TomDispatches for almost a decade, or the extraordinary contribution they've made to the American dialogue. Check out this bundle of some of the best from that time span."
—Rebecca Solnit, author of *Hope in the Dark* and *A Paradise Built in Hell*

"*They* may have Blackwater/Xe, Halliburton, aircraft-carrier battle groups, deadly drones by the score, and the world's largest military budget, but we have Tom Engelhardt—and a more powerful truth-seeking missile has seldom been invented. Longtime fans like me will be happy to see some of his most memorable pieces reprinted here, although woven together in a way that makes them still stronger; for anyone not yet familiar with his work, this is your chance to meet one of the most forceful analysts alive of our country's dangerous, costly addiction to all things military."
—Adam Hochschild, author of *To End All Wars* and *King Leopold's Ghost*

"Tom Engelhardt is the I. F. Stone of the post–9/11 age—seeing what others miss, calling attention to contradictions that others willfully ignore, insisting that Americans examine in full precisely those things that make us most uncomfortable."
—Andrew J. Bacevich, author of *Washington Rules: America's Path to Permanent War*

"Tom Engelhardt is among our most trenchant critics of American perpetual war. Like I. F. Stone in the 1960s, he has an uncanny ability to ferret out and see clearly the ugly truths hidden in government reports and statistics. No cynic, he always measures the sordid reality against a bright vision of an America that lives up to its highest ideals."

—Juan R. Cole, professor of history at the University of Michigan

"Like an extended Motown shuffle with some hard-hitting Stax breaks, and never devoid of an all-too-human sense of humor and pathos, Tom's book takes us for the ride. . . . [I]nvaluable in showing how the empire walks the walk and talks the talk."

—Pepe Escobar, *Asia Times*

"In *The American Way of War: How Bush's Wars Became Obama's*, Tom Engelhardt provides a clear-eyed examination of U.S. foreign policy in the Bush and Obama years, and details unsparingly how Obama has inherited—and in many cases exacerbated—the ills of the Bush era. . . . [A]n important book for anyone hoping to understand how the U.S. arrived at its current predicament during the Bush years, and how it remains in this predicament despite Obama's best efforts—or perhaps because of them."

—Inter Press Service

"Tom Engelhardt's biting look at United States militarism, *The American Way of War* . . . [is] pithy . . . [and] alarming. . . . He takes on our war-possessed world with clear-eyed, penetrating precision."

—*Mother Jones*

"Essential . . . seamlessly edited . . . establishes him as one of the grand chroniclers of the post-9/11 era."

—Dan Froomkin, *Huffington Post*

"These simple pleas for readers to reconsider an idea they might previously have taken for granted are one of the strengths of this book. Demonstrating Engelhardt's experience as a professional editor, he avoids the overly strident or self-righteous condescension that characterizes too much online political writing, instead using clear and unvarnished prose to attack the fundamental principles of the post–September 11 mindset."

—*Foreign Policy in Focus*

"American history does not begin with 9/11, yet the worldview of so many in the United States since then has been shaped by how the mainstream media had colored events following the terrorist attacks. But to break free from that distorted perception which bears little resemblance to reality—as people once knew it—one needs the help of a little imagination. In Tom Engelhardt's *The American Way of War: How Bush's Wars Became Obama's*, you could step back and see all the views that you had taken for granted challenged, as you indulge yourself in a world of ideas that are logical and straightforward but just were not quite visible to you before. All of course are backed by key facts, sound analysis and invaluable context."

—*Middle East Online*

"With an excellent mind and an equally fine pen, Engelhardt demonstrates true patriotism to the American founding. . . . Reading such good prose invigorates like little else in this world of sorrows. But one should not consider Engelhardt merely a writer of golden prose. This body has a soul as well, and Engelhardt convincingly presents evidence as well as argument throughout the book. . . . *The American Way of War* is brimming with insights."

—*American Conservative*

"Excellent. . . . Anyone who wants to rebuild an antiwar movement . . . should read *The American Way of War*. . . . Reading this book feels like poking around with a flashlight in the unexamined corners of the post-9/11 American imperial mindset. . . . Sharp wit runs throughout the book. The section about the lack of media coverage of air campaigns, for example, is wonderfully titled 'On Not Looking Up.' Not only does this humor make *The American Way of War* a surprisingly entertaining read given the subject matter, it reminds us of something all great antiwar movements have known—the war machine is not just evil, it's often absurd."

—*Socialist Worker*

## Praise for TomDispatch

"One of my favorite websites."

—Bill Moyers

"At a time when the mainstream media leave out half of what the public needs to know, while at the same time purveying oceans of official nonsense, the public needs an alternative source of news. Tom Engelhardt's TomDispatch has been that for me. With unerring touch, he finds the stories I need to read, prefacing them each day with introductions that in themselves form a witty, hugely enjoyable, brilliant running commentary on the times. He is my mainstream."

—Jonathan Schell

"Tom Engelhardt [is] the finest and hardest working essayist and editor of the post–9/11 era, who has kept a steady eye on Washington's 'baser' intentions since even before the 2003 invasion."

—Jim Lobe, Inter Press Service

"These are the traits of a TomDispatch essay: unapologetically intellectual, relentlessly original, a little bit dangerous. For many of us, these are the key pieces of analysis that make sense of our post-9/11 world. How odd that many of them have never actually been printed. Until now."

—Naomi Klein

"TomDispatch is one of the wonders of the electronic age. A touch of the finger and you get the juiciest, meatiest information and analysis, so rich a feast of intelligence and insight I often felt short of breath."

—Howard Zinn

"TomDispatch is essential reading. It is a one-stop shop where you can find the most provocative thinkers writing the most eloquent and hard-hitting articles about the most pressing issues of the day. Read, get mad, and take action."

—Amy Goodman

# The United States of Fear

**TOM ENGELHARDT**

Haymarket Books
Chicago, Illinois

© 2011 by Tom Engelhardt

Published in 2011 by Haymarket Books
PO Box 180165
Chicago, IL 60618
www.haymarketbooks.org
773-583-7884
info@haymarketbooks.org

ISBN: 978-1-60846-154-7

Trade distribution:
In the US, Consortium Book Sales and Distribution, www.cbsd.com
In Canada, Publishers Group Canada, www.pgcbooks.ca
In the UK, Turnaround Publisher Services, www.turnaround-uk.com
In Australia, Palgrave Macmillan, www.palgravemacmillan.com.au
All other countries, Publishers Group Worldwide, www.pgw.com

Cover design by Eric Ruder

Published with the generous support of Lannan Foundation
and the Wallace Global Fund.

Printed in the United States by union labor.

Library of Congress cataloging-in-publication data is available.

10 9 8 7 6 5 4 3 2 1

# CONTENTS

## INTRODUCTION

# American Warscapes

## A World Made by War

When you look at me, you can't mistake the fact that I'm of a certain age. But just for a moment, think of me as ten years old. You could even say that I celebrated my ninth birthday recently, without cake, candles, presents, or certainly joy.

I've had two mobilized moments in my life. The first was in the Vietnam War years; the second, the one that leaves me as a ten-year-old, began on the morning of September 11, 2001. I turned on the TV while doing my morning exercises, saw a smoking hole in a World Trade Center tower, and thought that, as in 1945 when a B-25 slammed into the Empire State Building, a terrible accident had happened.

Later, after the drums of war had begun to beat, after the first headlines had screamed their World War II–style messages ("The Pearl Harbor of the 21st Century"), I had another thought. And for a reasonably politically sophisticated guy, my second response was at least as off-base as the first. I thought that this horrific event taking place in my hometown might open Americans up to the pain of the world. No such luck, of course.

If you had told me then that we would henceforth be in a state of eternal war, as well as living in a permanent war state, that, to face a ragtag enemy of a few thousand stateless terrorists, the national security

1

establishment in Washington would pump itself up to levels not faintly reached when facing the Soviet Union—a major power with thousands of nuclear weapons and an enormous military—that "homeland"—a distinctly un-American word—would land in our vocabulary never to leave, and that a second Defense Department dubbed the Department of Homeland Security would be set up not to be dismantled in my lifetime, that torture (excuse me, "enhanced interrogation techniques") would become as American as apple pie and that some of those "techniques" would actually be demonstrated to leading Bush administration officials inside the White House, that we would pour money into the Pentagon at ever-escalating levels even after the economy crashed in 2008, that we would be fighting two potentially trillion-dollar-plus wars without end in two distant lands, that we would spend untold billions constructing hundreds of military bases in those same lands, that the CIA would be conducting the first drone air war in history over a country we were officially not at war with, that most of us would live in a remarkable state of detachment from all of this, and finally—only, by the way, because I'm cutting this list arbitrarily short—that I would spend my time writing incessantly about "the American way of war" and produce a book with that title, I would have thought you were nuts.

But every bit of that happened, making clear that, like human beings everywhere, I have no special knack for peering into the future. If it were otherwise, I would undoubtedly now be zipping through fabulous spired cities with a jetpack on my back (as I was assured would happen in my distant youth). But if prediction isn't our forte, then adaptability to changing circumstances may be—as my trajectory for the past ten years proves.

A decade ago, in response to the bizarre spectacle of this nation going to war while living at peace, even if in a spasmodic state of collective national fear, I did something I hardly understood at the time. I launched a nameless listserv of collected articles and my own expanding commentary that ran against the common wisdom of that October moment when our second Afghan War was just beginning. A little more than a year later, thanks to the Nation Institute, it became a website with the name TomDispatch.com. And because our leaders swore we were "a nation at war," because we were in fact killing people in quantity in distant lands, because the power of the state at home was being strengthened in startling ways, while everything still open about our society seemed to be shutting down, even as the military was being pumped up to Schwarzeneggerian dimensions, I started writing about war. At some level, I can't tell you how ridiculous that was. After all, I'm the most civilian and peaceable of guys. I've never even been in the military. I was, however, upset with the Bush administration, the connect-no-dots media coverage of that moment, and the repeated 9/11 rites that proclaimed us the planet's greatest victim, survivor, and dominator, leaving only one role, greatest Evildoer, open for the rest of the planet (and you know who auditioned for, and won, that part hands down).

## Things That Go Boom in the Night

I won't say, however, that I had no expertise whatsoever with a permanent state of war and a permanent war state, only that the expertise I had was available to anyone who had lived through the post–World War II era. I was reminded of this on a recent glorious Sunday when, from the foot of Manhattan, I set out, for the first time in more than half a century, on a brief ferry ride that proved, for me, as effective a time machine as anything H. G. Wells had ever imagined. That ferry was not, of course, taking me to a future civilization at the edge of time, but to Governor's Island, now a park and national monument in the eddying waters of New York harbor and to the rubble of a gas station my father, a World War II veteran, ran there in the early 1950s when the island was still a major U.S. Army base.

On many mornings in those years, I accompanied him on that short ride across the East River and found myself amid buzzing jeeps and drilling soldiers in a world of army kids with, among other wonders, access to giant swimming pools and kiddie-matinee Westerns. As a dyed-in-the-wool city boy, it was my only real exposure to the suburbs, and it proved an edenic one that also caught something of the exotically militarized mood of that Korean War moment.

As on that island, as for most Americans then, the worlds of the warrior and of abundance were no more antithetical than they were to the corporate executives, university research scientists, and military officers using a rising military budget and the fear of communism to create a new national security economy. An alliance between big industry, big science,

military had been forged during World War II that blurred the
es between the military and the civilian by fusing together a double set of desires: for technological breakthroughs leading to ever more
efficient weapons of destruction and to ever easier living. The arms race—
the race, that is, for future "good wars"—and the race for the good life
were being put on the same "war" footing.

In the 1950s, a military Keynesianism was already driving the U.S.
economy toward a consumerism in which desire for the ever larger car
*and* missile, electric range *and* tank, television console *and* submarine
were wedded in single corporate entities. The companies producing the
large objects for the American home—General Electric, General Motors,
and Westinghouse, among others—were also major contractors developing the big-ticket weapons systems ushering the Pentagon into its own
age of abundance.

More than half a century later, the Pentagon is still living a life of
abundance—despite one less-than-victorious, less-then-good war after
another—while we, increasingly, are not. In the years in between, the developing national security state of my childhood just kept growing, and
in the process the country militarized in the strangest of ways.

Only once in that period did a sense of actual war seem to hover over
the nation. That was, of course, in the Vietnam years of the 1960s and
early 1970s, when the draft brought a dirty war up close and personal,
driving it into American homes and out onto the streets, when a kind of
intermittent warfare seemed to break out in this country's cities and ghet-
tos, and when impending defeat drove the military itself to the edge of
revolt and collapse.

From the 1970s until 2001, as that military rebuilt itself as an all-
volunteer force and finally went back to war in distant lands, it seemed
to disappear from everyday life. There were no soldiers in sight, nothing
we would consider commonplace today—from uniforms and guns in
train stations to military flyovers at football games, and the repeated rites
of praise for American troops that are now everyday fare in a world
where, otherwise, we largely ignore our wars.

In 1989, for instance, in the *Progressive* magazine I described a country that seemed to me to be undergoing further militarization, even if in
a particularly strange way. Ours was, I wrote, an

America that conforms to no notions we hold of militarism. . . . Militarization is, of course, commonly associated with uniformed, usually exalted troops in evidence and a dictatorship, possibly military, in power. The United States, by such standards, still has the look of a civilian society. Our military is, if anything, less visible in our lives than it was a decade ago: No uniforms in the streets, seldom even for our traditional parades; a civilian-elected government; weaponry out of sight . . . the draft and the idea of a civilian army a thing of the past.

In the Reagan-Bush era, the military has gone undercover in the world that we see, though not in the world that sees us. For if it is absent from our everyday culture, its influence is omnipresent in corporate America, that world beyond our politics and out of our control—the world which, nonetheless, plans our high-tech future of work and consumption. There, the militarization of the economy and the corporatization of the military are processes so far gone that it seems reasonable to ask whether the United States can even be said to have a civilian economy.

Little did I know. Today, it seems, our country is triumphant in producing only things that go boom in the night: we have a near monopoly on the global weapons market and on the global movie market, where in the dark we're experts on explosions of every sort. When I wrote in 1989 that the process was "so far gone," I had no idea how far we still had to go. I had no idea, for instance, how far a single administration could push us when it came to war. Still, one thing that does remain reasonably constant about America's now perpetual state of war is how little we—the 99 percent of us who don't belong to the military or fight—actually see of it, even though it is, in a sense, all around us.

## Warscapes

From a remarkable array of possibilities, here are just a few warscapes—think of them as landscapes, only deadlier—that might help make more visible an American world of, and way of, war that we normally spend little time discussing, debating, or doing anything about.

As a start, let me try to conjure up a map of what "defense," as imagined by the Pentagon and the U.S. military, actually looks like. For a second just imagine a world map laid flat before you. Now divide it, the whole globe, like so many ill-shaped pieces of cobbler, into six servings—

you can be as messy as you want, it's not an exact science—and label them the U.S. European Command or Eucom (for Europe and Russia), the U.S. Pacific Command or Pacom (Asia), Centcom (the Greater Middle East and a touch of North Africa), Northcom (North America), Southcom (South America and most of the Caribbean), and Africom (almost all of Africa). Those are the "areas of responsibility" of the six U.S. military commands.

In case you hadn't noticed, that takes care of just about every inch of the planet, but—I hasten to add—not every bit of imaginable space. For that, if you were a clever cartographer, you would somehow need to include Stratcom, the U.S. Strategic Command charged with, among other things, ensuring that we dominate the heavens, and the newest of all the "geographic" commands, Cybercom, which oversees "1,000 elite military hackers and spies under one four-star general," all prepared to engage in preemptive war in cyberspace.

Some of these commands have crept up on us over the years. Centcom, which now oversees our wars in Afghanistan and Iraq, was formed in 1983, a result of the Carter Doctrine—that is, of President Jimmy Carter's decision to make the protection of Persian Gulf oil a military necessity, while both Northcom (2002) and Africom (2007) were creations of the Global War on Terror (GWOT).

From a mapping perspective, however, the salient point is simple enough: at the moment, there is no imaginable space on or off the planet that is not an "area of responsibility" for the U.S. military. That, not the protection of our shores and borders, is what is now meant by the word "defense" in the Department of Defense. And if you were to stare at that map for a while, I can't help but think it would come to strike you as abidingly strange. No place at all of no military interest to us? What does that say about our country—and us?

In case you think the map I've just described is cartographic hyperbole, consider this: we now have what is, in essence, a secret military inside the U.S. military. I'm talking about our special operations forces. These elite and largely covert forces were rapidly expanded in the Bush years as part of the Global War on Terror, but also thanks to Secretary of Defense Donald Rumsfeld's urge to bring covert activities that were once the province of the CIA under the Pentagon's wing.

By the end of George W. Bush's second term in office, special operations forces were fighting in, training in, or stationed in approximately sixty countries under the aegis of the Global War on Terror. Less than two years later, according to the *Washington Post*, thirteen thousand special operations troops were deployed abroad in approximately seventy-five countries as part of an expanding Global War on Terror (even if the Obama administration had ditched that name); in other words, special ops troops alone are now operating in close to 40 percent of the 192 countries that make up the United Nations.

And talking about what the Pentagon has taken under its wing, I'm reminded of a low-budget sci-fi film of my childhood, *The Blob*. In it, a gelatinous alien grows ever more humongous by eating every living thing in its path, with the exception of Steve McQueen in his debut screen role. By analogy, take what's officially called the U.S. Intelligence Community (IC), which Rumsfeld was so eager to militarize. It's made up of seventeen major agencies and outfits, including the Office of the Director of National Intelligence (ODNI). Created in 2004 in response to the intelligence dysfunction of 9/11, ODNI is already its own small bureaucracy, with 1,500 employees and next to no power to do the only thing it was ever really meant to do: coordinate the generally dysfunctional labyrinth of the IC itself.

You might wonder what kind of "intelligence" a country could possibly get from seventeen competing, bickering outfits—and that's not even the half of it. According to a *Washington Post* series "Top Secret America" by Dana Priest and William Arkin:

> In all, at least 263 organizations have been created or reorganized as a response to 9/11. . . . Some 1,271 government organizations and 1,931 private companies work on programs related to counterterrorism, homeland security and intelligence in about 10,000 locations across the United States. . . . In Washington and the surrounding area, 33 building complexes for top-secret intelligence work are under construction or have been built since September 2001. Together they occupy the equivalent of almost three Pentagons or 22 U.S. Capitol buildings—about 17 million square feet of space.

And keep in mind that more than two-thirds of the IC's intelligence programs are controlled by the Pentagon, which also means control over a major chunk of the combined intelligence budget, announced at $80 billion ("2 ½ times the size it was on Sept. 10, 2001," according to Priest and Arkin), but undoubtedly far larger. And when it comes to the Pentagon, that's just a start. Massive expansion in all directions has been its modus operandi since 9/11. Its soaring budget hit about $700 billion for fiscal year 2010 (when you include a war-fighting supplemental bill of $33 billion)—an increase of *only* 4.7 percent in budget-slashing times—and is projected to hit $726 billion in fiscal year 2011. Chris Hellman of the National Priorities Project crunched the numbers in 2010, however, and found that the full U.S. national security budget was actually more than $1.2 trillion.

Not surprisingly, the Pentagon has taken over a spectrum of previously State Department–controlled civilian activities, ranging from humanitarian relief and development (also known as "nation building") to actual diplomacy. And don't forget its growing roles as a domestic-disaster manager and a global arms dealer. You could certainly think of the Pentagon as the blob on the American horizon, and yet, looking around, you might hardly be aware of the ways in which your country continues to be militarized.

With that in mind, let's examine another warscape, particularly appropriate at a moment when numerous commentators are pointing out how the United States is morphing from a can-do into a can't-do nation, when the headlines are filled with exploding gas lines and grim reports on the country's aging infrastructure. Still, don't think that the old can-do American spirit of my childhood is dead. Quite the contrary, we still have our great building projects, our equivalents of pyramids and ziggurats— and in some cases we even build them near the ruins of actual ziggurats and pyramids. I'm talking about our military bases, especially those being constructed in our war zones.

No sooner had U.S. troops taken Baghdad in April 2003 than the Pentagon and the crony corporations it now can't go to war without began to pour billions of taxpayer dollars into the construction of well-fortified American towns in Iraq that included multiple bus routes, PXs, fast-food joints, massage parlors, Internet cafés, power plants, water-treatment plants, fire stations, sewage plants, you name it.

Hundreds of military bases, micro to mega, were built in Iraq alone, including the ill-named but enormous Victory Base Complex at the edge of Baghdad International Airport, with at least nine significant sub-bases nestled inside it, and Balad Air Base, which—sooner than you could say "Saddam Hussein's in captivity"—was handling air traffic on the scale of O'Hare International in Chicago, and bedding down forty thousand inhabitants, including hire-a-gun African cops, civilian defense employees, special ops forces, employees of private contractors, and tons of troops.

And all of this was nothing compared to the feat the Pentagon accomplished in Afghanistan, where the U.S. military now claims to have built four hundred bases of every sort from the smallest combat outposts to monster installations like Bagram Air Base. In a country without normal resources, adequate fuel, or much of anything else, just about all construction materials for those bases and the fuel to go with them had to be delivered over treacherous supply lines thousands of miles long—so treacherous and difficult, in fact, that, by the time a gallon of fuel reaches Afghanistan to keep our Humvees and Mine Resistant Ambush Protected vehicles rolling along, it's estimated to cost at least $400.

Of course, whatever skills we may lack when it comes to predicting the future, all things must end, including the American war state and our strange state of war. The question is: Can our over-armed global mission be radically downsized before it downsizes us? It will happen anyway and it won't take forever either, not the way things are going, but it will happen in a less harmful way, if you're involved, in whatever fashion you choose, in making it so. Had I had a birthday cake with candles on it for that ninth birthday of mine and blew them out, that, I think, would have been my wish.

## How the Movies Saved My Life

Every childhood has its own geography and every child is an explorer, as daring as any Peary or Amundsen or Scott. I was the mildest of children, such a picky eater that my parents called me a "quince" (a fruit sour enough, they insisted, to make your face pucker, as mine did when challenged by any food out of the ordinary). I was neither a daredevil nor a chance-taker, and by my teens scorned myself for being so boringly on the straight and narrow. I never raced a car, or mocked a cop, or lit out for the territories.

Still, by the luck of the draw, as a child of the 1950s, I was plunged into a landscape more exotic than most American kids could then have imagined. It was still devastated by war, populated to a startling extent by present and former enemies, and most amazingly, the Germans, Japanese, Italians, and Russians (not to speak of the French and English) I encountered there were thrillingly alive in a way everything in my life told me we Americans weren't.

Let me explain, geographically speaking and as personally as I can. I grew up at 40 East 58th Street, just off Madison Avenue, in the heart of Manhattan, two blocks from the Plaza Hotel, where Eloise got her hair cut. Apartment 6D—"as in David," we always said. My parents moved there in 1946, just after World War II. It was two doors down from the Plaza movie theater, and getting to 6D was an exotic affair. You exited a small, gated elevator into a modest-sized corridor, apartments on either side, only to find yourself on a catwalk in the open air looking down on what might have been the low roofs of Paris. A stroll along that catwalk and a right turn into another corridor got you to our rent-controlled duplex with its living-room skylight under which my mother—"New York's girl caricaturist," as she was known in the gossip columns of the war years—regularly set up her easel. My room was upstairs.

The fifties are now recalled as a golden age when Americans, white ones anyway, burst into the suburbs, while all the consumerist gratifications deferred by the Great Depression and World War II were sated. It was the age of the television set ("Bigger screen . . . Brighter picture . . . Better reception") and pop-up toasters, of Frigidaires and freezers big enough "for the whole family" ("holds 525 pounds!") of "extension" phones, wonder of wonders, ("I just couldn't get along without my kitchen telephone"), and cigarettes so "soothing to the nerves" that doctors and baseball players alike were proud to endorse them.

With good jobs and rising wages in a still war-battered world, the United States stood so much taller than the rest of the planet, manufacturing the large items of the peaceable life (cars, above all) and the advanced weaponry of war, often in the same dominant corporations. It was a world in which Bell Telephone, that purveyor of extension phones, could also run upbeat ads aimed at boys extolling its weapons work. (As one began: "Chip Martin, college reporter, sees a 'talking brain' for guided missiles. . . . 'Glad to see you, Chip. Understand you want to find out how our Air Force can guide a warhead a quarter of the way around the world. Well, look here . . . '")

Inexpensive gas, cheap well-marbled steaks, and reliable warheads that might end life as we knew it—that seems like a reasonable summary of the obvious in American life in those years. And if you were a kid and wanted more, Hollywood was there to deliver: it was a time when, on screen, the marines always advanced before the movie ended, and the sound of a bugle meant the bluecoats were coming to save the day. It was the moment when, for the first time in history, teenagers had money in their pockets and could begin to spend it on clothes, records, and other entertainment, propelling the country into a new age in which the Mad Men of that era would begin advertising directly to them.

I knew that world, of course, even if our little "icebox," which iced over easily, was no Frigidaire. Living in the middle of Manhattan, I could catch the all-American-ness of life by taking a three-block walk to the RKO 58th Street movie theater at the corner of Third Avenue where, popcorn in hand, I'd settle in for a double-feature version of the world as it was supposed to be. There, too, I could regularly see my father's war. Like so many of those we now call "the greatest generation," he was silent on the subject of his war experience (except for rare rants about "war profiteers" and "the Japs"), but that mattered little. After all, what did he have to say when the movies taught me everything I needed to know about what he had done in his war?

Because the then-liberal rag the *New York Post* assigned my mother to draw the Army-McCarthy hearings (being broadcast live on ABC); we got a TV for the first time in April 1954. Of course, the sitcoms I was allowed to watch, like Hollywood's war films, Westerns, and comedies, had a remarkable tendency to end tidily and on an upbeat note. Unlike movies about my father's war, however, I had something to compare those sitcoms to and, much as I loved *Father Knows Best*, it bore not the slightest resemblance to anything my hard-pressed mother, angry father, and I were living out. In it, I could find no hint of the messy psychic geography of my own childhood.

For my nuclear family in those first years of the nuclear age, it was bad times all the way. In the middle years of the decade, my father, a salesman, was out of work and drinking heavily; my mother brought home "the bacon" (really, that's the way they spoke about it then), which—I have her account book from those years—was excessively lean. They were struggling to keep up the appearance of a middle-class life while falling ever more deeply into debt. The fights about "Tommy's doctor bill" or "Tommy's school bill" began as soon as they thought I was asleep.

Among my most vivid memories was creeping out into the light of the hall, propping myself up by the stairs and listening, mesmerized, as my parents went at it below with startling verbal violence. Think of that as my first perch as a future writer.

Like most kids in most places, I assumed then that my life, including such eternally angry nights, was the way it was for everyone. My problems, as I saw it, didn't actually begin until I stepped out onto 58th Street, where, as far as I could tell, a landscape strangely empty of interest stretched as far as the eye could see. If America then sat atop the world, triumphant and alone, the blandness that aloneness bred, a kind of unnaturally fearful uniformity of everything, is difficult today to conjure up or even describe. At the time, though, I hardly understood why the world I was being promised struck me as so dull. I thought it was me. And above all, I didn't have a clue when or how *this* would end and life, whatever that was, would begin.

Fortunately for me, geography came to my rescue. My street, was— no hyperbole here—unique at that moment. You could have traveled a fair distance in 1950s America, hundreds or possibly thousands of miles, without stumbling upon a movie house dedicated to "foreign films," and yet between Sixth Avenue and Lexington Avenue, in fewer than three and a half city blocks, I had three of them—the Paris just west of Fifth Avenue, the Plaza by my house, and between Park and Lexington, the Fine Arts.

You would no more have wondered about why they were clustered there than why your parents duked it out each night. And yet how strange that was in a still remarkably white bread and parochial American world. Immigration, remember, had largely been shut down by act of Congress in 1924 (see, for example, the Asian Exclusion Act) and America's doors didn't begin to open again until the early 1950s. In a time when you can get bagels in El Paso and Thai, Japanese, or Mexican food in Anytown, USA, it's hard to remember just how rare the "foreign" in "foreign films" once was. In that earlier era of American fear and hysteria, that word and the dreaded phrase "Communist influence" were linked.

And so, to enter the darkness of one of those theaters and be suddenly transported elsewhere on Earth, to consort with the enemy and immerse yourself in lives that couldn't have seemed more alien (or attractive), under more empathetic circumstances—well, that was not a common experience. Think of those movie houses not simply as one confused and unhappy teenage boy's escape hatch from the world, but as *Star Trek*ian–style wormholes into previously unsuspected parallel universes that happened to exist on planet Earth.

By the time I was thirteen, the manager of the Plaza had taken a shine to me and was letting me into any movie I cared to see. *A Taste of Honey* (a coming-of-age story about a working-class English girl—Rita Tushingham with her soulful eyes—impregnated by a black sailor and cared for by a gay man), Alan Resnais's *Last Year at Marienbad* (a film of unparalleled murkiness, notable for a matchstick game the unnamed characters play that caused a minor cocktail party craze in its day), *Billy Liar* (a chance to fall in love with the young Julie Christie as a free spirit), Ingmar Bergman's *The Virgin Spring* (a medieval tale of rape and revenge), it didn't matter. I seldom had the slightest idea what I was walking into, and in that Internet-less world there was no obvious place to find out, nor was there anyone to guide me through those films or tell me what I should think, which couldn't have been more disorienting or glorious.

On any afternoon I might suddenly be French or Russian or—weirdest of all for a Jewish kid living in New York City—German. Each film was a shock all its own, a deep dive into some previously unimagined world. If I needed confirmation that these movies were from another universe, it was enough that, in an era of glorious Technicolor, they were still obdurately and inexplicably black and white, every one of them. What more evidence did I need that foreigners inhabited another planet?

The actors in those films, unlike Hollywood's, existed on a remarkably human scale. Sometimes, they even fought as fiercely and messily as my parents and they had genuinely bad times, worse than anything I had yet imagined. Above all—a particularly un-American trait in the movies then—everything did not always end for the best.

In fact, however puzzlingly, sometimes those films didn't seem to end at all, at least not in the way I then understood endings. As in the last frozen, agonizing, ecstatic image of a boy's face in Francois Truffaut's *The 400 Blows* (which I didn't see until college), it was easy to imagine that almost anything might happen within moments of such "endings," that life would go on—which was, for me, completely unexpected at the movies.

And don't forget that these films made you work. Except for the British movies, there were always subtitles, exotic in themselves, which made them seem like so many illustrated novels. And here was the strangest thing: that black-and-white world you had to read to decipher had an uncanny ability to suck the color out of Manhattan.

And those films offered history lessons capable of turning what I thought I knew upside down. In my American world, for instance, the atomic bomb was everywhere, just not in clearly recognizable form. If you went to the RKO to catch *Them!* or *This Island Earth*, for instance, you could see the bomb and its effects, after a fashion, via fantasies about alien superweapons and radioactive mutant monsters. Still, you could grow up in 1950s America, as I did, without ever learning much or seeing a thing about what two actual atomic bombs had done to Hiroshima and Nagasaki—unless, that is, your local movie theater happened to show Alain Resnais's 1959 film *Hiroshima Mon Amour* (scripted by the novelist Marguerite Duras).

But before I go on, a caveat. Perhaps the reason memoirs are so often written by the young these days is that, once you reach a certain age, only fiction might allow you to truly make your way back to childhood. I have not the slightest doubt that those hours in the dark profoundly affected my life, and yet I find it difficult indeed to conjure the boy who first slipped into those movie houses on his own. Much of the time, it seems to me, he belongs to someone else's novel, someone else's life. Trying to make my way back to whatever he thought when he first saw those films, I feel like an archeologist digging in the ruins of my own life. When I view the same films today, I sometimes get a chill of recognition and I'm still won over, but often I wonder just what he saw in them. What in the world could my teenage self have thought while watching *Hiroshima Mon Amour*, parts of which—apologies to Duras and Resnais—are unbearably pretentious? ("You saw nothing in Hiroshima. Nothing . . . Hiroshima, that's your name . . .")

A movie about a one-night stand between a French actress making a "peace" movie in the rebuilt city of Hiroshima (who had once loved a German soldier in wartime France and paid the price), and a married Japanese architect who had been in the army in World War II while his family lived (and perhaps died) in that city—what did I make of that? What did I know? There was flesh to be seen, however obliquely, in bed, in the shower—and back then that was something. But there were also those dismally incantatory lines from Duras.

Here's what I don't doubt, though: That film gave me a gut-level primer in nuclear politics and nuclear destruction available nowhere else in my world. No mutant monsters, spaceships, or alien superweapons, just grainy, graphic glimpses of the victims from the atomic bombing of Hiroshima and of other "victims" being made up—burn patterns and keloids being painted on bodies—for the actress's antinuclear "peace" movie, the film within the film. It was there that I watched my first antinuclear demonstration—again for that other movie—as protesters marched by with signs that offered a little lesson in atomic politics and some basic information about nuclear weapons. Above all, I was, however briefly, taken under the mushroom cloud to see something then essentially taboo in this country: the real results of our "victory weapon," of what we had done to *them*, of my father's war as I would never otherwise have seen it.

If the scenes of the two lovers titillated me, those brief glimpses under that cloud haunted me. Certainly, the dreams I had in those years, in which the bomb went off over a distant city while a blast of heat seared my body, or I found myself wandering through some bleak, atomically blasted landscape, owed something to that film.

Like all of us, I wonder what made me the way I am. What left me, as a book editor, able to slip inside the skin of someone else's words? What gave me, as a critic, the distance to see our world askew? What made me, as the creator of a website who has never been in the military, focus with a critical eye on the American way of war?

There are, of course, no answers to such questions, just guesses. But I wouldn't be writing this if I didn't believe that those hours in the dark had something to do with it. I wouldn't be focused on a movie I can now barely watch if I wasn't convinced that it had a hand in sending me, as a book editor, on my own Hiroshima journey. (In 1979, I would publish in translation a Japanese book, *Unforgettable Fire: Pictures Drawn by Atomic Bomb Survivors*, which, I believe, was the first time any sizable number of images of the experience under Hiroshima's mushroom cloud made it into mainstream American culture.)

Compare all this to the war I saw at my local RKO, the one John Wayne led, the one in which the highly decorated Audie Murphy played himself on-screen mowing down Germans by the score. And then, right down the block, there was the other war I sat in on, the one our enemies fought, the one that lacked my father. As a boy, I was undoubtedly typical in imagining the defeat of Hitler as essentially an American triumph in Europe—until, that is, I walked into the Fine Arts and saw Russian director Mikhail Kalatozov's *The Cranes Are Flying*.

Part of a post-Stalinist cinematic breakout moment, its heroine and hero, Veronica and Boris, are young, in love, filmed at arty angles, and in the movie's early scenes might as well be frolicking on the banks of the Seine. But that mood only lasts until the Nazis invade. Boris volunteers for the army and, finding himself and his unit in a swamp surrounded by Germans, dies heroically but miserably in the mud. The news of his death never reaches the waiting Veronica in Moscow, who goes into shock on finding her apartment destroyed and her parents dead from a German air raid, is raped (so the film implies) in that state during another air raid by Boris's cousin, a pianist and draft evader, and grimly marries him . . . and that's hardly halfway into the film.

There is also the child Veronica saves from being run over just as she's about to commit suicide, who also turns out to be named Boris. Yes, call it an absurd war melodrama, but it was also passionately filled to the brim with mud, fire, overcrowded living quarters, rooms full of wounded soldiers, slackers, and high-livers in a panorama of wartime Russia. Grim, shocking, and above all youthful, it was the Russian film that not only took Europe by storm and won the Palme d'Or at Cannes in 1958, but took me by storm as well. The Russians—the Reds, the Commies—were then our mortal enemies. So imagine my surprise on discovering, up close and personal, that they had fought a monumental, terrible war against the Nazis, and that they couldn't have been more human—or winning.

A year or two later, I would watch *Ballad of a Soldier*, another Russian war film, this time about a kid hardly older than I was then who gets a six-day pass from the front for wiping out a couple of German tanks (in a paroxysm of fear). In an odyssey through a devastated landscape—city buildings blasted, trains blown up, bridges down, amputees visible—he makes his way home just in time to greet his mother, kiss her goodbye, and head back to the front (where, you've learned as the film begins, he dies). You simply could not see such films and hate the Russians.

Then, on the theme of teenagers at war, there was *The Bridge*, a fierce 1959 antiwar film directed by Bernhard Wicki that genuinely shocked me, perhaps as much because I found myself identifying with those German boy soldiers as by the brutality of the fighting into which they were plunged. In the last days of World War II, a group of small-town, high-spirited high school classmates, no older than I was then, are ushered hurriedly into the army, given the briefest training, and (while Nazi officials flee) rushed to a bridge of absolutely no significance to stop advancing American tanks. They are patriotic and absurdly eager to defend their town and country. All but one of them die for nothing, as does an American trying to convince them to stop fighting. ("We don't fight kids!" he yells before one of them shoots him.) The film ends on these words, which then chilled me to the bone: "This happened on April 27, 1945. It was so unimportant that it was not mentioned in any war communiqué."

To see that war through German eyes, even briefly, was to enter forbidden territory. Nonetheless, those boys were, to me, as unnervingly human as the French pilot in Serge Bourguignon's 1962 film *Sundays and Cybele*, suffering from what we would now call post-traumatic stress disorder after killing a child in the French version of the Vietnam War. Back in Paris, he strikes up an "innocent" relationship with a twelve-year-old girl (which, I can now see, had surprisingly sexual overtones), is mistaken for someone out to kill her, and shot dead by the police, the sight of which passes his trauma on to her.

These films and others like them gave me a space apart where I was privileged to absorb secrets no one in my world knew (which, to a lost teen, was nothing less than life preserving). They confirmed in me a sense that the world was not as we were told, nor was ours the single most exceptional way of living on Earth. Like that perch by the stairs above my parents' fights, those films helped turn me into a critic—of Hollywood certainly, of our American world more generally, and of my own world more specifically. And the space they opened for a child who despaired of himself (and the triumphalist American future everyone assured him was rightfully his) would prove useful decades later. After all, I now write about our American wars without ever having visited a war zone—except, of course, in the movies. There, in the 1950s and early 1960s, I advanced with the marines *and* the Russians, bombed Tokyo but also experienced (however briefly) Hiroshima after it was atomized. I took out Panzers, but for two hours one afternoon was a German boy waiting to die at a bridge of no significance as American tanks bore down on him.

So let me now, for the first time, offer a small bow of gratitude to Alain Resnais, Mikhail Kalatozov, Serge Bourguignon, Bernhard Wicki, François Truffaut, and all the others I met at the movies so long ago who turned my world inside out. You saved my life.

# CHAPTER 1

# The United States of Fear

It's finally coming into focus, and it's not even a difficult equation to grasp. Take a country in the grips of an expanding national security state, and sooner or later your "safety" will mean your humiliation, your degradation. And by the way, it will mean the degradation of your country, too.

Just ask Rolando Negrin, a Transportation Security Administration (TSA) screener who passed through one of those new "whole body image" scanners in May 2009 as part of his training for airport security. His coworkers claimed to have gotten a look at his "junk" and mocked him mercilessly, evidently repeatedly asking, "What size are you?" and referring to him as "little angry man." In the end, calling it "psychological torture," he insisted that he snapped, which in his case meant that he went after a coworker, baton first, demanding an apology.

Consider that a little parable about just how low this country has sunk, how psychologically insecure we've become while supposedly guarding ourselves against global danger. There is no question that, at the height of Cold War hysteria, when superpower nuclear arsenals were out of this world and the planet seemed a hair trigger from destruction, big and small penises were in play, symbolically speaking. Only now, however, facing a ragtag set of fanatics and terrorists—not a mighty nation but a puny crew—are those penises perfectly real and, potentially, completely humiliating.

## Failed Bombs Do the Job

We live, it seems, in a national security "homeland" of little angry bureaucrats who couldn't be happier to define what safety means for you and big self-satisfied officials who can duck the application of those safety methods. Your government can now come up with any wacky solution to American "security" and you'll pay the price. One guy brings a failed shoe bomb onto an airplane, and you're suddenly in your socks. Word has it that bombs can be mixed from liquids in airplane bathrooms, and there go your bottled drinks. A youthful idiot flies toward Detroit with an ill-constructed bomb in his underwear, and suddenly they're taking naked scans of you or threatening to grope your junk.

Two bombs don't go off in the cargo holds of two planes and all of a sudden sending things around the world threatens to become more problematic and expensive. Each time, the price of safety rises and some set of lucky corporations, along with the lobbyists and politicians who support them, get a windfall. In each case, the terror tactic (at least in the normal sense) failed. In each case, the already draconian standards for our security were ratcheted up, while even more money was poured into new technology and human reinforcements that may, in the end, cause more disruption than any successful terror attack.

Directly or indirectly, you pay for the screeners and scanners and a labyrinthine intelligence bureaucracy that officially wields an $80 billion budget, and all the lobbyists and shysters and pitchmen who accompany our burgeoning homeland-security complex. And by the way, no one's the slightest bit nice about it either, which isn't surprising since it's a national security state we're talking about, which means its mentality is punitive. It wants to lock you down quietly and with your full acquiescence, if possible. Offer some trouble, though, or step out of line, and you'll be hit with a $10,000 fine or maybe put in cuffs. It's all for your safety, and fortunately they have a set of the most inept terror plots in history to prove their point.

## Taking Off the Gloves (and Everything Else)

Since the beginning of George W. Bush's second term, Americans have been remarkably quiet when it comes to the national security disasters being perpetuated in their name. America's wars, its soaring Pentagon budgets, its billion-dollar military bases, its giant new citadels still called embassies but actually regional command centers, its ever-escalating CIA drone war along the Pakistani tribal borderlands, the ever-expanding surveillance at home, and the incessant "night raids" and home razings thousands of miles away in Afghanistan, not to speak of Washington's stimulus-package spending in its war zones have caused no more than the mildest ripple of protest, much less genuine indignation, in this country. American safety has, in every case, trumped outrage. Now, for the first time in years, the oppressiveness of a national security state bent on locking down American life has actually gotten to some Americans. No flags are yet flying over mass protests with "Don't Scan on Me" emblazoned on them. Still, the idea that air travel may mean a choice between a spritz of radiation and a sorta naked snapshot or—thrilling option B— having some overworked, overaggressive TSA agent grope you, has caused outrage, at least among a minority of Americans, amid administration confusion.

But here's the thing: in our deluded state, Americans don't tend to connect what we're doing to others abroad and what we're doing to ourselves at home. We refuse to see that the more than one trillion dollars that continue to go into the Pentagon, the U.S. Intelligence Community, and the national security state yearly, as well as the stalemated or losing wars Washington insists on fighting in distant lands, have anything to do with the near collapse of the American economy, job devastation at home, or any of the other disasters of our age. As a result, those porno-scanners and enhanced pat-downs are indignities without a cause—except, of course, for the terrorists who keep launching their bizarre plots to take down our planes.

And yet whatever inconvenience, embarrassment, or humiliation you suffer in an airport shouldn't be thought of as something the terrorists have done to us. It's what the American national-security state that we've quietly accepted demands of its subjects, based on the idea that no degree of danger from a terrorist attack, however infinitesimal, is acceptable. When it comes to genuine safety, anything close to that principle is absent from other aspects of American life where—from eating to driving to drinking to working—genuine danger exists and genuine damage is regularly done.

We now live not just with all the usual fears that life has to offer, but in something like a United States of Fear.

When George W. Bush and his cronies decided to sally forth and smite the Greater Middle East, they exulted that they were finally "taking the gloves off." And so they were: aggressive war, torture, abuse, secret imprisonment, souped-up surveillance, slaughter, drone wars: there was no end to it. When those gloves came off, other people suffered first. But wasn't it predictable—since wars have a nasty habit of coming home— that, in the end, other things would come off, and sooner or later they would be on you: your hat, your shoes, your belt, your clothes, and of course, your job, your world?

The imposition of more draconian safety and security methods is, of course, being considered for buses, trains, and boats. Can trucks, taxis, cars, and bikes be far behind? After all, once begun, there can, by definition, be no end to the search for perfect security. And what happens when the first terrorist with a suppository bomb is found aboard one of our planes? After all, such weapons already exist.

### You Wanna Be Safer? Really?

You must have a friend who's extremely critical of everyone else but utterly opaque when it comes to himself. Well, that's this country, too.

Here's a singular fact to absorb: we now know that a bunch of Yemeni al-Qaeda adherents have a far better hit on just who we are, psychologically speaking, and what makes us tick than we do. They have a more accurate profile of us than our leading intelligence profilers undoubtedly do of them. In November 2010 they released an online magazine laying out just how much the two U.S.-bound cargo-bay bombs that caused panic cost them: a mere $4,200 and the efforts of "less than six brothers" over three months. They even gave their plot a name, Operation Hemorrhage (and what they imagined hemorrhaging, it seems, was not American blood, but treasure).

Now, they're laughing at us for claiming the operation failed because, reportedly thanks to a tip from Saudi intelligence, those bombs didn't go off. "This supposedly 'foiled plot,'" they wrote, "will without a doubt cost America and other Western countries billions of dollars in new security measures. That is what we call leverage." They are, they claim, planning to use the "security phobia that is sweeping America" not to cause major casualties, but to blow a hole in the U.S. economy. "We knew that cargo planes are staffed by only a pilot and a copilot, so our objective was not to cause maximum casualties but to cause maximum losses to the American economy." This is a new definition of asymmetrical warfare. The terrorists never have to strike an actual target. It's not even incumbent upon them to build a bomb that works. Just about anything will do. To be successful, they only have to repeatedly send things in our direction, inciting the Pavlovian reaction from the U.S. national security state, causing it to further tighten its grip (or grope) at yet greater taxpayer expense.

In a sense, both the American national security state and al-Qaeda are building their strength and prestige as our lives grow more constrained and our treasure vanishes.

So you wanna be safer? I mean, *actually* safer? Here's a simple formula for beginning to improve American safety and security at every level. End our trillion-dollar wars in Afghanistan and Iraq. Begin to shut down our global empire of bases. Stop building grotesque embassy-citadels abroad (one even has a decorative moat!). End our overseas war-stimulus packages and bring some of that money home. In short, stop going out of our way to tick off foreigners and then pouring our treasure into an American war machine intent on pursuing a generational global war against them.

Of course, the U.S. national security state has quite a different formula for engendering safety in America: fight the Afghan War until hell freezes over, keep the odd base or two in Iraq, dig into the Persian Gulf region, send U.S. Special Operations troops into any country where a terrorist might possibly lurk, and make sure those drones aren't far behind. In other words, reinforce our war state by ensuring that we're eternally in a state of war, and then scare the hell out of Americans by repeatedly insisting that we're in imminent danger, that shoe, underwear, and someday butt bombers will destroy our country, our lives, and our civilization. Insist that a single percent of risk is 1 percent too much when it comes to terror and American lives, and then demand that those who feel otherwise be dealt with punitively if they won't shut up.

It's a formula for leaving you naked in airports, while increasing the oppressive power of the state. And here's the dirty, little, distinctly

Orwellian secret: the national security state can't do without those Yemeni terrorists, as well as our homegrown variety (and vice versa). All of them profit from a world of war. You don't, however. And on that score, what happens in an airport line should be the least of your worries. The national security state is eager to cop a feel. As long as we don't grasp the connections between our war state and our "safety," things will only get worse and, in the end, our world will genuinely be in danger.

## Welcome to Postlegal America

Is the Libyan war legal? Was Osama bin Laden's killing legal? Is it legal for the president of the United States to target an American citizen for assassination? Were those "enhanced interrogation techniques" legal? Each of these questions would seem to call out for debate, for answers. Or perhaps not.

Now you couldn't call me a legal scholar. I've never set foot inside a law school, and in sixty-seven years only made it onto a single jury (dismissed before trial). Still, I feel at least as capable of responding to such questions as any constitutional law professor. My answer: they are irrelevant. Think of them as twentieth-century questions that don't begin to come to grips with twenty-first-century American realities. In fact, think of them, and the very idea of a nation based on the rule of law, as symptoms of nostalgia for a long-lost republic. At least in terms of what used to be called "foreign policy," and more recently "national security," the United States is now a post-legal society.

It's easy enough to explain what I mean. If, in a country theoretically organized under the rule of law, wrongdoers are never brought to justice and nobody is held accountable for possibly serious crimes, then you don't have to be a constitutional law professor to know that its citizens actually exist in a postlegal state. If so, Is it legal is the wrong question to be asking, even if we have yet to discover the right one.

### Pretzeled Definitions of Torture

Of course, when it came to a range of potential Bush-era crimes—the use of torture, the running of offshore "black sites," the extraordinary rendition of suspected terrorists to lands where they would be tortured, illegal domestic spying and wiretapping, and the launching of wars of aggression—it's hardly news that no one of the slightest significance has ever been brought to justice. On taking office, President Barack Obama offered a clear formula for dealing with this issue. He insisted that Americans should "look forward, not backward" and so turn the page on the whole period. Then he set his Justice Department to work on other matters—such as defending (and in some cases expanding) Bush-era positions on executive power. But honestly, did anyone anywhere doubt that no Bush-era official would ever be brought to trial here for such crimes?

Everyone knows that in the United States if you're a thief caught breaking into someone's house, you'll be brought to trial, but if you're caught breaking into someone else's country, you'll be free to take to the lecture circuit, write your memoirs, become a university professor, and appear regularly on Sunday talk shows.

Of all the "debates" over legality in the Bush and Obama years, the torture debate has perhaps been the most interesting and, in some ways, the most realistic. After 9/11, the Bush administration quickly turned to a crew of handpicked Justice Department lawyers to create the necessary rationale for what its officials most wanted to do—in their quaint phrase, "take the gloves off." And those lawyers responded with a set of pseudo-legalisms that put various methods of "information extraction" beyond the powers of the Geneva Conventions, the UN's Convention Against Torture (signed by President Ronald Reagan and ratified by the Senate), and domestic antitorture legislation, including the War Crimes Act of 1996 (passed by a Republican Congress).

In the process, they created infamously pretzled new definitions for acts previously accepted as torture. Among other things, they essentially left the definition of whether an act was torture or not to the torturer (that is, to what he believed he was doing at the time). In the process, acts that had historically been considered torture became "enhanced interrogation techniques." An example would be waterboarding, which had once been bluntly known as "the water torture" or "the water cure" and whose perpetrators had, in the past, been successfully prosecuted in American military and civil courts. Such techniques were signed off on after first reportedly being "demonstrated" in the White House to an array of top officials, including the vice president, the national security adviser, the attorney general, and the secretary of state.

In the United States, the very issue of legality fell away almost instantly. Newspapers rapidly replaced the word *torture*—when applied to what American interrogators did—with the term *enhanced interrogation techniques*, which was widely accepted as less controversial and more objective. At the same time, the issue of the legality of such techniques was superseded by a fierce national debate over their efficacy. It has lasted to this day, and returned with a bang with the bin Laden killing.

Nothing better illustrates the nature of our postlegal society. Antitorture laws were on the books in this country. If legality had truly mattered, it would have been beside the point whether torture was an effective way to produce "actionable intelligence" and so prepare the way for the killing of a bin Laden. By analogy, it's perfectly reasonable to argue that robbing banks can be a successful and profitable way to make a living, but who would agree that a successful bank robber hadn't committed an act as worthy of prosecution as an unsuccessful one caught on the spot? Efficacy wouldn't matter in a society whose central value was the rule of law. In a postlegal society in which the ultimate value espoused is the safety and protection a national security state can offer you, it means the world.

As if to make the point, the Supreme Court in May 2011 offered a postlegal ruling for our moment: it declined to review a lower court ruling that blocked a case in which five men, who had experienced extraordinary rendition (a fancy globalized version of kidnapping) and been turned over to torturing regimes elsewhere by the CIA, tried to get their day in court. No such luck. The Obama administration claimed (as had the Bush administration before it) that simply bringing such a case to court would imperil national security (that is, state secrets)—and won. As Ben Wizner, the American Civil Liberties Union lawyer who argued the case, summed matters up, "To date, every victim of the Bush administration's torture regime has been denied his day in court."

To no one's shock, in June 2011 Attorney General Eric Holder announced that the Obama administration, after looking into ninety-nine cases of potential official torture in the Bush years, would prosecute none of them. To put it another way, every CIA torturer, all those involved in acts of rendition, and all the officials who authorized such acts, as well as the lawyers who put their stamp of approval on them, are free to continue their lives untouched. Recently, the Obama administration even went to court to "prevent a lawyer for a former CIA officer convicted in Italy in the kidnapping of a radical Muslim cleric from privately sharing classified information about the case with a Federal District Court judge." (Yes, Virginia, elsewhere in the world a few Americans have been tried in absentia for Bush-era crimes.) In response, wrote Scott Shane of the *New York Times*, the judge "pronounced herself 'literally speechless.'"

The realities of our moment are simple enough: other than abusers too low level (see England, Lynndie, and Graner, Charles) to matter to our national security state, no one in the CIA, and certainly no official of any sort, is going to be prosecuted for the possible crimes Americans committed in the Bush years in pursuit of the Global War on Terror.

## On Not Blowing Whistles

It's beyond symbolic, then, that only one figure from the national security world seems to remain in the "legal" crosshairs: the whistleblower. If, as the president of the United States, you sign off on a system of warrantless surveillance of Americans—the sort that not so long ago was against the law in this country—or if you happen to run a giant telecom company and go along with that system by opening your facilities to government snoops, or if you run the National Security Agency (NSA) or are an official in it overseeing the kind of data mining and intelligence gathering that goes with such a program, then—as recent years have made clear—you are above the law.

If, however, you happen to be an NSA employee who feels that the agency has overstepped the bounds of legality in its dealings with Americans, that it is moving in Orwellian directions, and that government malfeasance should be exposed, and if you offer even unclassified information to a newspaper reporter, as was the case with Thomas Drake, be afraid. You may be prosecuted by the Bush and then Obama Justice Departments, and threatened with thirty-five years in prison under the Espionage Act (not for "espionage," but for having divulged the lowest of low-grade state secrets in a world in which, increasingly, everything having to do with the state is becoming a secret).

If you are a CIA employee who tortured no one but may have given information damaging to the reputation of the national security state—in this case, about a botched effort to undermine the Iranian nuclear program—to a journalist, watch out. You are likely, as in the case of Jeffrey Sterling, to find yourself in a court of law. And if you happen to be a journalist like James Risen who may have received that information, you are likely to be hit by a Justice Department subpoena attempting to force you to reveal your source, under threat of imprisonment for contempt of court.

If you are a private in the U.S. military with access to a computer with low-level classified material from the Pentagon's wars and the State Department's activities, if you've seen something of the grim reality of what the national security state looks like when superimposed on Iraq, and if you decide to shine some light on that world, as army private Bradley Manning is believed to have done, they'll toss you in prison and throw away the key. You'll be accused of having "blood on your hands" and tried under the Espionage Act by those who actually have blood on their hands and are beyond all accountability.

When it comes to acts of state today, there is only one law: don't pull up the curtain on the doings of any aspect of our spreading National Security Complex or the imperial executive that goes with it. And when someone in Congress actually moves to preserve some aspect of older notions of American privacy (versus American secrecy), as Senator Rand Paul did recently in reference to the Patriot Act, he is promptly smeared as potentially "giving terrorists the opportunity to plot attacks against our country, undetected."

### Enhanced Legal Techniques

This is the reality of postlegal America: since the attacks of September 11, 2001, the National Security Complex has engorged itself on American fears and grown at a remarkable pace. According to "Top Secret America," a *Washington Post* series written in mid-2010, 854,000 people have "top secret" security clearances, "51 federal organizations and military commands, operating in 15 U.S. cities, track the flow of money to and from terrorist networks . . . [and] some 1,271 government organizations and 1,931 private companies work on programs related to counterterrorism, homeland security, and intelligence in about 10,000 locations across the United States."

Just stop a moment to take that in. And then let this sink in as well: whatever any one of those employees does inside that national-security world, no matter how "illegal" the act, it's a double-your-money bet that he or she will never be prosecuted for it (unless it happens to involve letting Americans know something about just how they are being "protected").

The Intelligence Community, the National Security Complex, including the Pentagon and that post-9/11 creation, the Department of Homeland Security, and the imperial executive have thrived in these years. They have all expanded their powers and prerogatives based largely on the claim that they are protecting the American people from potential harm by terrorists out to destroy our world. Above all, however, they seem to have honed a single skill: the ability to protect themselves, as well as the lobbyists and corporate entities that feed off them. They have increased their funds and powers, even as they enveloped themselves as institutions in a penumbra of secrecy. The power of this complex of institutions is still on the rise, even as the power and wealth of the country it protects is visibly in decline.

The question Is it legal is obviously inapplicable in a land where the rule of law no longer applies to everyone. If you are an ordinary citizen, of course, it still applies to you, but not if you are part of the state apparatus that officially protects you. The institutional momentum behind this development is simple enough to demonstrate: it hardly mattered that, after George W. Bush took off those gloves, the next president elected was a former constitutional law professor. The National Security Complex is the King George of the present moment. In the areas that matter to that complex, Congress has ever less power and is generally ever more ready to cede what power it has left.

Democracy? The people's representatives? How quaint in a world in which our real rulers are unelected, shielded by secrecy, and supported by a carefully nurtured, almost religious attitude toward security and the U.S. military.

The National Security Complex has access to us, to our lives and communications, though we have next to no access to it. It has, in reserve, those enhanced interrogation techniques and when trouble looms, a set of what might be called enhanced legal techniques as well. It has the ability to make war at will (or whim). It has a growing post-9/11 secret army cocooned inside the military: twenty thousand or more troops in special operations outfits like the SEAL team that took down Osama bin Laden, also enveloped in secrecy. In addition, it has the CIA and an expanding fleet of armed drone aircraft ready to conduct its wars and operations globally in semisecrecy, without the permission or oversight of the American people or their representatives. And war, of course, is the ultimate aphrodisiac for the powerful.

Theoretically, the National Security Complex exists only to protect you. Its every act is done in the name of making you safer, even if the idea of safety and protection doesn't extend to your job, your foreclosed home, or aid in disastrous times.

Welcome to post-legal America. It's time to stop wondering whether its acts are illegal and start asking: Do you really want to be this "safe"?

## The 100 Percent Doctrine in Washington

Here's a scenario to chill you to the bone:

*Without warning, the network—a set of terrorist super cells—struck in northern Germany and Germans began to fall by the hundreds, then thousands. As panic spread, hospitals were overwhelmed with the severely wounded. More than twenty of the victims died.*

*No one doubted that it was al-Qaeda, but where the terrorists had come from was unknown. Initially, German officials accused Spain of harboring them (and the Spanish economy promptly took a hit). Then, confusingly, they retracted the charge. Alerts went off across Europe as fears spread. Russia closed its borders to the European Union, which its outraged leaders denounced as a "disproportionate" response. Even a small number of Americans visiting Germany ended up hospitalized.*

*In Washington, there was panic, though no evidence existed that the terrorists were specifically targeting Americans or that any of them had slipped into this country. Still, at a hastily called news conference, Secretary of Homeland Security Janet Napolitano raised the new terror alert system for the first time from its always "elevated" status to "imminent" (that is, "a credible, specific, and impending threat"). Soon after, a Pentagon spokesman an-*

*nounced that the U.S. military had been placed on high alert across Europe. Commentators on Fox News, quoting unnamed FBI sources, began warning that this might be the start of the "next 9/11"—and that the Obama administration was unprepared for it. Former vice president Dick Cheney, in a rare public appearance at the American Enterprise Institute, denounced the president for "heedlessly putting this country at risk from the terrorists." In Congress, members of both parties rallied behind calls for hundreds of millions of dollars of supplementary emergency funding for the Department of Homeland Security to strengthen airport safety. ("In such difficult economic times," said House Speaker John Boehner, "Congress will have to find cuts from nonmilitary discretionary spending at least equal to these necessary supplementary funds.")*

*Finally, as the noise in the media echo chamber grew, President Obama called a prime-time news conference and addressed the rising sense of hysteria in Washington and the country, saying: "Al-Qaeda and its extremist allies will stop at nothing in their efforts to kill Americans. And we are determined not only to thwart those plans, but to disrupt, dismantle, and defeat their networks once and for all." He then ordered a full review of U.S. security and intelligence capabilities and promised a series of "concrete steps to protect the American people: new screening and security for all flights, domestic and international; . . . more air marshals on flights; and deepening cooperation with international partners."*

### Terrorism Tops Shark Attacks

The first part of this scenario is, of course, a "terrorist" version of the 2011 *E. coli* outbreak in Germany—the discovery of an all-new, antibiotic-resistant "super-toxic variant" of the bacteria that caused death and panic in Europe. Although al-Qaeda and *E. coli* do sound a bit alike, German officials initially (and incorrectly) accused Spanish cucumbers, not terrorists in Spain or German bean sprouts, of causing the crisis. And the "disproportionate" Russian response was not to close its borders to the European Union, but to ban EU vegetables until the source of the outbreak was discovered.

Above all, the American overreaction was pure fiction. In fact, scientists here urged calm and midlevel government officials issued statements of reassurance on the safety of the country's food supply system.

No one attacked the government for inaction. Cheney did not excoriate the president, nor did Napolitano raise the terror alert level. And Obama's statement, quoted above, was actually given on January 5, 2010, in the panicky wake of the "underwear bomber's" failed attempt to blow a hole in a Christmas Day plane headed from Amsterdam to Detroit.

Ironically, non-super-toxic versions of *E. coli* now cause almost as much damage yearly in the United States as the super-toxic strain did in Europe. The Centers for Disease Control and Prevention (CDC) have estimated that earlier in the decade about sixty Americans died annually from *E. coli* infections and ensuing complications, and another 2,000 were hospitalized. More recently, the figure for *E. coli* deaths has dropped to about twenty a year. For food-borne disease more generally, the CDC estimates that 48 million (or one of every six) Americans get sick yearly, 128,000 are hospitalized, and about 3,000 die.

By comparison, in the near decade since 9/11, while hundreds of Americans died from *E. coli*, and at least 30,000 from food-borne illnesses generally, only a handful of Americans, perhaps fewer than twenty-five, have died from anything that might be considered a terror attack in this country, even if you include the assassination attempt against Congresswoman Gabrielle Giffords and the Piper Cherokee PA-28 that a disgruntled software engineer flew into an Austin, Texas, building containing an IRS office, killing himself and an IRS manager. ("Well, Mr. Big Brother IRS man, let's try something different; take my pound of flesh and sleep well," he wrote in his final note.)

In other words, in terms of damage since 9/11, terror attacks have ranked above shark attacks but below just about anything else that could possibly be dangerous to Americans, including car crashes, which have racked up between 33,800 and 43,500 deaths a year since 2001.

While *E. coli* deaths have dropped in recent years, no one expects them to get to zero, nor have steps been taken that might bring us closer to the 100 percent safety mark. As Gardiner Harris of the *New York Times* wrote, "A law passed by Congress last year gave the Food and Drug Administration new powers to mandate that companies undertake preventive measures to reduce the likelihood of such outbreaks, and the law called for increased inspections to ensure compliance. The agency requested additional financing to implement the new law, including hiring more inspectors next year. Republicans in the House have instead proposed cutting the agency's budget."

## Doctrines from One to One Hundred

Here, then, is one of the strange phenomena of our post-9/11 American age: in only one area of life are Americans officially considered 100 percent scared, and so 100 percent in need of protection: terrorism.

No one has been urging that a Global War on Food-Borne Illnesses be launched. In fact, at this moment, six strains of *E. coli* that do cause illness in this country remain unregulated. Department of Agriculture proposals to deal with them are "stalled" in the Office of Management and Budget. Meanwhile, the super-toxic *E. coli* strain that appeared in Europe remains officially unregulated here. On the other hand, send any doofus America-bound on a plane with any kind of idiotic device, and the politicians, the media, and the public promptly act as if the sky were falling or civilization itself were at risk.

This might be of only moderate interest if it weren't for the U.S. national security state. Having lost its Communist superenemy in 1991, it now lives, breathes, and grows on its self-proclaimed responsibility to protect Americans 100 percent of the time, 100 percent of the way, from any imaginable terror threat. The National Security Complex has, in fact, grown fat by relentlessly pursuing the promise of making the country totally secure from terrorism, even as life grows ever less secure for so many Americans when it comes to jobs, homes, finances, and other crucial matters. It is on this pledge of protection that the complex has managed to extort the tidal flow of funds that have allowed it to bloat to monumental proportions and encase itself in a cocoon of self-protective secrecy and immunity.

In the days after 9/11, Vice President Cheney proposed a new formula for American war policy. Its essence was this: even a 1 percent chance of an attack on the United States, especially involving weapons of mass destruction, must be dealt with as if it were a certainty. Journalist Ron Suskind dubbed it "the one percent doctrine." It may have been the rashest formula for "preventive" or "aggressive" war offered in the modern era and, along with the drumbeat of bogus information that Cheney and crew dished out about weapons of mass destruction in Iraq, it was the basis for the Bush administration's disastrous attempt to occupy that country and build a *Pax Americana* in the Greater Middle East.

There was, it turns out, a "homeland" equivalent, never quite formulated or given a name, but remarkably successful at feeding an increasingly all-encompassing domestic war state. Call it the 100 percent doctrine (for total safety from terrorism). While the 1 percent version never quite caught on, the 100 percent doctrine has already become part of the American credo. Thanks to it, the National Security Complex is a self-reinforcing, self-perpetuating mechanism. Any potential act of terrorism simply feeds the system, creating new opportunities to add yet more layers to one bureaucracy or another, or to promote new programs of surveillance and control—and the technology that goes with them. Every minor deviation from terror safety, even involving plots that failed dismally or never had the slightest chance of success, is but an excuse for further funding.

Meanwhile, the complex continually "mans up" (or drones up) and, from Pakistan to Yemen, launches attacks officially meant to put terrorists out of action but that create more of them in the process. In other words, consider it a terrorist-creating machine that needs—what else?—repeated evidence of or signs of terrorism to survive and thrive.

Though few here seem to notice, none of this bears much relationship to actual American security. But if the National Security Complex doesn't make you secure, its 100 percent doctrine is by no means a failure. On the basis of ensuring your security from terror, it has managed to make itself secure from bad times, the dangers of downsizing, most forms of accountability, or prosecution for acts that once would have been considered crimes.

In fact, terrorism is anything but the greatest of our problems or threats, which means that acquiescing to a state dedicated to expansion on the principle of keeping you safe from terror is like making a bargain with the devil.

So suck it up. Nothing is secure. No one is safe. Now eat your sprouts.

## Obama's Bush-League World

George W. who? I mean, the guy is so over. When he turned the big six-five, it was barely a footnote in the news. And Dick Cheney, tick-tick-

tick. Condoleezza Rice? She's already onto her next memoir, and yet it's as if she's been wiped from history. As for Donald Rumsfeld, he published his memoir in February 2011 and it hit the bestseller lists, but months later, where is he?

And can anyone be surprised? They were wrong about Afghanistan. They were wrong about Iraq. They were wrong about Saddam Hussein's weapons of mass destruction. They were wrong about what the U.S. military was capable of doing. The country imploded economically while they were at the helm. Geopolitically speaking, they headed the car of state for the nearest cliff. In fact, when it comes to pure wrongness, what weren't they wrong about?

Americans do seem to have turned the page on Bush and his cronies. (President Obama called it looking forward, not backward.) Still, glance over your shoulder and, if you're being honest, you'll have to admit that one thing didn't happen: they didn't turn the page on us.

They may have disappeared from our lives, but the post-9/11 world they had such a mad hand in creating hasn't. It's not just the Department of Homeland Security or that un-American word *homeland*, both of which are undoubtedly embedded in our lives forever. Or the Patriot Act, now as American as apple pie. Or Guantánamo which, despite a presidential promise, may never close. Or all the wild, overblown fears of terrorism and the new security world that goes with them, neither of which shows the slightest sign of abating. Or the National Security Agency's surveillance of and spying on Americans which, as far as we can tell, is ongoing. No, it's scores of Bush policies and positions that will clearly be with us until hell freezes over. Among them all, consider the Obama administration's updated version of that signature Bush invention, the Global War on Terror.

Yes, Obama's national security officials threw that term to the dogs back in 2009, and now pursue a no-name global strategy that's meant not to remind you of the Bush era. Recently, the White House released an unclassified summary of its 2011 "National Strategy for Counterterrorism," a nineteen-page document in prose only a giant bureaucracy with a desire to be impenetrable could produce. If it makes a feeble attempt to put a little rhetorical space between Obama-style counterterrorism and what the Bush administration was doing, it still manages to send one overwhelming message: George W. Bush, Dick Cheney, et al., are still striding amongst us, carrying big sticks and with that same crazed look in their eyes.

The Global War on Terror was the bastard spawn of the disorientation and soaring hubris of the days after the 9/11 attacks, which set afire the delusional geopolitical dreams of Bush, Cheney, their top national security officials, and their neocon supporters. And here's the saddest thing: the Bush administration's most extreme ideas when it comes to GWOT are now the humdrum norm of Obama administration policies—and hardly anyone thinks it's worth a comment.

### A History Lesson from Hell

It's easy to forget just how quickly GWOT was upon us or how strange it really was. On the night of September 11, 2001, addressing the nation, President Bush first spoke of winning "the war against terrorism." Nine days later, in an address to a joint session of Congress, the phrase "war on terror" was already being expanded. "Our war on terror," Bush said, "begins with al-Qaeda, but it does not end there. It will not end until every terrorist group of global reach has been found, stopped, and defeated."

In those early days, there were already clues aplenty as to which way the wind was gusting in Washington. Top administration officials immediately made it plain that a single yardstick was to measure planetary behavior from then on: Were you "with us or against us"? From the Gulf of Guinea to Central Asia, that question would reveal everything worth knowing, and terror would be its measure.

As the *New York Times* reported on September 14, Bush's top officials had "cast aside diplomatic niceties" and were giving Arab countries and "the nations of the world a stark choice: stand with us against terrorism or face the certain prospect of death and destruction." According to Pakistani dictator Pervez Musharraf, Deputy Secretary of State Richard Armitage took that message directly to his country's intelligence director: either ally with Washington in the fight against al-Qaeda, or prepare to be bombed "back to the Stone Age," as Armitage reportedly put it.

Global War on Terror? They weren't exaggerating. These were people shocked by what had happened to iconic buildings in the "homeland" and overawed by what they imagined to be the all-conquering power of the U.S. military. In their fever dreams, they thought that this was their moment and the apocalyptic winds of history were at their backs. And they weren't hiding where they wanted it to blow them, either. That was why they tried to come up with names to replace GWOT—World War IV (the third was the Cold War) and the Long War being two of them—that would be even blunter about their desire to plunge us into a situation from which none of us would emerge in our lifetimes. But to the extent anything stuck, GWOT did.

As journalist Ron Suskind reported in his book *The One Percent Doctrine*, in a "Presidential Finding" on September 17, 2011, only six days after the World Trade Center towers went down, Bush granted the CIA an unprecedented license to wage war globally. By then, the CIA had presented him with a plan whose name was worthy of a sci-fi film: the "Worldwide Attack Matrix." According to Suskind, it already "detailed operations [to come] against terrorists in 80 countries."

In other words, with less than two hundred countries on the planet, the president had declared open season on nearly half of them. Of course, the Pentagon wasn't about to be left out while the CIA was given the run of the globe. Soon enough, Secretary of Defense Rumsfeld began building up an enormous CIA-style secret army of elite special operations forces within the military. By the end of the Bush years, these had reportedly been deployed in—don't be surprised—sixty countries. In the Obama era, that number expanded to seventy-five—mighty close to the eighty in the Worldwide Attack Matrix.

And one more thing, there was a new weapon in the world, the perfect weapon to make mincemeat of all boundaries and a mockery of national sovereignty and international law (with little obvious danger to us): the pilotless drone. Surveillance drones already in existence were quickly armed with missiles and bombs and, in November 2002, one of these was sent out on the first CIA robot assassination mission—to Yemen, where six al-Qaeda suspects in a vehicle were obliterated without a by-your-leave to anyone.

### CT to the Horizon

That CIA strike launched the drone wars, which are now a perfectly humdrum part of our American world of war. In June 2011, the Obama administration leaked news that it was intensifying its military-run war against al-Qaeda in Yemen by bringing the CIA into the action. The agency is now to build a base for its drone air wing somewhere in the Middle East to hunt Yemeni terrorists (and assumedly those elsewhere in the region as well). Yemen functionally has no government to cooperate with, but in pure Bushian fashion, who cares?

At the same time, unnamed American officials leaked the news that, for the first time, a U.S. military drone had conducted a strike against al-Shabab militants in Somalia, with the implication that this was a "war" that would also be intensifying. Meanwhile, curious reports were emerging from Pakistan, where the CIA has been conducting an escalating drone war since 2004 (strikes viewed "negatively" by 97 percent of Pakistanis, according to a 2011 Pew poll). Top Pakistani officials were threatening to shut down the agency's drone operations at Shamsi air base in Baluchistan. Shamsi is the biggest of the three borrowed Pakistani bases from which the CIA secretly launches its drones. The Obama administration responded bluntly. White House counterterrorism chief John O. Brennan insisted that, whatever happened, the United States would continue to "deliver precise and overwhelming force against al-Qaida" in the Pakistani tribal areas.

As Spencer Ackerman of *Wired*'s *Danger Room* blog summed things up, "The harsh truth is that the Pakistanis can't stop the drone war on their soil. But they can shift its launching points over the Afghan border. And the United States is already working on a backup plan for a long-term drone war, all without the Pakistanis' help." In other words, permission from a beleaguered local ally might be nice, but it isn't a conceptual necessity.

If Bush's crew is long gone, the world they willed us is alive and well. After all, there are reasonable odds that, on the day you read this, somewhere in the free-fire zone of the Greater Middle East, a drone "piloted" from an air base in the western United States or perhaps a secret "suburban facility" near Langley, Virginia, will act as judge, jury, and executioner somewhere in the "arc of instability." It will take out a terrorist suspect or suspects, or a set of civilians mistaken for terrorists, or a "target" someone in Washington didn't like, or that one of our allies-cum-intelligence-assets had it in for, or perhaps a mix of all of the above. We can't be sure how many countries' American drones, military or CIA, are patrolling, but in at least six of them—Afghanistan, Pakistan, Yemen, Somalia, Libya, and Iraq—they have launched strikes in recent years that have killed more "suspects" than ever died in the 9/11 attacks.

And there is more—possibly much more—to come. In late June 2011, the Obama administration posted that unclassified summary of its 2011 National Strategy for Counterterrorism at the White House website. It's a document that carefully avoids using the term *war on terror*, even though counterterrorism adviser Brennan did admit that it "tracked closely with the goals" of the Bush administration.

The document tries to argue that, when it comes to counterterrorism (or CT), the Obama administration has actually pulled back somewhat from the expansiveness of Bush-era GWOT thinking. We are now, it insists, only going after "al-Qaeda and its affiliates and adherents," not every "terror group" on the planet. But here's the curious thing: when you check out its "areas of focus," other than "the Homeland" (always capitalized as if our country were the United States of Homeland), what you find is an expanded version of the Bush global target zone, including the Maghreb and Sahel (North Africa), East Africa, the Arabian Peninsula, Iraq, South Asia, Central Asia, and—thrown in for good measure—Southeast Asia. In most of those areas, Bush-style hunting season is evidently still open.

If you consider deeds, not words, when it comes to drones the arc of instability is expanding—and based on the new counterterrorism document, the next place for our robotic assassins to cross borders in search of targets could be the Maghreb and Sahel. There, we're told, al-Qaeda in the Lands of the Islamic Maghreb (AQIM), with roots in Algeria but operatives in northern Mali, among other places, potentially threatens "U.S. citizens and interests in the region."

Here's how the document puts the matter in its classically bureaucratese version of English: "[W]e must therefore pursue near-term efforts and at times more targeted approaches that directly counter AQIM and its enabling elements. We must work actively to contain, disrupt, degrade, and dismantle AQIM as logical steps on the path to defeating the group. As appropriate, the United States will use its CT tools, weighing the costs and benefits of its approach in the context of regional dynamics and perceptions and the actions and capabilities of its partners in the region."

That may not sound so ominous, but best guess: the GWOT is soon likely to be on the march across North Africa, heading south. And Obama national security appointments only emphasize how much the drone wars are on Washington's future agenda. After all, Leon Panetta, the man who since 2009 ran the CIA's drone wars, has moved over to the Pentagon as secretary of defense, while Bush's favorite general, David Petraeus, the war commander who loosed American air power (including drone power) in a massive way in Afghanistan, is moving on to the CIA.

On his first visit to South Asia as secretary of defense, Panetta made the claim that Washington was "within reach of strategically defeating al-Qaeda." Perhaps it won't surprise you that such news signals not a winding down, but a ratcheting up, of the Global War on Terror. Panetta, as Craig Whitlock of the *Washington Post* reported, "hinted of more to come, saying he would redouble efforts by the military and the spy agency to work together on counterterrorism missions outside the traditional war zones of Afghanistan and Iraq."

More to come, as two men switching their "civilian" and military roles partner up. Count on drone-factory assembly lines to rev up as well, and the military's special operations forces to be in expansion mode. And note that by the penultimate page of that CT strategy summary, the administration has left al-Qaeda behind and is muttering in bureau-speak about Hezbollah and Hamas, Iran and Syria ("active sponsors of terrorism"), and even the Revolutionary Armed Forces of Colombia.

On the Bush administration's watch, the United States blew a gasket, American power went into decline, and the everyday security of everyday Americans took a major hit. Still, give them credit. They were successful on at least one count: they made sure that we'd never stop fighting their war on terror. In this sense, Obama and his top officials are a drone national security team, carrying out the dreams and fantasies of their predecessors, while Bush and his men (and woman) give lucrative speeches and write books hundreds or thousands of miles away.

## CHAPTER 2

# Entering the Soviet Era

## Washington Drunk on War

Mark it on your calendar. It seems we've finally entered the Soviet era in America.

You remember the Soviet Union, now almost twenty years in its grave, but who gives it a second thought today? Even in its glory years, that "evil empire" was sometimes referred to as "the second superpower." In 1991, after seven decades, it suddenly disintegrated and disappeared, leaving the United States—the "sole superpower" or even the "hyperpower," on planet Earth—surprised but triumphant.

The USSR had been heading for the exits for quite a while, not that official Washington had a clue. At the moment it happened, Soviet "experts" like Robert Gates, then director of the CIA, still expected the Cold War to go on and on. In Washington, eyes were trained on the might of the Soviet military, which the Soviet leadership had never stopped feeding, even as its sclerotic bureaucracy was rotting, its economy (which had ceased to grow in the late 1970s) was tanking, budget deficits were soaring, indebtedness to other countries was growing, and social welfare payments were eating into what funds remained. Not even a vigorous reformist leader like Mikhail Gorbachev could stanch the rot, especially when, in the late 1980s, the price of Russian oil fell drastically.

Looking back, the most distinctive feature of the last years of the Soviet Union may have been the way it continued to pour money into its military—and its military adventure in Afghanistan—when it was already going bankrupt and the society it had built was beginning to collapse around it. In the end, its aging leaders made a devastating miscalculation. They mistook military power for power on this planet. Armed to the teeth and possessing a nuclear force capable of destroying the Earth many times over, the Soviets nonetheless remained the vastly poorer, weaker, and (except when it came to the arms race) far less technologically innovative of the two superpowers.

In December 1979, perhaps taking the bait of the Carter administration, whose national security adviser was eager to see the Soviets bloodied by a "Vietnam" of their own, the Red Army invaded Afghanistan to support a weak Communist government in Kabul. When resistance in the countryside, led by Islamic fundamentalist guerrillas and backed by the other superpower, only grew, the Soviets sent in more troops, launched major offensives, called in air power, and fought on brutally and futilely for a decade until, in 1989, long after they had been whipped, they withdrew in defeat.

Gorbachev had dubbed Afghanistan "the bleeding wound," and when the wounded Red Army finally limped home, it was to a country that would soon cease to exist. For the Soviet Union, Afghanistan had literally proven "the graveyard of empires." If, at the end, its military remained standing, the empire didn't.

If you don't already find this description just a tad eerie, given the present moment in the United States, you should.

In Washington, the Bush administration—G. H. W.'s, not G. W.'s—declared victory and then left the much ballyhooed "peace dividend" in the nearest ditch. Caught off guard by the collapse of the Soviet Union, Washington's consensus policy makers drew no meaningful lessons from it, just as they had drawn few that mattered from their Vietnam defeat sixteen years earlier.

Quite the opposite: successive administrations would blindly head down the very path that had led the Soviets to ruin. They would serially agree that, in a world without significant enemies, the key to global power was still the care and feeding of the U.S. military and the military-industrial complex that went with it. As the years passed, that military would be sent regularly into the far reaches of the planet to fight frontier wars, establish military bases, and finally impose a global *Pax Americana* on the planet.

This urge, delusional in retrospect, seemed to reach its ultimate expression in the second Bush administration, whose infamous "unilateralism" rested on a belief that no country or even bloc of countries should ever again be allowed to come close to matching United States military power. (As its National Security Strategy of 2002 put the matter—and it couldn't have been blunter on the subject—the United States was to "build and maintain" its military power "beyond challenge.") Bush's military fundamentalists firmly believed that, in the face of the most technologically advanced, bulked-up, destructive force around, hostile states would be "shocked and awed" by a simple demonstration of U.S. power, and friendly ones would have little choice but to come to heel. After all, as the president said in front of a Veterans of Foreign Wars convention in 2007, the U.S. military was "the greatest force for human liberation the world has ever known."

In this way, far more than the Soviets, the top officials of the Bush administration mistook military power for power, a gargantuan misreading of the economic position of the United States in the world.

### Boundless Military Ambitions

The attacks of September 11, 2001, that "Pearl Harbor of the twenty-first century," clinched the deal. In the space the Soviet Union had deserted, which had been occupied for years by minor outlaw states like North Korea, there was now a new shape-shifting enemy, al-Qaeda (also known as Islamic extremism or the new "totalitarianism"), which could be just as big as you wanted to make it. Suddenly, we were in what the Bush administration dubbed "the Global War on Terror"—and this time there would be nothing "cold" about it.

Bush administration officials promptly suggested that they were prepared to use a newly agile American military to "drain the swamp" of global terrorism. ("While we'll try to find every snake in the swamp, the essence of the strategy is draining the swamp," insisted Deputy Secretary of Defense Paul Wolfowitz two weeks after 9/11.) They were prepared, they made clear, to undertake these draining operations against Islamic "terrorist networks" in no less than sixty countries around the planet.

Their military ambitions, in other words, knew no bounds; nor, it seemed, did the money and resources that began to flow into the Pentagon, the weapons industries, the country's increasingly militarized intelligence services, mercenary companies like Blackwater and KBR that grew fat on a privatizing administration's war plans and the multi-billion-dollar no-bid contracts it was eager to proffer, the new Department of Homeland Security, and a ramped-up, ever more powerful national security state.

As the Pentagon expanded, taking on ever newer roles, the numbers would prove staggering. By the end of the Bush years, Washington was doling out almost twice what the next nine nations combined were spending on their militaries, while total U.S. military expenditures came to just under half the world's total. Similarly, by 2008, the United States controlled almost 70 percent of the global arms market. It also had eleven aircraft-carrier battle groups capable of patrolling the world's seas and oceans at a time when no power that could faintly be considered a possible future enemy had more than one.

By then, private contractors had built for the Pentagon almost three hundred military bases in Iraq, ranging from tiny combat outposts to massive "American towns" holding tens of thousands of troops and private contractors. They were in the process of doing the same in Afghanistan and, to a lesser extent, in the Persian Gulf region generally. This, too, represented a massive investment in what looked like a permanent occupation of the oil heartlands of the planet. As right-wing pundit Max Boot put it after a flying tour of America's global garrisons, the United States possessed military bases that add up to "a virtual American empire of Wal-Mart-style PXs, fast-food restaurants, golf courses, and gyms."

Depending on just what you counted, there were anywhere from seven hundred to twelve hundred or more of those bases, micro to macro, acknowledged and unacknowledged, around the globe. Meanwhile, the Pentagon was pouring money into the wildest blue-skies thinking at its advanced research arm, the Defense Advanced Research Projects Agency (DARPA), whose budget grew by 50 percent.

Through DARPA, well-funded scientists experimented with various ways to fight wars in the near and distant future (at a moment when no one was ready to put significant government money into blue-skies thinking about, for instance, how to improve education). The Pentagon was also pioneering a new form of air power, drone warfare, in which "we" wouldn't be anywhere near the battlefield, and the battlefield would no longer necessarily be in a country with which we were at war.

It was additionally embroiled in two disastrous, potentially trillion-dollar wars (and various global skirmishes), all this at top dollar at a time when next to no money was being invested in bridges, tunnels, water-works, and the like that made up an aging American infrastructure. Except when it came to victory, the military stood ever taller, while its many missions expanded exponentially, even as the domestic economy was spinning out of control.

In other words, in a far wealthier country, another set of leaders, having watched the Soviet Union implode, decisively embarked on the Soviet path to disaster.

### Military Profligacy

In fall 2008, the abyss opened under the U.S. economy, which the Bush administration had been blissfully ignoring, and millions of people fell into it. Giant institutions wobbled or crashed, foreclosures happened on a mind-boggling scale, infrastructure began to buckle, state budgets were caught in a death grip, teachers' jobs, another kind of infrastructure, went down the tubes in startling numbers, and the federal deficit soared.

A new president also entered the Oval Office, someone (many voters believed) intent on winding down Bush's wars and the delusions of military omnipotence and technological omniscience that went with them. If George W. Bush had pushed this country to the edge of disaster, at least his military policies, as many of his critics saw it, were as extreme and anomalous as the cult of executive power his top officials fostered.

But here was the strange thing. In the midst of the Great Recession, under a new president with supposedly far fewer illusions about American omnipotence and power, war policy continued to expand in just about every way. The Pentagon budget rose by Bushian increments, and while the Iraq War began to wind down, the new president doubled down in Afghanistan soon after entering office, and then again before the end of 2009. There, he "surged" in multiple ways. At best, the United States was only drawing down one war, in Iraq, to feed the flames of another.

As in the Soviet Union before its collapse, the exaltation of the military at the expense of the rest of society and the economy had by now become the new normal, so much so that hardly a serious word could be said—lest you not "support our troops"—when it came to ending the American way of war or downsizing the global mission. Even when, after years of astronomical growth, Secretary of Defense Robert Gates began to talk about cost-cutting at the Pentagon, it was in the service of the reallocation of that money to war-fighting.

Here was how the *New York Times* summed up what reduction actually meant for our ultimate supersized institution in tough times: "Current budget plans project growth of only 1 percent in the Pentagon budget, after inflation, over the next five years." *Only* 1 percent growth— at a time when state budgets, for instance, are being slashed to the bone. Like the Soviet military, the Pentagon is planning to remain obese whatever else goes down.

Meanwhile, the "antiwar" president has been overseeing the expansion of the new normal on many fronts, including the expanding size of the army itself. In fact, when it comes to the Global War on Terror—even with the name now in disuse—the profligacy can still take your breath away.

Consider, for instance, the $2.2 billion Host Nation Trucking contract the Pentagon uses to pay protection money to Afghan security companies which, in turn, slip some part of those payments to the Taliban to let American supplies travel safely on Afghan roads. Or consider the $683,000 the Pentagon spent, according to the *Washington Post*, to "renovate a café that sells ice cream and Starbucks coffee" at its base/prison in Guantánamo Bay, Cuba. Or the $773,000 used there "to remodel a cinder-block building to house a KFC/Taco Bell restaurant," or the $7.3 million spent on baseball and football fields, or the $60,000 batting cage, or a promised $20,000 soccer cage, all part of the approximately $2 billion that have gone into the American base and prison complex that Barack Obama promised to close but hasn't.

Or what about the U.S. Embassy in Baghdad, that 104-acre, almost three-quarters-of-a-billion-dollar, twenty-one-building homage to the American-mall-as-fortified-citadel? It costs more than $1.5 billion a year to run, and bears about as much relationship to an "embassy" as McDonald's does to a neighborhood hamburger joint. According to a recent audit, millions of dollars in "federal property" assigned to what is essentially a vast command center for the region, including 159 of the embassy's 1,168 vehicles, are missing or unaccounted for.

Or consider a particularly striking example of military expansion under President Obama, superbly reported by the *Washington Post*'s Karen DeYoung and Greg Jaffe in a piece headlined, "U.S. 'Secret War' Expands Globally as Special Operations Forces Take Larger Role." As a story, it sank without a trace in a country evidently unfazed by the idea of having its forces garrisoned and potentially readying to fight everywhere on the planet. Here's how the piece began: "Beneath its commitment to soft-spoken diplomacy and beyond the combat zones of Afghanistan and Iraq, the Obama administration has significantly expanded a largely secret U.S. war against al-Qaeda and other radical groups, according to senior military and administration officials. Special operations forces have grown both in number and budget, and are deployed in seventy-five countries, compared with about sixty at the beginning of last year."

Now, without opening an atlas, just try to name *any* seventy-five countries on this planet. And yet U.S. special operatives are now engaging in war, or preparing for war, or training others to do so, or covertly collecting intelligence in that many countries across Asia, Africa, the Middle East, and Latin America.

Whatever it is or isn't called, this remains Bush's Global War on Terror on an expansionist trajectory. DeYoung and Jaffe quote an unnamed "senior military official" saying that the Obama administration has allowed "things that the previous administration did not," and report that special operations commanders are now "a far more regular presence at the White House" than in the Bush years. Not surprisingly, those special operations forces have themselves expanded in the first year and a half of the Obama presidency and, for fiscal year 2011, the administration has requested a 5.7 percent hike in their budget to $6.3 billion.

Once upon a time, special operations forces got their name because they were small and "special." Now, they are, in essence, being transformed into a covert military within the military and, as befits their growing size, reports Noah Shachtman of *Wired's Danger Room*, the Army

Special Forces alone are slated to get a new $100 million "headquarters" in northern Afghanistan. It will cover about 17 acres and will include a "communications building, Tactical Operations Center, training facility, medical aid station, Vehicle Maintenance Facility . . . dining facility, laundry facility, and a kennel to support working dogs. . . . Supporting facilities include roads, power production system and electrical distribution, water well, non-potable water production, water storage, water distribution, sanitary sewer collection system, communication manhole/duct system, curbs, walkways, drainage and parking." This headquarters, adds Shachtman, will take a year to build, "at which point, the U.S. is allegedly supposed to begin drawing down its forces in Afghanistan."

### Creeping Gigantism

The first year and a half of the Obama administration has seen a continuation of what could be considered the monumental socialist-realist era of American war-making (including a decision to construct another huge, Baghdad-style "embassy" in Islamabad, Pakistan). This sort of creeping gigantism, with all its assorted cost overruns and private perks, would undoubtedly have seemed familiar to the Soviets. Certainly no less familiar will be the near decade the U.S. military has spent in the Afghan graveyard.

Drunk on war as Washington may be, the United States in 2011 is still not the Soviet Union in 1990—not yet. But it's not the triumphant "sole superpower" anymore, either. Its global power is visibly waning, its ability to win wars distinctly in question, its economic viability open to doubt. Its airports are less shiny and more Third World–like every year. Unlike France or China, it has not a mile of high-speed rail. And when it comes to the future, especially the creation and support of innovative industries in alternative energy, it's chasing the pack. It is increasingly a low-end service economy, losing good jobs that will never return. And if its armies come home in defeat, watch out.

In 1991, the Soviet Union suddenly evaporated. The Cold War was over. Like many wars, it seemed to have an obvious winner and an obvious loser. Nearly twenty years later, as the United States heads down the Soviet road to disaster—even if the world can't imagine what a bankrupt America might mean—it's far clearer that, in the titanic struggle of the two superpowers that we came to call the Cold War, there were actually two losers, and that, when the "second superpower" left the scene, the first was already heading for the exits, just ever so slowly and in a state of self-intoxicated self-congratulation. Nearly every decision in Washington since then, including Barack Obama's to expand both the Afghan War and the war on terror, has only made what was, in 1991, one possible path seem like fate itself.

Call up the Politburo in Washington. We're in trouble.

## The Urge to Surge

Just as 2010 ended, the U.S. military's urge to surge resurfaced in a significant way. "Leaders" in the Obama administration and "senior American military commanders" in Afghanistan slipped information to *New York Times* reporters Mark Mazzetti and Dexter Filkins about secret planning to increase pressure on the Pakistani tribal borderlands via cross-border raids by U.S. Special Operations forces in the new year. In the front-page story those two reporters produced, you could practically slice with a dull knife American military frustration over a war going terribly wrong, over an enemy (shades of Vietnam) with "sanctuaries" for rest, recuperation, and rearming just over an ill-marked, only half-existent border.

You could practically taste the chagrin of the military that their war wasn't proceeding exactly swimmingly. You could practically reach out and be seared by their anger at the Pakistanis for continuing to take American bucks by the billions while playing their own game, rather than an American one, in the region.

If you were of a certain age, you could practically feel (shades of Vietnam again!) that eerily hopeful sense that the next step in spreading the war, the next escalation, could be the decisive one—the familiar conviction that, when things are going badly, the answer is never less, always more.

From this single *New York Times* piece, you can sense just how addictive war is for the war planners. Once you begin down the path of invasion and occupation, turning back is as difficult as an addict going cold turkey. It's easy to forget that war is a drug. When you're high on it, your decisions undoubtedly look as rational, even practical, as the public language you tend to use to describe them. But don't believe it for a second.

Once you've shot up this drug, your thinking is impaired. Through its dream-haze, unpleasant history becomes bunk; what others couldn't do, you fantasize that you can.

Forget the fact that crossing similar borders to get similar information and wipe out similar sanctuaries in Cambodia and Laos in the Vietnam War years led to catastrophe for American planners and the peoples of the region. It only widened that war into what in Cambodia would become auto-genocide. Forget the fact that, no matter whom American raiders might capture, they have no hope of capturing the feeling of nationalism (or the tribal equivalent) that, in the face of foreign invaders or a foreign occupation, keeps the under-armed resilient against the mightiest of forces.

In what the Bush administration used to call "the Greater Middle East," Washington is now in its third and grimmest surge iteration. The first took place in the 1980s during the Reagan administration's anti-Soviet jihad in Afghanistan and proved the highest of highs. The second got rolling as the last century was ending and culminated in the first years of the twenty-first century amid what can only be described as delusions of grandeur or even imperial megalomania. It focused on a global *Pax Americana* and the wars that would extend it into the distant future.

The third started in 2006 in Iraq and is still playing itself out in Afghanistan in 2011. Three decades after the American urge to surge in Afghanistan helped destabilize one imperial superpower, the Soviet Union, the present plans seem to be destabilizing the other superpower of the Cold War era. And what our preeminent group of surgers welcomed as an "unprecedented strategic opportunity" as this century dawned may, in its later stages, be seen as an unprecedented act of strategic desperation.

That, of course, is what drugs, taken over decades, do to you: they give you delusions of grandeur and then leave you on the street, strung out and without much to call your own. Perhaps it's fitting that Afghanistan, the country we helped turn into the planet's leading narco-state, has given us a thirty-year high from hell.

### Getting High in Afghanistan

If you have any doubts, then I suggest you spend some time looking at secret Soviet documents from the USSR's Afghan debacle of the 1980s. It gives you chills to run across Communist Party general secretary Mikhail

Gorbachev at a Politburo meeting in October 1985, almost six years after Soviet troops first flooded into Afghanistan, reading letters aloud to his colleagues from embittered Soviet citizens. ("The Politburo had made a mistake and must correct it as soon as possible—every day precious lives are lost.") Or, in November 1986, insisting to those same colleagues that the Afghan War must be ended in a year, "at maximum, two."

Yet, with the gut-wrenching sureness history offers, you can't help but know that, even two years later, even with a strong desire to leave (which has yet to surface among the Washington elite a decade into our own Afghan adventure), imperial pride and fear of loss of "credibility" would keep the Soviets fighting on to 1989. Or what about Marshal Sergei Akhromeyev offering that same Politburo meeting an assessment that any honest American military commander might offer a quarter century later about our own Afghan adventure: "There is no single piece of land in this country that has not been occupied by a Soviet soldier. Nevertheless, the majority of the territory remains in the hands of the rebels."

Or General Boris Gromov, the commander of the Soviet 40th Army in Afghanistan, boasting "on his last day in the country that '[n]o Soviet garrison or major outpost was ever overrun.'" Or Andrei Gromyko, chairman of the presidium of the Supreme Soviet, emphasizing in 1986 the strategic pleasure of their not-so-secret foe, that other great imperial power of the moment: "Concerning the Americans, they are not interested in the settlement of the situation in Afghanistan. On the contrary, it is to their advantage for the war to drag out." The same might today be said of a far less impressive foe, al-Qaeda.

Or in 1988, with the war still dragging on, to read a "closed" letter the Communist Party distributed to its members explaining how the Afghan fiasco happened (again, the sort of thing that any honest American leader could say of our Afghan War): "In addition, [we] completely disregarded the most important national and historical factors, above all the fact that the appearance of armed foreigners in Afghanistan was always met with arms in the hands [of the population]. . . . One should not disregard the economic factor either. If the enemy in Afghanistan received weapons and ammunition for hundreds of millions and later even billions of dollars, the Soviet-Afghan side also had to shoulder adequate expenditures. The war in Afghanistan costs us 5 billion rubles a year."

Or finally the pathetic letter the Soviet Military Command delivered to the head of the UN mission in Afghanistan on February 14, 1989, arguing (just as the American military high command would do of our war effort) that it was "not only unfair but even absurd to draw . . . parallels" between the Soviet Afghan disaster and the American war in Vietnam. That was, of course, the day the last of one hundred thousand Soviet soldiers— just about the number of American soldiers there in mid-2011—left Afghan soil heading home to a sclerotic country bled dry by war, its infrastructure aging, its economy crumbling. Riddled by drugs and thoroughly demoralized, the Red Army limped home to a society led by a Communist Party significantly delegitimized by its disastrous Afghan adventure, and with its Islamic territories from Chechnya to Central Asia in increasing turmoil. In November of that same year, the Berlin Wall would be torn down, and not long after, the Soviet Union would disappear.

Reading those documents, you can almost imagine CIA director William Webster and "his euphoric 'Afghan Team'" toasting the success of the agency's ten-year effort, its largest paramilitary operation since the Vietnam War. The Reagan administration's surge in Pakistan and Afghanistan had been profligate, involving billions of dollars and a massive propaganda campaign, as well as alliances with the Saudis and a Pakistani dictator and his intelligence service to fund and arm the most extreme of the anti-Soviet jihadists of that moment—"freedom fighters" as they were then commonly called in Washington.

It's easy to imagine the triumphalist mood of celebration among those who had intended to give the Soviet Union a full blast of the Vietnam effect. They had used the "war" part of the Cold War to purposely bleed the less powerful and less wealthy of the two superpowers dry. As President Reagan would write in his memoirs: "The great dynamic of capitalism had given us a powerful weapon in our battle against Communism—money. The Russians could never win the arms race; we could outspend them forever."

By 1990, the urge to surge seemed a success beyond imagining. Forget that it had left more than a million Afghans dead (and more dying), that one-third of that impoverished country's population had been turned into refugees, or that the most extreme of the jihadists, including a group calling itself al-Qaeda, had been brought together, funded, and empowered through the Afghan War. More important, the urge to surge in the region was now in the American bloodstream. And who could ever imagine that, in a new century, "our" freedom fighters would become our sworn enemies, or that the Afghans, that backward people in a poor land, could ever be the sort of impediment to American power that they had been to the Soviets?

The Cold War was over. The surge had it. We were supreme. And what better high could there be than that?

## Fever Dreams of Military Might

Of course, with the Soviet Union gone, there was no military on the planet that could come close to challenging the American one, nor was there a nascent rival on the horizon. Still, a question remained: After centuries of great power rivalry, what did it mean to have a sole superpower on planet Earth, and what path should that triumphant power head down? It took a few years, including passing talk about a possible "peace dividend"—that is, the investment of monies that would have gone into the Pentagon and the military in infrastructural and other domestic projects—for this question to be settled, but settled it was, definitively, on September 12, 2001.

And for all the unknown paths that might have been taken in this unique situation, the one chosen was familiar. It was, of course, the very one that had helped lead the Soviet Union to implosion, the investment of vast national treasure in military power above all else. However, to those high on the urge to surge and now eager to surge globally, when it came to an American future, the fate of the Soviet Union seemed no more relevant than what the Afghans had done to the Red Army. In those glory years, analogies between the greatest power the planet had ever seen and a defeated foe seemed absurd to those who believed themselves the smartest, clearest-headed guys in the room.

Previously, the Cold War arms race, like any race, had involved at least two, and sometimes more, great powers. Now, it seemed, there would be something new under the sun, an arms race of one, as the United States prepared itself for utter dominance into a distant, highly militarized future. The military-industrial complex would, in these years, be further embedded in the warp and woof of American life, the military expanded and privatized (which meant being firmly embraced by crony corporations and hire-a-gun outfits of every sort), and the U.S. "global presence"—from military bases to aircraft-carrier task forces—ballooned until, however briefly, the United States became a military presence unique in the annals of history.

Thanks to the destructive acts of nineteen jihadists, the urge to surge would with finality overwhelm all other urges in the fall of 2001, and there would be a group ready for just such a moment, for (as the newspaper headlines screamed) a "Pearl Harbor of the twenty-first century." To take full stock of that group, however, we would first have to return to June 3, 1997, the day a confident crew of Washington think-tank, academic, and political types calling themselves the Project for the New American Century (PNAC) posted a fin de siècle "statement of principles." In it, they called for "a military that is strong and ready to meet both present and future challenges; a foreign policy that boldly and purposefully promotes American principles abroad; and national leadership that accepts the United States' global responsibilities." Crucially, they were demanding that the Clinton administration, or assumedly some future administration with a better sense of American priorities, "increase defense spending significantly."

The twenty-three men and two women who signed the initial PNAC statement urging the United States to go for the military option in the twenty-first century would, however, prove something more than your typical crew of think-tank types. After all, not so many years later, after a disputed presidential election settled by the Supreme Court, Dick Cheney would be vice president; I. Lewis ("Scooter") Libby would be his right-hand man; Donald Rumsfeld would be secretary of defense, and Paul Wolfowitz would be deputy secretary of defense; Zalmay Khalilzad, head of the Bush-Cheney transition team at the Department of Defense and then the first post-invasion U.S. ambassador to Afghanistan, as well as ambassador to Iraq and the UN; Elliott Abrams, special assistant to the president with a post on the National Security Council; Paula Dobriansky, under secretary of state for democracy and global affairs; Aaron Friedberg, deputy assistant for national security affairs and director of policy planning in the office of the vice president; and Jeb Bush, governor of Florida. (Others like John Bolton, who signed on to PNAC later, would be no less well employed.)

This may, in fact, be the first example in history of a think tank coming to power and actually putting its blue-sky suggestions into operation as government policy, or perhaps it's the only example so far of a government-in-waiting masquerading as think tank. In either case, more than thirteen years later, the success of that group can still take your breath away, as can both the narrowness—and scope—of their thinking, and of their seminal document, "Rebuilding America's Defenses," published in September 2000, two months before George W. Bush took the presidency. This crew of surgers extraordinaires was considering a global situation that, as they saw it, offered Americans an "unprecedented strategic opportunity." Facing a new century, their ambitions were caught by James Peck in his book *Ideal Illusions: How the U.S. Government Co-opted Human Rights*, in this way: "In the [Reagan] era, Washington organized half the planet; in the [Bush era] it sought to organize the whole."

"Rebuilding America's Defenses," if remembered at all today, is recalled mainly for a throwaway sentence that looked ominous indeed in retrospect: "Further, the process of transformation [of the military], even if it brings revolutionary change, is likely to be a long one, absent some catastrophic and catalyzing event—like a new Pearl Harbor." It remains, however, a remarkable document for other reasons. In many ways canny about the direction war would take in the near future, ranging from the role of drones in air war to the onrushing possibility that cyberwar (or "Net-War," as they called it) would be the style of future conflict, it was a clarion call to ensure this country's "unchallenged supremacy" into the distant future by military means alone.

In 1983, in an address to the National Association of Evangelicals, President Ronald Reagan famously called the Soviet Union an "evil empire." It wanted, as he saw it, what all dark empires (and every evildoer in any James Bond film) desires: unchallenged dominion over the planet—and it pursued that dominion in the name of a glorious "world revolution." Now, in the name of American safety and the glories of global democracy, we were—so the PNAC people both pleaded and demanded—to do what only evil empires did and achieve global dominion beyond compare over planet Earth.

We could, they insisted, enforce an American peace, a *Pax Americana*, for decades to come, if only we poured our resources, untold billions (they refused to estimate what the real price might be) into war preparations and, if necessary, war itself, from the seven seas to the heavens, from manifold new "forward operating bases on land" to space and cyberspace. Pushing "the American security perimeter" ever farther into the distant reaches of the planet (and "patrolling" it via "constabulary missions") was, they claimed, the only way that "U.S. military supremacy" could be translated into "American geopolitical preeminence." It was also the only way that the "homeland"—yes, unlike 99.9 percent of Americans before 9/11, they were already using that term—could be effectively "defended."

In making their pitch, they were perfectly willing to acknowledge that the United States was already a military giant among midgets, but they were also eager to suggest that our military situation was "deteriorating" fast, that we were "increasingly ill-prepared" or even in "retreat" on a planet without obvious enemies. They couldn't have thought more globally. (They were, after all, visionaries, as druggies tend to be.) Nor could they have thought longer term. And on military matters, they couldn't have been more up to date.

Yet on the most crucial issues, they—and their documents—couldn't have been dumber or more misguided. They were fundamentalists when it came to the use of force and idolaters on the subject of the U.S. military. They believed it capable of doing just about anything. As a result, they made a massive miscalculation, mistaking military destructiveness for global might. Nor could they have been less interested in the sinews of global economic power (though they did imagine our future enemy to be China). Nor were they capable of imagining that the greatest military power on the planet might be stopped in its tracks—in the Greater Middle East, no less—by a ragtag crew of Iraqis and Afghans. To read "Rebuilding America's Defenses" today is to see the rabbit hole down which, as if in a fever dream, we would soon disappear.

It was a genuine tragedy that they came to power and proceeded to put their military-first policies in place; that, on September 12 of the year that "changed everything," the PNAC people seized the reins of defense and foreign policy, mobilized for war, began channeling American treasure into the military solution they had long desired, and surged. That urge to surge was infamously caught in notes based on Secretary of Defense Donald Rumsfeld's comments taken on September 11, 2001.

"[B]arely five hours after American Airlines Flight 77 plowed into the Pentagon. . . . Rumsfeld was telling his aides to come up with plans for striking Iraq," even though he was already certain that al-Qaeda had launched the attack. ("'Go massive,' the notes quote him as saying. 'Sweep it all up. Things related and not.'") And so they did. They swept up everything and then watched as their dreams and geopolitical calculations were themselves swept into the dustbin of history. And yet the urge to surge, twisted and desperate, did not abate.

To one degree or another, we have been on the Soviet path for years and yet, ever more desperately, we continue to plan additional surges. Our military, like the Soviet one, has not lost a battle and has occupied whatever ground it chose to take. Yet, in the process, it has won less than nothing at all. Our country, still far wealthier than the Soviet Union ever was, has nonetheless entered its Soviet phase. At home, in the increasing emphasis on surveillance of every sort, there is even a hint of what made "soviet" and "totalitarian" synonymous.

The U.S. economy looks increasingly sclerotic as state and city governments are laying off teachers, police, even firefighters, Americans are unemployed in near record numbers, global oil prices are ominously on the rise, and yet taxpayer money continues to pour into the military and into its foreign wars. It has recently been estimated, for instance, that after spending $11.6 billion in 2011 on the training, supply, and support of the Afghan army and police, the U.S. government will continue to spend an average of $6.2 billion a year at least through 2015—and that's but one expense in the estimated $120 billion a year being spent at present on the Afghan War, what can only be described as part of our war stimulus package abroad.

Sooner than later, Washington, the Pentagon, and the U.S. military will have to enter rehab. They desperately need a twelve-step program for recovery. Until then, the delusions and the madness that go with surge addiction are not likely to end.

## Osama bin Laden's American Legacy

Back in the 1960s, Senator George Aiken of Vermont offered two American presidents a plan for dealing with the Vietnam War: declare victory and go home. Roundly ignored at the time, it's a plan worth considering again today for a war in Afghanistan and Pakistan now more than a decade old.

Osama bin Laden has, of course, been eliminated. Literally. By Navy SEALS. Or as one of a crowd of revelers who appeared in front of the White House the night his killing was announced put it on an impromptu sign riffing on *The Wizard of Oz*: "Ding, Dong, Bin Laden Is Dead." And wouldn't it be easy if he had indeed been the Wicked Witch of the West and all we needed to do was click those ruby slippers three times, say "there's no place like home," and be back in Kansas. Or if this were V-J day and a sailor's kiss said it all.

Unfortunately, in every way that matters for Americans, it's an illusion that Osama bin Laden is dead. In every way that matters, he will fight on, barring a major Obama administration policy shift in Afghanistan, and it's we who will ensure that he remains on the battlefield that George W. Bush's administration once so grandiosely labeled the Global War on Terror.

Admittedly, the Arab world had largely left bin Laden in the dust even before he took that bullet to the head. There, the focus was on the Arab Spring, the massive, ongoing, largely nonviolent protests that shook the region and its autocrats to their roots. In that part of the world, his death was, as Tony Karon of *Time* magazine wrote, "little more than a historical footnote," and his dreams are now essentially meaningless.

Consider it an insult to irony, but the world bin Laden really changed forever wasn't the Greater Middle East. It was here. Cheer his death, bury him at sea, don't release any photos, and he'll still carry on as a ghost as long as Washington continues to fight its deadly, disastrous wars in his old neighborhood.

### The Tao of Terrorism

If analogies to *The Wizard of Oz* were in order, bin Laden might better be compared to that film's wizard rather than the wicked witch. After all, he was, in a sense, a small man behind a vast screen on which his frail frame took on, in the United States, the hulking proportions of a supervillain, if not a rival superpower. In actuality, al-Qaeda, his organization, was, at best, a ragtag crew that, even before it was embattled and on the run, had the most limited of operational capabilities. Yes, it could mount spectacularly murderous actions, but only one of them every year or two.

Bin Laden was never "Hitler," nor were his henchmen the Nazis, nor did they add up to Stalin and his minions. The nearest thing al-Qaeda had to a state was the impoverished, ravaged, Taliban-controlled part of Afghanistan where some of its camps were once sheltered. Even the money available to bin Laden, while significant, wasn't much to brag about. The 9/11 attacks were estimated to cost $400,000 to $500,000, which in superpower terms is pure chump change.

Despite the apocalyptic look of the destruction bin Laden's followers caused in New York and at the Pentagon, he and his crew of killers represented a relatively modest, distinctly non-world-ending challenge to the United States. And had the Bush administration focused the same energies on hunting him down that it put into invading and occupying Afghanistan and then Iraq, can there be any question that almost ten years wouldn't have passed before he was killed or, as will now never happen, was brought to trial?

It was our misfortune and Osama bin Laden's good luck that Washington's dreams were not those of a global policeman intent on bringing a criminal operation to justice, but of an imperial power whose leaders wanted to lock the oil heartlands of the planet down for decades to come. After all, while bin Laden only had the ability to launch major operations every couple of years, Washington—with almost unlimited amounts of money, weapons, and troops at its command—was capable of launching operations every day.

In a sense, after 9/11, bin Laden commanded Washington by taking possession of its deepest fears and desires and turning them to his own ends, the way a bot takes over a computer. It was he who ensured that the invasion and occupation of Afghanistan would be put into motion. It was he who also ensured that the invasion and occupation of Iraq would be launched. It was he who brought America's Afghan War to Pakistan, and American aircraft, bombs, and missiles to Somalia and Yemen to fight that Global War on Terror. And for the last near-decade, he did all this the way a Tai Chi master fights: using not his own minimal strength but our massive destructive power to create the sort of mayhem in which he undoubtedly imagined that an organization like his could thrive.

Don't be surprised, then, that prior to his death, bin Laden seems to have been sequestered in a walled compound in a resort area just north of the Pakistani capital, Islamabad, doing next to nothing. Think of him as practicing the Tao of Terrorism. And the less he did, the fewer operations he was capable of launching, the more the American military did for him in creating what collapsing Chinese dynasties used to call "chaos under heaven."

### Dead and Alive

As is now obvious, bin Laden's greatest wizardry was performed on us, not on the Arab world, where the movements he spawned from Yemen to North Africa have proven remarkably peripheral and unimportant. He helped open us up to all the nightmares we could visit upon ourselves (and others). In many ways, he broke us not on 9/11 but in the months and years thereafter. As a result, if we don't have the sense to follow Senator Aiken's advice, the wars we continue to fight with disastrous results will prove to be bin Laden's monument, and our imperial graveyard.

Now that the celebrations and partying over his death have long faded, we are once again left with the tattered American world bin Laden willed us, and it's easier to see just how paltry a thing this "victory" of his killing was. For all the print devoted to the operation that took him out, all the hosannas lavished on American Special Ops forces, the president, his planners, and various intelligence outfits, this was hardly a glorious American moment. If anything, we should probably be in mourning for what we buried long before we had bin Laden's body, for what we allowed him (and our own imperial greed) to goad us into doing to ourselves, and what, in the course of so doing, we did, in the name of fighting him, to others.

Those chants of "U-S-A! U-S-A!" on the announcement of his death were but faint echoes of the ones at Ground Zero on September 14, 2001, when President George W. Bush picked up a bullhorn and promised "the people who knocked these buildings down will hear all of us soon!" That would be the beginning of a brief few years of soaring American hubris and fantasies of domination wilder than those of any caliphate-obsessed

Islamic fundamentalist terrorist, and soon enough they would leave us high and dry in our present world.

Unless we set aside the special ops assaults and the drone wars and take a chance, unless we're willing to follow the example of all those non-violent demonstrators across the Greater Middle East and begin a genuine and speedy withdrawal from the Af-Pak theater of operations, Osama bin Laden will never die.

On September 17, 2001, President Bush was asked whether he wanted bin Laden dead. He replied: "There's an old poster out West, as I recall, that said 'wanted dead or alive.'" Dead or alive. Now, it turns out that there was a third option. Dead and alive.

The chance exists to put a stake through the heart of Osama bin Laden's legacy. After all, the man who officially started it all is gone. We could declare victory, Toto, and head for home. But why do I think that, on this score, the malign wizard is likely to win?

## Goodbye to All That

As we watched the dramatic events of the Arab Spring of 2011 in the Middle East, you would hardly have known that we had a thing to do with them. Oh, yes, in the name of its War on Terror, Washington had for years backed most of the thuggish governments that were under siege. When it came to Egypt in particular, there was initially much polite (and hypocritical) discussion in the media about how our "interests" and our "values" were in conflict, about how far the United States should back off its support for the regime of Egyptian autocrat Hosni Mubarak, and about what a "tightrope" the Obama administration was walking. While the president and his officials flailed, the mildest of questions were raised about how much we should chide our erstwhile allies, or encourage the massed protestors, and about whether we should "take sides" (as though we hadn't done so decisively in the previous decades).

With popular cries for "democracy" and "freedom" sweeping the Middle East, it's curious to note that the Bush-era's now-infamous "democracy agenda" has been nowhere in sight. In its brief and disastrous life, it was used as a battering ram for regimes Washington loathed and offered as a soft pillow of future possibility to those it loved.

Still, there's a story in a Washington stunned and "blindsided," in an administration visibly toothless and in disarray as well as dismayed over the loss of its Egyptian ally, "the keystone of its Middle Eastern policy," that's so big it should knock your socks off: Almost twenty years after the lesser superpower of the Cold War left the world stage, the "victor" is now lurching down the declinist slope. So don't mark the end of the Cold War in 1991 as our conventional histories do. Mark it in the early days of 2011, which served as a symbolic goodbye-to-all-that for the planet's "sole superpower."

### Abroads, Near and Far

The proximate cause of Washington's defeat is a collapse of its imperial position in a region that, ever since President Jimmy Carter proclaimed his Carter Doctrine in 1980, has been considered the crucible of global power. Today, "people power" has shaken the pillars of that American position in the Middle East, while—despite the staggering levels of military might the Pentagon still has embedded in the area—the Obama administration has found itself standing by helplessly and in grim confusion.

As a spectacle of imperial power on the decline, we haven't seen anything like it since 1989 when the Berlin Wall came down. Then, too, people power stunned the world. It swept like lightning across the satellite states of Eastern Europe, those "pillars" of the old Soviet Empire, most of which had (like the Middle East) seemed quiescent for years. It was an invigorating time. After all, such moments often don't come once in a life, no less twice in twenty years. If you don't happen to live in Washington, the Arab Spring is proving no less remarkable, unpredictable, and earthshaking than its predecessor.

What we're dealing with is, in a sense, the story of two "abroads." In 1990, in the wake of a disastrous war in Afghanistan, in the midst of a people's revolt, the Russians lost what they came to call their "near abroad," the lands from Eastern Europe to Central Asia that had made up the Soviet Empire. The United States had something the Soviets never possessed. Call it a "far abroad." Now, in the midst of another draining, disastrous Afghan War, in the face of another people's revolt, a critical part of its far abroad is being shaken to its core.

In the Middle East, the two pillars of American imperial power and control have long been Egypt and Saudi Arabia—along, of course, with obdurate Israel and little Jordan. In previous eras, the chosen bulwarks of "stability" and "moderation," terms much favored in Washington, had been the shah of Iran in the 1960s and 1970s (and you remember his fate), and Saddam Hussein in the 1980s (and you remember his, too). In the larger region the Bush administration liked to call "the Greater Middle East" or "the arc of instability," another key pillar has been Pakistan, a country now in destabilization mode under the pressure of a disastrous American war in Afghanistan.

The question is: How did this happen? And the answer, in part, is: blame it on the way the Cold War officially ended, the mood of unparalleled hubris in which the United States emerged from it, and the unilateralist path its leaders chose in its wake.

### Second-Wave Unilateralism

When the Soviet Union dissolved, Washington was stunned—the collapse was unexpected despite all the signs that something monumental was afoot—and then thrilled. The Cold War was over and we had won. It didn't take long for the talk to begin about how our power and glory would outshine even the Roman and British Empires. The conclusion that this victory—as in World War II—would have its benefits, that the world was now our oyster, led to two waves of American "unilateralism" or go-it-alone-ism that essentially drove the car of state directly toward the nearest cliff and helped prepare the way for the sudden eruption of people power in the Middle East.

The second of those waves began with the fateful post-9/11 decision of George W. Bush, Dick Cheney, Donald Rumsfeld, and company to "drain the global swamp." They would, that is, pursue al-Qaeda (and whomever else they decided to label an enemy) by full military means. That included the invasion of Afghanistan and the issuing of a with-us-or-against-us diktat to Pakistan, which reportedly included the threat to bomb that country "back to the Stone Age." It also involved a full-scale militarization, Pentagonization, and privatization of American foreign policy, and above all else, the crushing of Iraqi dictator Saddam Hussein and the occupation of his country. All that and more came to be associated with the term "unilateralism," with the idea that U.S. military power was so overwhelming Washington could simply go it alone in the world with any "coalition of the billing" it might muster and still get exactly what it wanted.

That second wave of unilateralism, now largely relegated to the memory hole of history by the mainstream media, helped pave the way for the upheavals in Tunisia, Egypt, and possibly elsewhere. As a start, from Pakistan to North Africa, the Bush administration's Global War on Terror, along with its support for thuggish rule in the name of fighting al-Qaeda, helped radicalize the region. Remember, for instance, that while Washington was pouring billions of dollars into the American-equipped Egyptian Army and the American-trained Egyptian officer corps, Bush administration officials were delighted to enlist the Mubarak regime as War on Terror warriors and use Egypt's jails as places to torture terror suspects rendered off streets anywhere on Earth.

In the process, by sweeping an area from North Africa to the Chinese border that it dubbed the Greater Middle East into that War on Terror, the Bush administration undoubtedly gave the region a newfound sense of unity, a feeling that the fate of its disparate parts was somehow bound together. In addition, Bush's top officials, fundamentalists all when it came to U.S. military might, had immense power at their command. They gave that power the snappy label "shock and awe," and then used it to blow a hole in the heart of the Middle East by invading Iraq. In the process, they put that land, already on the ropes, on life support.

It's never really come off. In the wars, civil and guerrilla, set off by the American invasion and occupation, hundreds of thousands of Iraqis undoubtedly died and millions more were sent into exile abroad or in their own land. Today, Iraq remains a barely breathing carcass of a nation, unable to deliver something as simple as electricity to its restive people or pump enough oil to pay for the disaster.

At the same time, the Bush administration sat on its hands while Israel had its way, taking Palestinian lands via its settlement policies and blowing its own hole in southern Lebanon with American backing (and weaponry) in the summer of 2006, and a smaller hole of utter devastation through Gaza in 2009. In other words, from Lebanon to Pakistan, the Greater Middle East was destabilized and radicalized. The acts of Bush's officials couldn't have been rasher, or more destructive. They managed, for instance, to turn Afghanistan into the globe's foremost narco-state, even as they gave new life to the Taliban—no small miracle for a movement that, in 2001, had lost its last vestige of popularity. Most crucial of all, they, and the Obama administration after them, spread the war irrevocably to populous, nuclear-armed Pakistan.

To their mad plans and projects you can trace, at least in part, the rise to power of Hezbollah in Lebanon and Hamas in the Gaza Strip (the only significant result of Bush's "democracy agenda," since Iraq's elections arrived, despite Bush administration opposition, due to the prestige of Ayatollah Ali al-Sistani). You can credit them with an Iran-allied Shiite government in Iraq and a resurgent Taliban in Afghanistan, as well as with the growth of a version of Taliban in Pakistan's tribal borderlands. You can also credit them with the disorganization and impoverishment of the region. In summary, when the Bush unilateralists took control of the car of state, they souped it up, armed it to the teeth, and sent it careering off to catastrophe.

How hollow the neocon quip of 2003 now rings: "Everyone wants to go to Baghdad. Real men want to go to Tehran." But remember too that, however much the Bush administration accomplished (in a manner of speaking), there was a wave of unilateralism, no less significant, that preceded it.

## Our Financial Jihadists

Though we all know this first wave well, we don't usually think of it as "unilateralist," or in terms of the Middle East at all, or speak about it in the same breath with the Bush administration and its neocon supporters. I'm talking about the globalists, sometimes called the neoliberals, who were let loose to do their damnedest in the good times of the post–Cold War Clinton years. They, too, were dreamy about organizing the planet and about another kind of American power that was never going to end: economic power. (And, of course, they would be called back to power in Washington in the Obama years to run the U.S. economy into the ground yet again.) They believed deeply that we were the economic superpower of the ages, and they were eager to create their own version of a *Pax Americana*. Intent on homogenizing the world by bringing American economic power to bear on it, their version of shock-and-awe tactics involved calling in institutions like the International Monetary

Fund (IMF) to discipline developing countries into a profitable kind of poverty and misery.

In the end, as they gleefully sliced and diced subprime mortgages, they drove a different kind of hole through the world. They were financial jihadists with their own style of shock-and-awe tactics and they, too, proved deeply destructive, even if in a different way. The irony was that, in the economic meltdown of 2008, they finally took down the global economy they had helped "unify." And that occurred just as the second wave of unilateralists were facing the endgame of their dreams of global domination. In the process, for instance, Egypt, the most populous of Arab countries, was economically neoliberalized and, except for a small elite who made out like the bandits, they were impoverished.

Talk about "creative destruction." The two waves of American unilateralists nearly took down the planet. They let loose demons of every sort, even as they ensured that the world's first experience of a sole superpower would prove short indeed. Heap onto the rubble they left behind the global disaster of rising prices for the basics—food and fuel—and you have a situation so combustible that no one should have been surprised when a Tunisian match lit it aflame.

Nobody today remembers how, in September 2004, Amr Musa, the head of the Arab League, described the post-invasion Iraqi situation. "The gates of hell," he said, "are open in Iraq." This was not the sort of language we were used to hearing in the United States, no matter what you felt about the war. It read like an over-the-top metaphor, but it could as easily be taken as a realistic depiction of what happened not just in Iraq, but in the Greater Middle East and, to some extent, in the world.

Our unilateralists twice drove blithely through those gates, imagining that they were the gates to paradise. The results are now clear for all to see. And the gates of hell remain open.

# CHAPTER 3

# Their Dead and Ours

## The View from Mount Olympus

The Greeks had it right. When you live on Mount Olympus, your view of humanity is qualitatively different. The Greek gods, after all, lied to, stole from, lusted for, and punished humanity without mercy while taking the planet for a spin. And it didn't bother them a bit. They felt—so Greek mythology tells us—remarkably free to intervene from the heights in the affairs of whichever mortals caught their attention and, in the process, to do whatever took their fancy without thinking much about the nature of human lives. If they sometimes felt sympathy for the mortals whose lives they repeatedly threw into havoc, they were incapable of real empathy. Such is the nature of the world when your view is the Olympian one and what you see from the heights are so many barely distinguishable mammals scurrying about.

In early April 2010, a modern example of what it means to act from the heights was available for all to see when the website WikiLeaks released a decrypted July 2007 video of two U.S. Apache helicopters attacking Iraqis on a street in Baghdad. At least twelve Iraqis, including two employees of the Reuters news agency, a photographer and his driver, were killed in the incident, and two children in the vehicle of a good Samaritan who stopped to pick up casualties and died in the process were also wounded.

Without a doubt, that video is a remarkable seventeen-minute demonstration of how to efficiently slaughter tiny beings from on high. There is no way American helicopter crews could know just who was walking down there—Sunni or Shiite, insurgent or shopper, Baghdadis with intent to harm Americans or Baghdadis paying little attention to two of the helicopters then so regularly buzzing the city. Were they killers, guards, bank clerks, unemployed idlers, Baathist Party members, religious fanatics, café owners? Who could tell from such a height? But the details mattered little.

The Reuters cameraman crouches behind a building looking, camera first, around a corner, and you hear an American in an Apache yell, "He's got an RPG!"—mistaking his camera with its long-range lens for a rocket-propelled grenade launcher. The pilot, of course, doesn't know that it's a Reuters photographer down there. Only we do. (And when his death did become known, the military carefully buried the video.) Along with that video comes a soundtrack in which you hear the Americans check out the rules of engagement, request permission to fire, and banter about the results. ("Hahaha. I hit 'em"; "Oh yeah, look at those dead bastards . . ."; and of the two wounded children, "Well, it's their fault bringing their kids into a battle.") Such callous chitchat is explained away in media articles here by the need of those whose job it is to kill for "psychological distance," but in truth that's undoubtedly the way you talk when you, and only you, have godlike access to the skies and can hover over the rest of humanity making preparations to wipe out lesser beings.

Another example of our Olympian detachment came in predawn darkness on February 12, 2010, in Paktia Province, eastern Afghanistan, when a U.S. Special Operations team dropped from the skies into a village near Gardez. There, in a world that couldn't be more distant from their lives, possibly based on an informant's bad tip, American snipers on rooftops killed an Afghan police officer ("head of intelligence in one of Paktia's most volatile districts"), his brother, and three women—a pregnant mother of ten, a pregnant mother of six, and a teenager. They then evidently dug the bullets out of the women's bodies, bound and gagged them, and filed a report claiming that the dead men were Taliban militants who had murdered the women—"honor killings"—before they arrived.

That was how the American press, generally reliant on military handouts, initially reported the story. Fortunately, in the face of some good on-the-spot journalism by an unembedded British reporter, this cover-up story ingloriously disintegrated, while U.S. military spokespeople retreated step by step in a series of partial admissions of error, leading to an in-person apology, including the sacrifice of a sheep and $30,000 in compensation payments.

## Ceremonial Evisceration

Both incidents elicited shock and anger from critics of American war policies. And both incidents are shocking. Probably the most shocking aspect of them, however, is just how humdrum they actually were. Start with one detail in those Afghan murders, reported in most accounts but little emphasized: what the Americans descended on was a traditional family ceremony. More than twenty-five guests had gathered for the naming of a newborn child.

In fact, over the past decade, Afghan and Iraqi ceremonies of all sorts have regularly been blasted away. Keeping a partial tally of wedding parties eradicated by American air power at TomDispatch.com, I had counted five such "incidents" between December 2001 and July 2008. A sixth in July 2002 in which possibly forty Afghan wedding celebrants died and many more were wounded has since come to my attention, as has a seventh that took place in August 2008. Other kinds of rites where significant numbers of Afghans gather have not been immune from attack, including funerals, and now, naming ceremonies. And keep in mind that these are only the reported incidents in a rural land where much undoubtedly goes unreported.

Even General Stanley McChrystal, former commander of U.S. forces in Afghanistan, expressed surprise at a tally of at least thirty Afghans killed and eighty wounded at checkpoints when U.S. soldiers opened fire on cars. He said: "We have shot an amazing number of people, but to my knowledge, none has ever proven to be a threat."

Take thirty-six-year-old Mohammed Yonus, a popular imam of a mosque on the outskirts of Kabul, who was killed in his car by fire from a passing NATO convoy, which considered his vehicle "threatening." His seven-year-old son was in the back seat. Or while on the subject of

Reuters employees, recall reporter Mazen Tomeizi, a Palestinian producer for the al-Arabiya satellite network of Dubai, who was killed on Haifa Street in central Baghdad in September 2004 in a U.S. helicopter attack. He was on camera at the time and his blood spattered the lens. Seif Fouad, a Reuters cameraman, was wounded in the same incident, while a number of bystanders, including a girl, were killed.

Or remember the seventeen Iraqi civilians infamously murdered when Blackwater employees in a convoy began firing in Nissour Square in Baghdad on September 16, 2007. Or the missiles regularly shot from U.S. helicopters and unmanned aerial drones into the heavily populated Shiite slum of Sadr City back in 2007 and 2008. Or the Iraqis regularly killed at checkpoints in the years since the invasion of 2003. Or, for that matter, the first moments of that invasion on March 20, 2003, when, according to Human Rights Watch, "dozens" of ordinary Iraqi civilians were killed in the fifty aerial "decapitation strikes" the Bush administration launched against Saddam Hussein and the rest of the Iraqi leadership, missing every one of them.

This is the indiscriminate nature of killing, no matter how "precise" and "surgical" the weaponry, when war is made by those who command the heavens and descend, as if from Mars, into alien worlds, convinced that they have the power to sort out the good from the bad, even if they can't tell villagers from insurgents. Under these circumstances, death comes in a multitude of disguises—from a great distance via cruise missiles or Predator drones to close up at checkpoints where armored American troops, fingers on triggers, have no way of telling a suicide bomber from a confused or panicked local with a couple of kids in the backseat.

It comes repetitively when U.S. Special Operations forces helicopter into villages after dark looking for terror suspects based on tips from unreliable informants who may be settling local scores of which the soldiers are dismally ignorant. It comes repeatedly to Afghan police or army troops mistaken for the enemy.

It came not just to a police officer and his brother and family in Paktia Province, but to a "wealthy businessman with construction and security contracts with the nearby American base at Shindand airport" who, along with up to seventy-six members of his extended family, was slaughtered in such a raid on the village of Azizabad in Herat Province in August 2008. It came to the family of Awal Khan, an Afghan army artillery commander (away in another province) whose "schoolteacher wife, a seventeen-year-old daughter named Nadia, a fifteen-year-old son, Aimal, and his brother, employed by a government department" were killed in April 2009 in a U.S.-led raid in Khost Province in eastern Afghanistan. (Another daughter was wounded and the pregnant wife of Khan's cousin was shot five times in the abdomen.)

It came to twelve Afghans by a roadside near the city of Jalalabad in April 2007 when marine special operations forces, attacked by a suicide bomber, let loose along a ten-mile stretch of road. Victims included a four-year-old girl, a one-year-old boy, and three elderly villagers. According to a report by Carlotta Gall of the *New York Times*, a "16-year-old newly married girl was cut down while she was carrying a bundle of grass to her family's farmhouse. . . . A 75-year-old man walking to his shop was hit by so many bullets that his son did not recognize the body when he came to the scene."

It came in November 2009 to two relatives of Majidullah Qarar, the spokesman for the minister of agriculture, who were shot down in cold blood in Ghazni City in another special operations night raid. It came in Uruzgan Province in February 2010 when U.S. Special Forces troops in helicopters struck a convoy of minibuses, killing up to twenty-seven civilians, including women and children. And it came on April 5, 2010, in an airstrike in Helmand Province in southern Afghanistan in which a residence was hit and four civilians—two women, an elderly man, and a child—were killed along with four men, immediately identified in a NATO press release as "suspected insurgents." And it came one week later on the outskirts of Kandahar, when U.S. troops opened fire on a bus, killing five civilians (including a woman), wounding more, and sparking angry protests.

## Planetary Predators

Whether in the skies or patrolling on the ground, Americans know next to nothing of the worlds they are passing above or through. This is, of course, even more true of the "pilots" who fly our latest wonder weapons, the Predators, Reapers, and other unmanned drones over American battle zones, while sitting at consoles somewhere in the United States. They are clearly engaged in the most literal of video-game wars, while living the most prosaic of godlike lives. A sign at Creech Air Force Base in Nevada warns such a drone pilot to "drive carefully" on leaving the base after a work shift "in" Afghanistan or Iraq. This, it says, is "the most dangerous part of your day."

One instructor of drone pilots has described this form of warfare vividly: "Flying a Predator is like a chess game.... Because you have a God's-eye perspective, you need to think a few moves ahead." However much you may "think ahead," though, the tiny, barely distinguishable creatures you're deciding whether or not to eradicate certainly don't inhabit the same universe as you, with your own looming needs, troubles, and concerns.

Here's the fact of the matter: in the cities, towns, and villages of the distant lands where Americans tend to make war, civilians die regularly and repeatedly at our hands. Each death may contain its own uniquely nightmarish details, but the overall story remains remarkably repetitious. Such "incidents" are completely predictable. Even General McChrystal, determined to "protect the population" in Afghanistan as part of his counterinsurgency war, has proven remarkably incapable of changing the nature of our style of warfare. Curtail air strikes, rein in special operations night attacks—none of it will, in the long run, matter. Put in a nutshell: If you arrive from the heavens, they will die.

Having watched the death of his son, the twenty-two-year-old Reuters photographer Namir Noor-Eldeen, in that July 2007 video, his father said: "At last the truth has been revealed, and I'm satisfied God revealed the truth.... If such an incident took place in America, even if an animal were killed like this, what would they do?" Noor-Eldeen may not have gone far enough. For that helicopter crew, his son was indeed the wartime equivalent of a hunted animal. An article on the front page of the *New York Times* captured this perspective, however inadvertently, when, speaking of the CIA's aerial war over Pakistan's tribal borderlands, it described the agency's unmanned drones as "observing and tracking targets, then unleashing missiles on their quarry." The word *quarry* has quite a straightforward definition: "a hunted animal; prey." Indeed, the al-Qaeda leaders, Taliban militants, and local civilians in the region are all "prey" which, of course, makes us the predators. That the majority of drones cruising those skies 24-7 and repeatedly launching their Hellfire missiles are named "Predators" should come as no surprise.

Americans are unused to being the prey in war and so essentially incapable of imagining what that actually means, day in, day out, year after year. We prefer to think of *their* deaths as so many accidents or mistakes—"collateral damage"—when they are the norm, not what's collateral in such wars. We prefer to imagine ourselves bringing the best of values and intentions to a backward, ignorant world and so invariably make ourselves sound far kindlier than we are. Like the gods of Olympus, we have a tendency to flatter ourselves, even as we continually remake the "rules of engagement" to suit our changing tastes and needs, while creating a language of war that suits our tender sensibilities about ourselves.

In this way, for instance, assassination-by-drone has become an ever more central part of the Obama administration's foreign and war policy, and yet the word *assassination*—with all its negative implications, legal and otherwise—has been displaced by the far more anodyne, bureaucratic term *targeted killing*. In a sense, in fact, what "enhanced interrogation techniques" were to the Bush administration, "targeted killing" is to the Obama administration.

For the gods, anything is possible. In the language of Olympian war, for instance, even sitting at a console thousands of miles from the not-quite-humans you are preparing to obliterate can become an act worthy of Homeric praise. As Greg Jaffe of the *Washington Post* reported, Colonel Eric Mathewson, the air force officer with the most experience with unmanned aircraft, has a new notion of "valor," a word "which is a part of almost every combat award citation." "Valor to me is not risking your life," he says. "Valor is doing what is right. Valor is about your motivations and the ends that you seek. It is doing what is right for the right reasons."

What the gods do is, by definition, glorious.

## Descending from on High

It's not only the American way of war, but the American way of statecraft that arrives as if from the heavens, ready to impose its own definitions of the good and necessary on the world. American officials, civilian and military, constantly fly into the embattled (and let's be blunt: Muslim) regions of the planet to make demands, order, chide, plead, wheedle, cajole, intimidate, threaten, twist arms, and bluster to get our "allies" to do what we most want.

Our special plenipotentiaries, our envoys, our secretary of state, our chairman of the Joint Chiefs, our Centcom commander, and our secretary of defense descend from the clouds on Islamabad, Kabul, or Baghdad frequently. Our vice president careens Iraq-wards to help mediate disputes, and even our president, the "heaviest political artillery" (as one analyst called him), dropped in for a six-hour visit to "Afghanistan" (actually the hanger of a large American air base and the presidential palace in Kabul) in 2010. While there—as American papers reported quite proudly—he chided and "pressed" Afghan president Hamid Karzai, offered "pointed criticism" on corruption, and delivered "a tough message." He then returned to the United States to find, to the surprise and frustration of his top officials, that Karzai—almost immediately accused of being unstable, possibly on drugs, and prone to childlike tantrums—responded by lashing out at his American minders.

We are, of course, the rational ones, the grown-ups, the good governance team, the incorruptible crew who bring enlightenment and democracy to the world, even if, as practical gods, in support of our Afghan War we're perfectly willing to shore up a corrupt autocrat elsewhere who is willing to lend us an air base (for $60 million a year in rent) to haul in troops and supplies—until he falls.

All of this is par for the course for the Olympians from North America. It all seems normal, even benign, except in the rare moments when videos of slaughter begin to circulate. Viewed from the ground up, however, we undoubtedly seem as petulant as the gods or demiurges of some malign religion, or as the aliens and predators of some horrific sci-fi film— heartless, unfeeling, and murderous. As Safa Chmagh, the brother of one of the Reuters employees who died in the 2007 Apache attack, reportedly said: "The pilot is not human, he's a monster. What did my brother do? What did his children do? Does the pilot accept his kids to be orphans?"

As with tales humans tell of the gods, there's a moral here: If you want it to be otherwise, don't descend on strange lands armed to the teeth, prepared to occupy, and ready to kill.

## The Perfect American Weapon

Before George W. Bush had his fever dream, the United States had already put its first unmanned aerial vehicles (UAVs) or drone surveillance planes in the skies over Kosovo in the late 1990s. By November 2001, it had armed them with missiles and was flying them over Afghanistan. In November 2002, a Predator drone would loose a Hellfire missile on a car in Yemen, a country with which we weren't at war. Six suspected al-Qaeda members, including a suspect in the bombing of the USS *Cole*, would be turned into twisted metal and ash—the first "targeted killings" of the American robotic era.

Just two months earlier, in September 2002, as the Bush administration was "introducing" its campaign to sell an invasion of Iraq to Congress and the American people, CIA director George Tenet and Vice President Dick Cheney "trooped up to Capitol Hill" to brief four top Senate and House leaders on a hair-raising threat to the country. A "smoking gun" had been uncovered. According to "new intelligence," Iraqi dictator Saddam Hussein had in his possession unmanned aerial vehicles advanced enough to be armed with biological and chemical weaponry. Worse yet, these were capable—so the CIA director and vice president claimed—of spraying those weapons of mass destruction over cities on the East Coast of the United States.

It was just the sort of evil plan you might have expected from a man regularly compared to Adolf Hitler in our media, and the news evidently made an impression in Congress. Democratic senator Bill Nelson of Florida, for example, said that he voted for the administration's resolution authorizing force in Iraq because "I was told not only that [Saddam had weapons of mass destruction] and that he had the means to deliver them through unmanned aerial vehicles, but that he had the capability of transporting those UAVs outside of Iraq and threatening the homeland here in America, specifically by putting them on ships off the eastern seaboard."

In a speech in October 2002, President Bush offered a version of this apocalyptic nightmare to the American public. Of course, like Saddam's supposed ability to produce "mushroom clouds" over American cities, the Iraqi autocrat's advanced UAVs (along with the ships needed to position them off the U.S. coast) were a feverish fantasy of the Bush era and would soon enough be forgotten.

Instead, in the years to come, it would be American pilotless drones that would repeatedly attack Iraqi urban areas with Hellfire missiles and bombs. In those years, our drones would also strike repeatedly in Afghanistan, and especially in the tribal borderlands of Pakistan, where in an escalating "secret" or "covert" war, which has been no secret to anyone, multiple drone attacks often occur weekly. They are now considered so much the norm that, with humdrum headlines slapped on ("U.S. missile strike kills 12 in NW Pakistan"), they barely make it out of summary articles about war developments in the American press.

And yet those robotic planes, with their young "pilots" (as well as the camera operators and intelligence analysts who make up a drone "crew") sitting in front of consoles 7,000 miles away from where their missiles and bombs are landing, have become another kind of American fever dream. The drone is our latest wonder weapon and a bragging point in a set of wars where there has been little enough to brag about. CIA director Leon Panetta has, for instance, called the agency's drones flying over Pakistan "the only game in town" when it comes to destroying al-Qaeda.

A typically anonymous U.S. official in a *Washington Post* report claimed of drone missile attacks, "We're talking about precision unsurpassed in the history of warfare." Or as Gordon Johnson of the Pentagon's Joint Forces Command told author Peter Singer, speaking of the glories of drones: "They don't get hungry. They are not afraid. They don't forget their orders. They don't care if the guy next to them has been shot. Will they do a better job than humans? Yes."

Seven thousand of them, the vast majority of the surveillance variety, are reportedly already being operated by the military, and that's before swarms of "mini-drones" come online. Our American world is being redefined accordingly.

### Smoking Drones

These days, CIA and administration officials troop up to Capitol Hill to offer briefings to Congress on the miraculous value of pilotless drones: in disrupting al-Qaeda, destroying its leadership or driving it "deeper into hiding," and taking out key figures in the Taliban. Indeed, what started as a 24-7 assassination campaign against al-Qaeda's top leadership has already widened considerably. The "target set" has by now reportedly expanded to take in ever lower-level militants in the tribal borderlands. In other words, a drone assassination campaign is morphing into the first full-scale drone war. And, as in all wars from the air, civilians are dying in unknown numbers.

If the temperature is again rising in Washington when it comes to these weapons, this time it's a fever of enthusiasm for the spectacular future of drones. The air force has in fact, plotted out that future to the year 2047, to a time when single pilots should be able to handle multiple drones in operations in the skies over some embattled land, and both to a far more distant moment when those drones should be able to handle themselves, flying, fighting, and making key decisions about just who to take out without a human being having to intervene.

When *we* possess such weaponry, it turns out, there's nothing unnerving or disturbing, apocalyptic or dystopian about it. Today, in the American homeland, not a single smoking drone is in sight.

Now it's the United States whose drones are ever more powerfully weaponized. It's the United States that is developing a twenty-two ton, tail-less drone twenty times larger than a Predator that can fly at Mach 7 and (theoretically) land on the pitching deck of an aircraft carrier. It's the Pentagon that is planning to increase the funding of drone development by 700 percent over the next decade.

Admittedly, there is a modest counter-narrative to all this enthusiasm for our robotic prowess and "precision." It involves legal types like Philip Alston, the United Nations special representative on extrajudicial executions. He issued a twenty-nine-page report criticizing Washington's "ever-expanding entitlement for itself to target individuals across the globe." Unless limits are put on such claims, and especially on the CIA's drone war over Pakistan, he suggests, soon enough a plethora of states will follow in America's footprints, attacking people in other lands "labeled as terrorists by one group or another." Such mechanized, long-distance warfare, he also suggests, will breach what respect remains for the laws of war.

"Because operators are based thousands of miles away from the battlefield," he wrote, "and undertake operations entirely through computer screens and remote audio-feed, there is a risk of developing a 'PlayStation' mentality to killing." Similarly, the ACLU has filed a freedom of information act lawsuit against the U.S. government, demanding that it "disclose the legal basis for its use of unmanned drones to conduct targeted killings overseas, as well as the ground rules regarding when, where, and against whom drone strikes can be authorized, and the number of civilian casualties they have caused."

But pay no mind to all this. The arguments may be legally compelling, but not in Washington, which has mounted a half-hearted claim to legitimate "self-defense," but senses that it's already well past the point where legalities matter. The die is cast, the money committed. The momentum for drone war and yet more drone war is overwhelming. It's a done deal. Drone war is, and will be, us.

## A Pilotless Military

If there are zeitgeist moments for products, movie stars, and even politicians, then such moments can exist for weaponry as well. The robotic drone is the Lady Gaga of this Pentagon moment.

It's a moment that could, of course, be presented as an apocalyptic nightmare in the style of the *Terminator* movies (with the United States as the soul-crushing Skynet) or as a remarkable tale of how "networking technology is expanding a home front that is increasingly relevant to day-to-day warfare" (as Christopher Drew put it in the *New York Times*). It could be described as the arrival of a dystopian fantasy world of one-way slaughter verging on entertainment or as the coming of a generation of homegrown video warriors who work "in camouflage uniforms, complete with combat boots, on open floors, with four computer monitors on each desk . . . and coffee and Red Bull help[ing] them get through the 12-hour shifts." It could be presented as the ultimate in cowardice—the killing of people in a world you know nothing about from thousands of miles away—or a new form of "valor."

The drones—their use expanding exponentially, with ever newer generations on the drawing boards, and the planes even heading for "the homeland"—could certainly be considered a demon spawn of modern warfare, or (as is generally the case in the United States) a remarkable example of American technological ingenuity, a problem solver of the first order at a time when few American problems seem capable of solution. Thanks to our technological prowess, it's claimed that *we* can now kill *them*, wherever they may be lurking, at absolutely no cost to ourselves, other than the odd malfunctioning drone. Not that even all CIA operatives involved in the drone wars agree with that one. Some of them understand perfectly well that there's a price to be paid.

As it happens, the enthusiasm for drones is as much a fever dream as the one President Bush and his associates offered back in 2002, but it's also distinctly us. Drone warfare fits us like a glove. With its consoles, chat rooms, and "single shooter" death machines, it certainly fits the skills of a generation raised on the computer, Facebook, and video games. That our valorous warriors, their day of battle done, can increasingly leave war behind and head home to the barbecue (or, given American life, the foreclosure) also fits an American mood.

If the drone presents the most extreme version thus far of the detachment of human beings from the battlefield (on only one side, of course) and so launches a basic redefinition of what war is all about, it also catches something important about the American way of war. After all, while this country garrisons the world, invests its wealth in its military, and fights unending, unwinnable frontier wars and skirmishes, most Americans are remarkably detached from all this. If anything, since the Vietnam War era, when an increasingly rebellious citizens' army proved disastrous for Washington's global aims, such detachment has been the goal of American war-making.

As a start, with no draft and so no citizens' army, war and the toll it takes is now the professional business of a tiny percentage of Americans (and their families). It occurs thousands of miles away and, in the Bush years, also became a heavily privatized, for-profit activity. As Pratap Chatterjee notes, "[E]very U.S. soldier deployed to Afghanistan and Iraq is matched by at least one civilian working for a private company. All told, about 239,451 contractors work for the Pentagon in battle zones around the world." And a majority of those contractors aren't even U.S. citizens.

If drones have entered our world as media celebrities, they have done so largely without debate. In a sense, our wars abroad could be thought of as the equivalent of so many drones. We send our troops off and then go home for dinner and put them out of mind.

## The Globalization of Death

Maybe what we need is the return of George W. Bush's fever dream from the American oblivion in which it's now interred. He was beyond wrong, of course, when it came to Saddam Hussein and Iraqi drones, but he wasn't completely wrong about the dystopian Drone World to come. There are now reportedly more than fifty countries that have purchased or are developing versions of those pilotless planes. In early 2010, the Iranians announced that they were starting up production lines for both armed and unarmed drones. Hezbollah used them against Israel in the 2006 summer war, years after Israel began pioneering their use in targeted killings of Palestinians.

Right now, in what still remains largely a post–Cold War arms race of one, the United States is racing to produce ever more advanced drones to fight our wars, with few competitors in sight. We're also obliterating classic ideas of national sovereignty, and of who can be killed by whom under what circumstances. We may not just be obliterating enemies, but creating them wherever our drones buzz overhead and our missiles strike. We are also creating the (il)legal framework for future war on a frontier where we won't long be flying solo. And when the first Iranian, or Russian, or Chinese missile-armed drones start knocking off their chosen sets of "terrorists," we won't like it one bit. When the first "suicide drones" appear, we'll like it even less. And if drones with the ability to spray chemical or biological weapons finally do make the scene, we'll be truly unnerved.

In the 1990s, we were said to be in an era of "globalization," which was widely hailed as good news. Now, the United States and its detached populace are pioneering a new era of killing that respects no boundaries, relies on the self-definitions of whoever owns the nearest drone, and establishes planetary free-fire zones. It's a nasty business, this globalization of death.

## Whose Hands? Whose Blood?

Consider the following statement offered by Admiral Mike Mullen, chairman of the Joint Chiefs of Staff, at a news conference on Thursday, June 24, 2010. He was discussing Julian Assange, the founder of WikiLeaks as well as the person who had taken responsibility for the vast Afghan War document release at that site. "Mr. Assange," Mullen commented, "can say whatever he likes about the greater good he thinks he and his source are doing, but the truth is they might already have on their hands the blood of some young soldier or that of an Afghan family."

Now, if you were the proverbial fair-minded visitor from Mars (who, in school civics texts of my childhood, always seemed to land on

Main Street, U.S.A., to survey the wonders of our American system), you might be a bit taken aback by Mullen's statement. After all, a crucial revelation in the trove of leaked documents Assange put online had to do with how much blood from innocent Afghan civilians was already on American hands.

The British *Guardian* was one of three publications given early access to the leaked archive, and it began its main article this way: "A huge cache of secret U.S. military files today provides a devastating portrait of the failing war in Afghanistan, revealing how coalition forces have killed hundreds of civilians in unreported incidents. They range from the shootings of individual innocents to the often massive loss of life from air strikes." Or as the paper added in a piece headlined "Secret CIA Paramilitaries' Role in Civilian Deaths": "Behind the military jargon, the war logs are littered with accounts of civilian tragedies. The 144 entries in the logs, recording some of these so-called 'blue on white' events, cover a wide spectrum of day-by-day assaults on Afghans, with hundreds of casualties." Or as it also reported, when exploring documents related to Task Force 373, an "undisclosed 'black' unit" of U.S. Special Operations forces focused on assassinating Taliban and al-Qaeda "senior officials": "The logs reveal that TF 373 has also killed civilian men, women, and children and even Afghan police officers who have strayed into its path."

Admittedly, the events recorded in the WikiLeaks archive took place between 2004 and the end of 2009, and so don't cover the Obama administration's across-the-board surge in Afghanistan. Then again, Admiral Mullen became chairman of the Joint Chiefs in October 2007, and so has been at the helm of the American war machine for more than two of the years in question. He was, for example, chairman in July 2008, when an American plane or planes took out an Afghan bridal party—seventy to ninety strong and made up mostly of women—on a road near the Pakistani border. They were "escorting the bride to meet her groom as local tradition dictates." The bride, whose name we don't know, died too, as did at least twenty-seven other members of the party, including children. Mullen was similarly chairman in August 2008 when a memorial service for a tribal leader in the village of Azizabad in Afghanistan's Herat Province was hit by repeated U.S. air strikes that killed at least ninety civilians, including perhaps fifteen women and up to sixty children.

Mullen was still chairman when, in November 2009, two relatives of Majidullah Qarar, the spokesman for the minister of agriculture, were shot down in cold blood in Ghazni City in a special operations night raid; as he was—and here we move beyond the WikiLeaks time frame—when, in February 2010, U.S. Special Forces troops in helicopters struck a convoy of minibuses, killing up to twenty-seven civilians, including women and children. He was no less chairman in July of 2010 when residents of a small town in Helmand Province in southern Afghanistan claimed that a NATO missile attack had killed fifty-two civilians, an incident that, like just about every other one mentioned above and so many more, was initially denied by U.S. and NATO spokespeople.

And this represents only a grim, minimalist highlight reel among rafts of such incidents, including repeated killings or woundings of innocent civilians at checkpoints. In other words, if your basic Martian visitor were to take the concept of command responsibility at all seriously, he might reasonably weigh actual blood (those hundreds of unreported civilian casualties of the American war the *Guardian* highlighted, for example) against prospective blood (possible Afghan informers killed by the Taliban via names combed from the WikiLeaks documents) and arrive at quite a different conclusion from Chairman Mullen.

In fact, being from another planet, he might even have picked up on something that most Americans would be unlikely to notice—that, with only slight alterations, Mullen's blistering comment about Assange could be applied remarkably well to Mullen himself. "Chairman Mullen," that Martian might have responded, "can say whatever he likes about the greater good he thinks he is doing, but the truth is he already has on his hands the blood of some young soldiers and that of many Afghan families."

### Killing Fields, Then and Now

Fortunately, there are remarkably few Martians in America, as was apparent when the WikiLeaks story broke in June 2010. Certainly, they were in scarce supply in the upper reaches of the Pentagon and, it seemed, hardly less scarce in the mainstream media. If, for instance, you read the version of the WikiLeaks story produced—with the same several weeks of special access—by the *New York Times*, you might have been forgiven for thinking that the *Times* reporters had accessed a different archive of documents than had the *Guardian* crew.

While the *Guardian* led with the central significance of those unreported killings of Afghan civilians, the *Times* led with reports (mainly via Afghan intelligence) of a Pakistani double-cross of the American war effort—of the ties, that is, between Pakistan's intelligence agency, the ISI, and the Taliban. The paper's major sidebar piece concerned the experiences and travails of Outpost Keating, an isolated American base in Afghanistan. To stumble across the issue of civilian deaths at American hands in the *Times* coverage, you had to make your way off the front page and through two full four-column WikiLeaks-themed pages and deep into a third.

With rare exceptions, this was typical of initial American coverage of that initial document dump. The WikiLeaks story, in fact, remained a remarkably bloodless saga in the United States until Admiral Mullen and Secretary of Defense Robert Gates (who oversaw the Afghan War since being confirmed in his post in December 2006) took control of it and began focusing directly on blood, specifically, the blood on Julian Assange's hands. Within a few days, that had become the WikiLeaks story, as headlines like CNN's "Top Military Official: WikiLeaks Founder May Have 'Blood' on His Hands" indicated. On ABC News, for instance, in a typical "bloody hands" piece of reportage, the secretary of defense told interviewer Christiane Amanpour that, whatever Assange's legal culpability might be, when it came to "moral culpability . . . that's where I think the verdict is guilty on WikiLeaks."

Moral culpability. From the Martian point of view, it might have been considered a curious phrase from the lips of the man responsible for the previous three and a half years of two deeply destructive wars that have accomplished nothing and have been responsible for killing, wounding, or driving into exile millions of ordinary Iraqis and Afghans. Given the reality of those wars, our increasingly wide-eyed visitor, now undoubtedly camping out on the Washington Mall, might have been struck by the selectivity of our sense of what constitutes blood and what constitutes collateral damage.

## Collateral Damage in America

Here, then, is a fact that our Martian (but few Americans) might notice: in a decade of futile and brutal war in Afghanistan and more than eight years of the same in Iraq, the United States has filled metaphorical tower upon tower with the exceedingly unmetaphorical bodies of civilian innocents, via air attacks, checkpoint shootings, night raids, artillery and missile fire, and, in some cases, the direct act of murder. Afghans and Iraqis have died in numbers impossible to count (though some have tried).

Among those deaths was that of a good Samaritan who stopped his minivan on a Baghdad street in July 2007 to help transport Iraqis wounded by an American Apache helicopter attack to the hospital. In repayment, he and his two children were gunned down by that same Apache crew. (The children survived; the event was covered up; typically, no American took responsibility for it; the case was not further investigated, and no one was punished or even reprimanded.) That was one of hundreds, or thousands, of similar events in both wars that Americans have known little or nothing about.

Now, Private Bradley Manning, a twenty-two-year-old intelligence analyst deployed to eastern Baghdad, who reportedly leaked the video of the event to WikiLeaks and may have leaked those ninety-two thousand documents as well, is preparing to face a court-martial, was branded a "traitor" by a U.S. senator, his future execution endorsed by the ranking minority member of the House of Representatives' subcommittee on terrorism, and is almost certain to find himself behind bars for years or decades to come. As for the men who oversaw the endless wars that produced that video (and, without doubt, many similar ones cloaked in the secrecy of "national security"), their fates are no less sure.

When Admiral Mullen relinquishes his post and retires, he will undoubtedly have his choice of lucrative corporate boards to sit on, and, if he cares to, lucrative consulting to do for the Pentagon or eager defense contractors, as well as an impressive pension to take home with him. Secretary of Defense Gates will undoubtedly leave his post with a wide range of job offers to consider, and if he wishes, he will probably get a multimillion-dollar contract to write his memoirs. Both will be praised, no matter what happens in or to their wars. Neither will be considered in any way responsible for those tens of thousands of dead civilians in distant lands.

Moral culpability? It doesn't apply. Not to Americans—not unless they leak military secrets. None of the men responsible will ever look at their hands and experience an "out, damned spot!" moment. That's a guarantee. However, a young man who, it seems, saw the blood and didn't want it on his hands, who found himself "actively involved in something that I was completely against," who had an urge to try to end two terrible wars, hoping his act would cause "worldwide discussion, debates, and reforms," will pay the price for them. He will be another body not to count in the collateral damage their wars have caused. He will also be collateral damage to the Afghan antiwar movement that wasn't.

The men who led us down this path, the presidents who presided over our wars, the military figures and secretaries of defense, the intelligence chiefs and ambassadors who helped make them happen, will have libraries to inaugurate, books to write, awards to accept, speeches to give, honors to receive, talk shows to go on. They will be treated with great respect, while Americans—once we have finally left the lands we insistently fought over—will undoubtedly feel little culpability either. And if blowback comes to the United States, and the first suicide drones arrive, everyone will be deeply puzzled and angered, but one thing is certain, we will not consider any damage done to our society "collateral" damage.

So much blood. So many hands. So little culpability. No remorse.


## One November's Dead

Remember how, as the invasion of Iraq was about to begin, the Bush administration decided to seriously enforce a Pentagon ban, in existence since the first Gulf War, on media coverage and images of the American dead arriving home at Dover Air Force Base in Delaware? In fact, the Bush-era ban did more than that. As the *Washington Post*'s Dana Milbank wrote, it "ended the public dissemination of such images by banning news coverage and photography of dead soldiers' homecomings on all military bases."

For those whose lives were formed in the crucible of the Vietnam years, including the civilian and military leadership of the Bush era, the dead, whether ours or the enemy's, were seen as a potential minefield when it came to antiwar opposition or simply the loss of public support in the opinion polls. Admittedly, many of the so-called lessons of the Vietnam War were based on half-truths or pure mythology, but they were no less powerful or influential for that.

In the Vietnam years, the Pentagon had, for instance, been stung by the thought that images of the American dead coming home in body bags had spurred on that era's huge antiwar movement (though, in reality, those images were rare). Nor were they likely to forget the effect of the "body count," offered by U.S. military spokesmen in late afternoon press briefings in Saigon, the South Vietnamese capital. Among disillusioned reporters, these became known as "the Five O'clock Follies." They were supposedly accurate counts of enemy dead, but everyone knew otherwise.

In a guerrilla war in which the taking of territory made next to no difference, the body count was meant as a promissory note against future success. As it became apparent that there would be no light at the end of the tunnel, however, that count began to look more barbaric to growing numbers of Americans.

## Body Bags and Body Counts

At the time of the first Gulf War, as part of a larger effort to apply the "lessons" of Vietnam, the Pentagon attempted to prevent any images of the American dead from reaching the home front. More than a decade later, top officials of George W. Bush's administration, focused on ensuring that the invasion of Iraq would be a "cakewalk" and a triumph, consciously played an opposites game with their version of Vietnam. That included, for instance, secretly counting the enemy dead but keeping mum about them for fear of re-creating the dreaded "body count."

General Tommy Franks, who directed the invasions of both Afghanistan and Iraq, bluntly insisted, "We don't do body counts." But it wasn't true, and in the end, President Bush couldn't help himself: his frustration with disaster in Iraq led him to start complaining about being unable to mention how successful U.S. forces were in killing the enemy. Finally, compulsively, he began to offer his own presidential body counts.

But an irony should be noted here. There was another lesson from Vietnam that didn't quite fit with those drawn from body bags and the body count. American troops had been treated terribly by the American public—so went the postwar tale—and particularly by the antiwar movement that reviled them as "baby killers" when they came home and regularly spat upon them. Often ignored in this mythic version of the antiwar movement was the fact that, as the 1970s began, it was being energized by significant numbers of Vietnam vets and active duty GIs. Nonetheless, all this was deeply believed, even by many who had been in that movement, and everyone, whatever their politics, vowed that it would never happen again. Hence, the troops, and especially the dead, were to be treated across the board and in a blanket way as "American heroes," and elevated to almost godlike status.

So, while President Bush carefully avoided making public appearances at Dover Air Force Base as the coffins were being unloaded (lest someone confuse him with Vietnam-era president Lyndon Johnson), much publicity was given to the way he met privately and emotionally— theoretically beyond the view of the media—with the families of the dead.

In a sense, whatever proscriptions were placed on imagery of the dead, the American dead were all over. For one thing, no sooner did the Bush administration shut down those images than war critics, following their own Vietnam "lessons," began complaining about his doing so. And even if they hadn't, every newspaper seemed to have its own "wall of heroes," those spreads filled with tiny images of the faces of the American dead, while their names were repeatedly read in somber tones on television. Similarly, antiwar activists toured the country with displays of empty combat boots or set up little cemeteries honoring the war dead, even while making the point that they should never have died.

No less significantly, dying Americans were actually news. I mean front-page news. If American troops died in a firefight or because of a suicide bomber or went down in a helicopter, it was often in the headlines. Whatever else you knew, you did know that Americans were dying in the wars Washington was fighting in distant lands.

## A Premature Graveyard of American Inattention

Well, that was Iraq, this is Afghanistan. That was the Bush era, these are the Obama years. And, with rare exceptions, the dead seldom make much news anymore.

Now, except in small towns and local communities where the news of a local death or the funeral of a dead soldier is dealt with as a major event, American deaths, often dribbling in one or two at a time, are generally acknowledged in the last paragraphs of summary war pieces buried deep inside papers (or far into the TV news). The American dead have, it seems, like the war they are now fighting, generally gone into the dustbin of news coverage.

Take the month of November 2010 in Afghanistan. You might have thought that American deaths would make headline news. After all, according to the website icasualties.org, there were fifty-eight allied deaths in that thirty-day period, fifty-three of them American. While those numbers were undoubtedly small if compared to, say, fatal traffic accidents, they were distinctly on the rise. Along with much other news coming out of the planet's number one narco-state, ranging from raging corruption to a rise in Taliban attacks, they trended terribly.

In understanding how this relative lack of attention was possible, it's worth noting that the American dead tend to come disproportionately from easy-to-ignore, tough-luck regions of the country, and disproportionately as well from small town and rural America, where service in the armed forces may be more valued, but times are also rougher, unemployment rates higher, and opportunities fewer. In this context, consider those November dead. If you look through the minimalist announcements released by the Pentagon, you discover that they were almost all men in their twenties, and that none of them seem to have come from our giant metropolises. Among the hometowns of the dead there was no Chicago, New York, Los Angeles, or Houston. There were a range of second-level cities including Flagstaff (Arizona), Rochester (New York), San Jose (California), Tallahassee (Florida), and Tucson (Arizona).

For the rest of the hometown names the Pentagon lists, from Aroostook, Maine, to Mesquite, Texas, whether they represent rural areas, small towns, parts of suburbs, or modest-sized cities, they read like a dirge for places you've never heard of unless you yourself were born there or lived in the vicinity. Here, for instance, are the hometowns of the six U.S. trainers who died in a single incident in late November when a "trusted" Afghan policeman opened fire on them: Athens, Ohio (pop. 21,909), Beaver Dam, Wisconsin (pop. 15,169), Mexico, Maine (pop. 2,959), Quartz Hill, California (pop. 9,890), Senoia, Georgia (pop. 3,720), Tell City, Indiana (pop. 7,845). Here, as well, are some, but hardly all, of the other hometowns of the November dead: Chesterfield, Michigan, Chittenango, New York, Conroe, Texas, Dalzell, South Carolina, Davie, Florida, Fort Smith, Arkansas, Freeman, Missouri, Frostburg, Maryland, Greenfield, Wisconsin, Greenwood, Louisiana, Mills River, North Carolina, Pago Pago, American Samoa, Sierra Vista, Arizona, Thomasville, Georgia, and Wyomissing, Pennsylvania.

Back in early 2007, demographer William O'Hare and journalist Bill Bishop, working with the University of New Hampshire's Carsey Institute, which specializes in the overlooked rural areas of our country, crunched the numbers on the rural dead from America's recent wars. According to their study, the death rate "for rural soldiers (twenty-four per million adults aged eighteen to fifty-nine) is 60 percent higher than the death rate for those soldiers from cities and suburbs (fifteen deaths per million)." More recently, sociologist Katherine Curtis arrived at similar conclusions in a study using data on U.S. troop deaths in Iraq through 2007. There's no reason to believe that much has changed in the last few years.

Keep in mind that a number of the soldiers who died in November 2010 had undoubtedly been in Afghanistan before, probably more than once, and had they lived (and stayed in the military), they would surely have been there again. The reason is simple enough: the full weight of the American war state and its seemingly eternal state of war lands squarely on the relatively modest numbers of "volunteers," often from out-of-the-way places, who make up the American fighting force. Multiple tours of duty are now the norm.

Given the modest attention focused on American deaths here in the United States, you might almost imagine that, from the Washington elite on down, Americans preferred not to know the price being paid for a war, already in its tenth year—and which the Obama administration has officially extended through 2014 for U.S. "combat troops" and possibly years beyond for tens of thousands of noncombat trainers and other forces who will be in no less danger.

In October 2009, six months after the Pentagon rescinded its ban on coverage of the arrival of the war dead, in an obvious rebuke to his predecessor, President Obama traveled to Dover Air Base. There, inside the plane that brought the dead home, he reportedly prayed over the coffins and was later photographed offering a salute as one of them was carried off the plane. (Eighteen were unloaded that day, including three containing dead agents from the Drug Enforcement Administration.) It was a moving ceremony and, as Byron York, columnist for the conservative *Washington Times*, pointed out not long after, the president wasn't alone. Thirty-five media outlets were there to cover him. Like so much in the Obama era, as York also noted, this particular post-Bush version of a sunshine policy didn't last long in practice.

Now that the dead can be covered, with rare exceptions few seem to care. For those who want to keep a significant American presence in Iraq, continue our war in Afghanistan until hell freezes over, and expand the Global War on Terror (stripped of its name in the Obama years but bolstered in reality), it's undoubtedly more convenient if the dead, like their war, remain in those shadows. In the Bush years, the dead, despite bans, seemed to be everywhere. In the Obama years, except to the spouses and children, parents, relatives, friends, and neighbors they leave behind, they seem to have disappeared into the netherworld like the "shadows" we sometimes imagine them to be. In this, they have followed the war in which they fought to a premature graveyard of American inattention.

## Top Guns No More

When men first made war in the air, the imagery that accompanied them was of knights jousting in the sky. Just check out movies like *Wings*, which won the first Oscar for Best Picture in 1927 (or any Peanuts cartoon in which Snoopy takes on the Red Baron in a literal "dogfight"). As late as 1986, five years after two American F-14s shot down two Soviet MiGs flown by Libyan pilots over the Mediterranean's Gulf of Sidra, it was still possible to make the movie *Top Gun*. In it, Tom Cruise played "Maverick," a U.S. naval aviator triumphantly involved in a similar incident. (*He* shoots down three MiGs.)

Admittedly, by then American air-power films had long been in decline. In Vietnam, the United States had used its air superiority to devastating effect, bombing the North and blasting the South, but go to American Vietnam films and, while that U.S. patrol walks endlessly into

a South Vietnamese village with mayhem to come, the air is largely devoid of planes.

Consider *Top Gun* an anomaly. Anyway, it's been twenty-five years
since that film topped the box office—and don't hold your breath for a
repeat at your local multiplex. After all, there's nothing left to base such
a film on. To put it simply, it's time for Americans to take the "war" out
of "air war." These days, we need a new set of terms to explain what U.S.
air power actually does.

American "air superiority" in any war the United States now fights
is total. In fact, the last time American jets met enemy planes of any sort
in any skies was in the first Gulf War in 1991, and since Saddam Hussein's
once powerful air force didn't offer much opposition—most of its planes
fled to Iran—that was brief. The last time U.S. pilots faced anything like
a serious challenge in the skies was in North Vietnam in the early 1970s.
Before that, you have to go back to the Korean War in the early 1950s.

This, in fact, is something American military types take great pride
in. Addressing the cadets of the Air Force Academy in March 2011, for
example, Secretary of Defense Robert Gates stated: "There hasn't been a
U.S. Air Force airplane lost in air combat in nearly forty years, or an
American soldier attacked by enemy aircraft since Korea." And he's probably right, though it's also possible that the last American plane shot
down in aerial combat was U.S. Navy pilot Michael Scott Speicher's jet
in the first Gulf War. (The navy continues to claim that the plane was
felled by a surface-to-air missile.)

As an F-117A Stealth fighter was downed by a surface-to-air missile
over Serbia in 1999, it's been more than eleven years since such a plane
was lost due to anything but mechanical malfunction. Yet in those years,
the U.S. military has remained almost continuously at war somewhere
and has used air power extensively, as in its "shock and awe" launching
of the invasion of Iraq, which was meant to "decapitate" Saddam Hussein
and the rest of the Iraqi leadership. No plane was lost, nor was an Iraqi
leader of any sort taken out in those fifty decapitation attacks, though
dozens of Iraqi civilians died.

You might even say that air power, now ramping up again in
Afghanistan, has continued to be the American way of war. From a military point of view, this is something worth bragging about. It's just that

the obvious conclusions are never drawn from it.

## The Valor of Pilots

To be a "top gun" in the U.S. military today is to be in staggeringly less danger than any American who gets into a car and heads just about anywhere, given this country's annual toll of about 34,000 fatal car crashes. In addition, there is far less difference than you might imagine between piloting a drone aircraft from a base thousands of miles away and being inside the cockpit of a fighter jet.

Articles are now regularly written about drone aircraft "piloted" by teams sitting at consoles in places like Creech Air Force Base in Nevada. Meanwhile, their planes are loosing Hellfire missiles thousands of miles away in Afghanistan (or, in the case of CIA "pilots," in the Pakistani tribal borderlands). When it comes to pilots in planes flying over Afghanistan, we imagine something quite different—and yet we shouldn't. Based on the record, those pilots might as well be in Nevada, since there is no enemy that can touch them. They are inviolate unless their own machines betray them and, with the rarest of imaginable exceptions, will remain so.

Nor does anyone here consider it an irony that the worst charge lodged by U.S. military spokespeople against their guerrilla enemies, whose recruits obviously can't take to the skies, is that they use "human shields" as a defense. This transgression against "the law of war" is typical of any outgunned guerrilla force that, in Mao Zedong's dictum, sees immense benefit in "swimming" in a "sea" of civilians. If they didn't do so and fought like members of a regular army, they would, of course, be slaughtered. This is considered, however implicitly, a sign of ultimate cowardice. On the other hand, while a drone pilot cannot (yet) get a combat award citation for "valor," a jet fighter pilot can and no one—here at least—sees anything strange or cowardly about a form of warfare that guarantees the American side quite literal, godlike invulnerability.

War by its nature is often asymmetrical. The retreat that turns into a rout that turns into a slaughter is a relative commonplace of battle. But it cannot be war, as anyone has ever understood the word, if one side is *never* in danger. And yet that is American air war as it has developed since World War II.

It's a long path from knightly aerial jousting to air war as . . . well, what? We have no language for it, because accurate labels would prove deflating, pejorative, and exceedingly uncomfortable. You would perhaps need to speak of cadets at the Air Force Academy being prepared for "air slaughter" or "air assassination," depending on the circumstances.

From those cadets to the secretary of defense to reporters covering our wars, no one here is likely to accept the taking of the "war" out of air war. And because of that, it is—conveniently—almost impossible for Americans to imagine how American-style war must seem to those in the lands where we fight. From the point of view of Afghans, Pakistanis, or other potential target peoples, those drones buzzing in the sky must seem very much like real-life versions of the Predator, that sci-fi alien hunter of human prey, or a Terminator, that machine version of the same. They must, that is, seem alien and implacable like so many malign gods. After all, the weaponry from those planes is loosed without recourse. No one on the ground can do a thing to prevent it and little to defend themselves. And often enough the missiles and bombs kill the innocent along with those our warriors consider the guilty.

To take one example, among many, consider the story behind this *New York Times* headline: "Nine Afghan Boys Collecting Firewood Killed by NATO Helicopters." On March 1, 2011, in Afghanistan's Kunar Province, ten boys, including two sets of brothers, were collecting wood for their families when the predators—this time American helicopters evidently looking for insurgents who had rocketed a nearby American base—arrived. Only one of the boys survived. He described the experience as one of being "hunted"—as the Predator hunts humans or human hunters stalk animals. They "hovered over us," he said, "scanned us, and we saw a green flash." Then the helicopters rose and began firing. For this particular nightmare, war commander General David Petraeus apologized directly to Afghan president Hamid Karzai, who has for years fruitlessly denounced U.S. and NATO air operations that have killed Afghan civilians. When an angered Karzai refused to accept his apology, Secretary of Defense Gates, on a surprise visit to the country, apologized as well, as did President Obama. And that was that—for the Americans.

Forget for a moment what this incident tells us about a form of warfare in which helicopter pilots, reasonably close to the ground (and modestly more vulnerable than pilots in planes), can't tell boys with sticks from insurgents with guns. The crucial thing to keep in mind is that, no matter how many apologies may be offered afterwards, this can't stop. According to the *Wall Street Journal*, death by helicopter is, in fact, on the rise. It's in the nature of this kind of warfare. In fact, Afghan civilians have repeatedly, even repetitiously, been blown away from the air, with or without apologies, since 2001.

In the weeks that preceded the killing of those boys, for instance, a "NATO"—these are usually American—air attack took out four Afghan security guards protecting the work of a road construction firm and wounded a fifth, according to the police chief of Helmand Province. A similar "deeply regrettable incident" took out an Afghan army soldier, his wife, and his four children in Nangarhar Province. And a third, also in Kunar Province, wiped out 65 civilians, including women and children, according to Afghan government officials. Visiting a hospital afterward, Karzai wept as he held a child whose leg had been amputated after being wounded in the attack.

The U.S. military did not weep. Instead, it rejected this claim of civilian deaths, insisting as it often does that the dead were "insurgents." It simply announced—and this is typical—that it was "investigating" the incident. General Petraeus managed to further offend Afghan officials when he visited the presidential palace in Kabul and reportedly claimed that some of the wounded children might have suffered burns not in an air attack but from their parents as punishment for bad behavior and were being counted in the casualty figures only to make them look worse.

Over the years, Afghan civilian casualties from the air have waxed and waned, depending on how much air power American commanders were willing to call in, but they have never ceased. As history tells us, air power and civilian deaths are inextricably bound together. They can't be separated, no matter how much anyone talks about "surgical" strikes and precision bombing. It's simply the barbaric essence, the very nature of this kind of war, to kill noncombatants.

One question sometimes raised about such casualties in Afghanistan is this: according to UN statistics, Taliban fighters (via roadside bombs and suicide bombers) kill far more civilians, including women and children, than do NATO forces, so why do the U.S.-caused deaths stick so in

Afghan craws when we periodically investigate, apologize, and even pay survivors for their losses? *New York Times* reporter Alissa J. Rubin, puzzling over this, offered the following answer: "[T]hose that are caused by NATO troops appear to reverberate more deeply because of underlying animosity about foreigners in the country." This seems reasonable as far as it goes, but don't discount what air power adds to the foreignness of the situation.

Consider what the twenty-year-old brother of two of the dead boys from the Kunar helicopter attack told the *Wall Street Journal* in a phone interview: "The only option I have is to pick up a Kalashnikov, RPG [rocket-propelled grenade], or a suicide vest to fight."

Whatever the Taliban may be, they remain part of Afghan society. They are there on the ground. They kill and they commit barbarities, but they suffer, too. In our version of air "war," however, the killing and the dying are perfectly and precisely, even surgically, separated. We kill, they die. It's that simple. Sometimes the ones we target to die do so, sometimes others stand in their stead. But no matter. We then deny, argue, investigate, apologize, and continue. We are, in that sense, implacable.

And one more thing: since we are incapable of thinking of ourselves as predators, no less emotionless Terminators, it becomes impossible for us to see that our air "war" on terror is, in reality, a machine for creating what we then call "terrorists." It is part of an American Global War *for* Terror. In other words, although air power has long been held up as part of the solution to terrorism, and though the American military now regularly boasts about the enemy body counts it produces, and the precision with which it does so, all of that, even when accurate, is also a kind of delusion.

So count on this: there will be no more Top Guns. No knights of the air. No dogfights and sky-jousts. No valor. Just one-sided slaughter and targeted assassinations. That is where air power has ended up. Live with it.

# CHAPTER 4

# Obama's Flailing Wars

## Obama's Af-Pak Flip-Flop

On stage, it would be farce. In Afghanistan and Pakistan, it's bound to play out as tragedy.

In March 2010 Barack Obama flew into Afghanistan for six hours, essentially to read the riot act to Afghan president Hamid Karzai, whom his ambassador had only months before termed "not an adequate strategic partner." Chairman of the Joint Chiefs admiral Mike Mullen followed within a day to deliver his own "stern message." While still on Air Force One, National Security Adviser James Jones offered reporters a version of the tough talk Obama was bringing with him. Karzai would later see one of Jones's comments and find it insulting. Brought to his attention as well would be a newspaper article that quoted an anonymous senior U.S. military official as saying of his half-brother, Ahmed Wali Karzai, a reputedly corrupt power broker in the southern city of Kandahar: "I'd like him out of there. . . . But there's nothing that we can do unless we can link him to the insurgency, then we can put him on the [target list] and capture and kill him." This was tough talk indeed. (As it turned out, in July 2011 Ahmed Wali Karzai was assassinated at his home in Kandahar by a former bodyguard.)

At the time, the media repeatedly pointed out that President Obama, unlike his predecessor, had consciously developed a standoffish relationship with Karzai. Meanwhile, both named and anonymous officials regularly castigated the Afghan president in the press for stealing an election and running a hopelessly corrupt, inefficient government that had little power outside Kabul, the capital. A previously planned Karzai visit to Washington was put on hold to emphasize the toughness of the new approach.

The administration was clearly intent on fighting a better version of the Afghan War with a new commander, a new plan of action, and a tamed Afghan president, a client head of state who would finally accept his lesser place in the greater scheme of things. A little blunt talk, some necessary threats, and the big stick of American power and money were sure to do the trick.

Meanwhile, across the border in Pakistan, the administration was in an all-carrots mood when it came to the local military and civilian leadership—billions of dollars of carrots, in fact. Our top military and civilian officials had all but taken up residence in Islamabad. By March 2010, for instance, Admiral Mullen had already visited the country fifteen times and U.S. dollars (and promises of more) were flowing in. Meanwhile, U.S. Special Operations forces were arriving in the country's wild borderlands to train the Pakistani Frontier Corps and the skies were filling with CIA-directed unmanned aerial vehicles pounding those same borderlands, where the Pakistani Taliban, al-Qaeda, and other insurgent groups involved in the Afghan War were located. In Pakistan, it was said, a crucial "strategic relationship" was being carefully cultivated.

Skip ahead to mid-May 2010 and somehow, like so many stealthy insurgents, the carrots and sticks had crossed the poorly marked, porous border between Afghanistan and Pakistan heading in opposite directions. On May 12, Karzai was in Washington being given "the red carpet treatment" as part of what was termed an Obama administration "charm offensive" and a "four-day love fest." The president set aside a rare stretch of hours to entertain Karzai and the planeload of ministers he brought with him.

At a joint news conference, Obama insisted that "perceived tensions" between the two men had been "overstated." Specific orders went out from the White House to curb public criticism of the Afghan president and give him "more public respect" as "the chief U.S. partner in the war effort." Secretary of State Hillary Clinton assured Karzai of Washington's long-term "commitment" to his country, as did Obama and then war commander General Stanley McChrystal. Praise was the order of the day.

John Kerry, chairman of the Senate Foreign Relations Committee, interrupted a financial reform debate to invite Karzai onto the Senate floor (an honor not bestowed on a head of state since 1967), where he was mobbed by senators eager to shake his hand. He was once again our man in Kabul. It was a stunning turnaround: a president almost without power in his own country had somehow tamed the commander in chief of the globe's lone superpower.

Meanwhile, Clinton, who had shepherded the Afghan president on a walk through a "private enclave" in Georgetown and hosted a "glittering reception" for him, appeared on CBS's *60 Minutes* to flay Pakistan. In the wake of an inept failed car bombing in New York City's Times Square, she had this stern message to send to the Pakistani leadership: "We want more, we expect more. . . . We've made it very clear that if, heaven forbid, an attack like this that we can trace back to Pakistan were to have been successful, there would be very severe consequences." Such consequences would evidently include a halt to the flow of U.S. aid to a country in economically disastrous shape. So much for the carrots.

According to the *Washington Post*, General McChrystal delivered a "similar message" to the chief of staff of the Pakistani army. To back up Clinton's public threats and McChrystal's private ones, hordes of anonymous American military and civilian officials were ready to pepper reporters with leaks about the tough love that might now be in store for Pakistan. The same *Post* story, for instance, spoke of "some officials . . . weighing in favor of a far more muscular and unilateral U.S. policy. It would include a geographically expanded use of drone missile attacks in Pakistan and pressure for a stronger U.S. military presence there."

According to similar accounts, "more pointed" messages were heading for key Pakistanis and "new and stiff warnings" were being issued. Americans were said to be pushing for expanded special operations training programs in the Pakistani tribal areas, while insisting that the Pakistani military launch a major campaign in North Waziristan, the heartland of various resistance groups including possibly al-Qaeda. "The element of threat" was now in the air, according to Tariq Fatemi, a former Pakistani ambassador, while in press reports you could hear rumblings about an "internal debate" in Washington that might result in more American "boots on the ground."

## Helpless Escalation

In other words, in the space of two months the Obama administration had flip-flopped when it came to who exactly was to be pressured and who reassured. A typically anonymous "former U.S. official who advises the administration on Afghan policy" caught the moment well in a comment to the *Wall Street Journal*. "This whole bending over backwards to show Karzai the red carpet," he told journalist Peter Spiegel, "is a result of not having had a concerted strategy for how to grapple with him."

On a larger scale, the flip-flop seemed to reflect tactical and strategic incoherence—and not just in relation to Karzai. To all appearances, when it comes to the administration's two South Asian wars, one open, one more hidden, Obama and his top officials were flailing around. For all the policy reviews and shuttling officials, the surging troops, extra private contractors, and new bases, Obama's wars were worsening. Lacking was any coherent regional policy or semblance of real strategy—counterinsurgency being only a method of fighting and a set of tactics for doing so. In place of strategic coherence there was just one knee-jerk response: escalation. As unexpected events gripped the Obama administration by the throat, its officials increasingly acted as if further escalation were their only choice, their fated choice.

This response was eerily familiar. It permeated Washington's mentality in the Vietnam War years. In fact, one of the strangest aspects of that war was the way America's leaders—including President Lyndon Johnson—felt increasingly helpless and hopeless even as they committed themselves to further steps up the ladder of escalation.

We don't know what the main actors in Obama's war have been feeling. We don't have their private documents or their secret taped conversations. Nonetheless, it should ring a bell when, as wars devolve, the only response Washington can imagine is further escalation.

## Pragmatism Goes to War

One thing can be said about the Bush administration: it had a grand strategic vision to go with its wars. Its top officials were convinced that the American military, a force they saw as unparalleled on planet Earth, would be capable of unilaterally shock-and-awing America's enemies in the oil heartlands of the planet. Its two wars would bring not just Afghanistan and Iraq, but Iran and Syria to their knees, leaving Washington to impose a *Pax Americana* on the Middle East and Central Asia (in the process of which groups like Hamas and Hezbollah would be subdued and anti-American jihadism ended).

They couldn't, of course, have been more wrong, something quite apparent to the Obama team. Now, however, we have a crew in Washington that seems to have no vision, great or small, when it comes to American foreign or imperial policy, and that seems, in fact, to lack any sense of strategy at all. What they have is a set of increasingly discredited tactics and an approach that might pass for good old American see-what-works "pragmatism."

The vision may be long gone, but the wars live on with their own inexorable momentum. Add into the mix American domestic politics, which could discourage any president from changing course and de-escalating a war, and you have what looks like a fatal—and fatally expensive—brew.

We've moved from Bush's visionary disasters to Obama's flailing wars, while the people of Afghanistan, Pakistan, and Iraq continue to pay the price. If only we could close the curtain on this strange mix of farce and tragedy, but evidently we're still stuck in act four of a five-act nightmare.

### The Question Mark Over Afghanistan

All of this leaves the massive American investment of its most precious resources, including lives, in Afghanistan an ongoing mystery that is never addressed. Somewhere in that country's vast stretches of poppy fields or in the halls of Washington's national security bureaucracy, lurks a great unasked question. It's a question asked almost half a century ago regarding the war in Vietnam, the lost war to which David Petraeus turned in 2006 to produce the army counterinsurgency manual that became the basis for his surge strategy.

The question then was: Why are we in Vietnam? It even became the title of a Norman Mailer novel. In 1965, President Lyndon Johnson's administration produced a government propaganda film solely in response to that question, which was already threatening to drive down his polling figures and upend his Great Society at home. The film was called *Why Viet-Nam*. While it had no question mark after the title, the question of whether to add one was actually argued out in the most literal way inside the administration. The film began with the president quoting a letter he had received from a mother "in the Midwest" whose son was stationed in Vietnam. You hear the president, in his homey twang, pick up that woman's question as if it were his own. "Why Viet-Nam?" he repeats three times as the title appears on the screen, after which, official or not, a question mark seems to hover over every scene, as it did over the war itself.

In a sense, the same question mark appeared both before and after the 2003 invasion of Iraq, but it has never been associated with Afghanistan. Because of 9/11, Afghanistan remained for years the (relatively) good (and largely forgotten) war, until visible failure visibly tarnished it.

It's far past time to ask that question, even as the Obama administration repeats the al-Qaeda mantra of the Bush years almost word for word and lets any explanation go at that. Why *are* we in Afghanistan? Why is our treasure being wasted there when it's needed here?

## Clueless in Afghanistan—and Washington

Have you ever thought about just how strange this country's version of normal truly is? Let me make my point with a single, hardly noticed *Washington Post* news story. It represents the sort of reporting that, in our world, zips by with next to no reaction, despite the true weirdness buried in it.

The piece by Craig Whitlock appeared on June 19, 2010, and was headlined, "U.S. Military Criticized for Purchase of Russian Copters for Afghan Air Corps." Maybe that's strange enough for you right there. Russian copters? Of course, we all know, at least vaguely, that U.S. spending on its protracted Afghan War and nation-building project is by now in the many hundreds of billions of dollars. And, of course, those dollars have to go somewhere.

Admittedly, these days in parts of the United States, state and city governments are having a hard time finding the money just to pay teachers or the police. The Pentagon, on the other hand, hasn't hesitated to use at least $25 billion to "train" and "mentor" the Afghan military and police—and after each round of training failed to produce the expected results, to ask for even more money, and train them again. That includes the Afghan National Army Air Corps which, in the Soviet era of the 1980s, had nearly 500 aircraft and a raft of trained pilots. The last of that air force—little used in the Taliban era—was destroyed in the U.S. air assault and invasion of 2001. As a result, the "Afghan air force" (with about fifty helicopters and transport planes) is now something of a misnomer, since it is, in fact, the U.S. Air Force.

Still, there are a few Afghan pilots, mostly in their forties, trained long ago on Russian Mi-17 transport helicopters, and it's on a refurbished version of these copters, Whitlock tells us, that the Pentagon has already spent $648 million. The Mi-17 was specially built for Afghanistan's difficult flying environment back when various Islamic jihadists, some of whom we're now fighting under the rubric of "the Taliban," were allied with us against the Russians.

Here's the first paragraph of Whitlock's article: "The U.S. government is snapping up Russian-made helicopters to form the core of Afghanistan's fledgling air force, a strategy that is drawing flak from members of Congress who want to force the Afghans to fly American choppers instead." So various congressional representatives are upset over the lack of a buy-American plan when it comes to the Afghan air force. That's the story Whitlock sets out to tell, because the Pentagon has been planning to purchase dozens more of the Mi-17s over the next decade, and that, it seems, is what's worth being upset about when perfectly good American arms manufacturers aren't getting the contracts.

But let's consider three aspects of Whitlock's article that no one is likely to spend an extra moment on, even if they do capture the surpassing strangeness of the American way of war in distant lands—and in Washington.

1. The Little Training Program That Couldn't: There are some 450 U.S. personnel in Afghanistan training the Afghan air force. Unfortunately, there's a problem. There may be no "buy American" program for that air force, but there is a "speak American" one. To be an Afghan air force pilot, you must know English—"the official language of the cockpit," Whitlock assures us (even if to fly Russian helicopters). As he points

out, however, the trainees, mostly illiterate, take two to five years simply to learn the language. (Imagine a U.S. Air Force in which, just to take off, every pilot needed to know Dari.)

Thanks to this language barrier, the U.S. military can train endlessly and next to nothing is guaranteed to happen. "So far," reports Whitlock, "only one Afghan pilot has graduated from flight school in the United States, although dozens are in the pipeline. That has forced the air corps to rely on pilots who learned to fly Mi-17s during the days of Soviet and Taliban rule." In other words, despite the impressive Soviet performance in the 1980s, the training of the Afghan Air Force has been re-imagined by Americans as a Sisyphean undertaking.

And this offers but a hint of how bizarre U.S. training programs for the Afghan military and police have proven to be. In fact, sometimes it seems as if exactly the same scathing report, detailing the same training problems and setbacks, has been recycled yearly without anyone who mattered finding it particularly odd—or being surprised that the response to each successive piece of bad news is to decide to pour yet more money and trainers into the project. For example, in 2005, at a time when Washington had already spent $3.3 billion training and mentoring the Afghan army and police, the U.S. Government Accounting Office (GAO) issued a report indicating that "efforts to fully equip the increasing number of [Afghan] combat troops have fallen behind, and efforts to establish sustaining institutions, such as a logistics command, needed to support these troops have not kept pace." Worse yet, the report fretted, it might take "up to $7.2 billion to complete [the training project] and about $600 million annually to sustain [it]."

In 2006, according to the *New York Times*, "a joint report by the Pentagon and the State Department . . . found that the American-trained police force in Afghanistan is largely incapable of carrying out routine law enforcement work, and that managers of the $1.1 billion training program cannot say how many officers are actually on duty or where thousands of trucks and other equipment issued to police units have gone." At best, stated the report, fewer than half of the officially announced number of police were "trained and equipped to carry out their police functions."

In 2008, by which time $16.5 billion had been spent on army and police training programs, the GAO chimed in again, indicating that only two of 105 army units were "assessed as being fully capable of conducting their primary mission," while "no police unit is fully capable." In 2009, the U.S. special inspector general for Afghan reconstruction reported that "only 24 of 559 Afghan police units are considered ready to operate without international help."

Such reports, as well as repeated (and repetitive) news investigations and stories on the subject, invariably are accompanied by a litany of complaints about corruption, indiscipline, illiteracy, drug use, staggering desertion rates, Taliban infiltration, ghost soldiers, and a host of other problems. In 2009, however, the solution remained as expectable as the problems: "The report called for more U.S. trainers and more money."

In June 2010, a U.S. government audit, again from the Special Inspector General, reported that "the standards used to appraise the Afghan forces since 2005 were woefully inadequate, inflating their abilities." The usual litany of training woes followed. Yet, according to Reuters, President Obama was asking for another $14.2 billion for the training project "for this year and next." And on July 22, 2010, the *Wall Street Journal*'s Julian Barnes reported that war commander General David Petraeus was planning to "retool" U.S. strategy to include "a greater focus on how Afghanistan's security forces are being trained."

When it comes to U.S. training programs then, you might conclude that Afghanistan has proved to be the land where time stood still—and so, evidently, has the Washington national security establishment's collective brain. For Washington, there seems to be no learning curve in Afghanistan, not when it comes to "training" Afghans anyway.

And here is the oddest thing of all, though no one even bothers to mention it in this context: the Taliban haven't had tens of billions of dollars in foreign training funds; they haven't had years of advice from the best U.S. and NATO advisers money can buy; they haven't had private contractors like DynCorp teaching them how to fight and police, and strangely enough, they seem to have no problem fighting. They are not undermanned, infiltrated by followers of Hamid Karzai, or particularly corrupt. They may be illiterate and may not be fluent in English, but they are ready, in up-to platoon-sized units, to attack heavily fortified U.S. military bases, Afghan prisons, a police headquarters, and the like with hardly a foreign mentor in sight.

It appears then, as a modern miracle in reverse that the United States has proven incapable of training a competent Afghan force in a country where arms are the norm, fighting has for decades seldom stopped, and the locals are known for their martial traditions. Similarly, it's abidingly curious that the United States has so far failed to train a modest-sized air force, even flying refurbished Italian light transport planes from the 1980s and those Russian helicopters, when the Soviet Union, the last imperial power to try this, proved up to creating an Afghan force able to pilot aircraft ranging from helicopters to fighter planes.

2. Non-Exit strategies: Now, let's wade a little deeper into the strangeness of what Whitlock reported by taking up the question of when we're actually planning to leave Afghanistan. Consider this passage from the Whitlock piece: "U.S. military officials have estimated that the Afghan air force won't be able to operate independently until 2016, five years after President Obama has said he intends to start withdrawing U.S. troops from Afghanistan. But [U.S. Air Force Brig. Gen. Michael R.] Boera said that date could slip by at least two years if Congress forces the Afghans to fly U.S. choppers." In other words, while Americans argue over what the president's drawdown date really means, and while Afghan president Hamid Karzai suggests that Afghan forces will take over the country's security duties by 2014, Whitlock's anonymous "U.S. military officials" are clearly operating on a different clock, on, in fact, Pentagon time, and so are planning for a 2016–2018 target date for that force simply to "operate independently" (which by no means indicates "without U.S. support").

If you were of a conspiratorial mind-set, you might almost think that the Pentagon preferred not to create an effective Afghan air force and instead wanted to remain the substitute Afghan air force forever and a day—as has also been the case in Iraq, a country that once had the world's sixth largest air force and now, after years of U.S. mentoring, has next to nothing.

3. Who Are the Russians Now?: Okay, let's move even deeper into American strangeness with a passage that makes up most of the twentieth and twenty-first paragraphs of Whitlock's twenty-five-paragraph piece: "In addition," he reports, "the U.S. Special Operations Command would like to buy a few Mi-17s of its own, so that special forces carrying out

clandestine missions could cloak the fact that they are American. 'We would like to have some to blend in and do things,' said a senior U.S. military official, speaking on condition of anonymity to discuss the clandestine program." No explanation follows on just how—or where—those Russian helicopters will help "cloak" American Special Operations missions, or what they are to "blend" into, or the "things" they are to do. There's no further discussion of the subject at all. In other words, the special op urge to Russianize its air transport has officially been reported, and as far as I know, not a single congressional representative has made a fuss over it, no mainstream pundit has written a curious or angry editorial challenging its appropriateness, and no reporter has followed up.

As just another little factoid of no great import buried deep in an article focused on other matters, undoubtedly no one has given it a thought. But it's worth stopping a moment and considering just how odd this tiny bit of news-that-won't-ever-rise-to-the-level-of-news actually is. One way to do this is to play the sort of opposites game that never quite works on this still one-way planet of ours.

Just imagine a similar news item coming out of another country.

*Hot off the wires from Tehran: Iranian special forces teams are scouring the planet for old American Chinook helicopters so they can be well "cloaked" in planned future forays into Afghanistan and Pakistan's Baluchistan Province.*

That might be a little hard to imagine right now, but I guarantee you one thing: had some foreign news source reported such a plan, or had Craig Whitlock somehow uncovered it and included it in a piece—no matter how obscurely nestled—there would have been pandemonium in Washington. Congress would have held hearings. Pundits would have opined on the infamy of Iranian operatives masking themselves in our choppers. The company or companies that sold the helicopters would have been investigated. And you can imagine what Fox News commentators would have had to say.

When we do such things, however, and a country like Pakistan reacts with what's usually described as "anti-Americanism," we wonder at the nationalistic hair-trigger they're on. We comment on their over-emotionalism, we highlight their touchy "sensibilities," and our reporters and pundits then write empathetically about the difficulties American military and civilian officials have dealing with such edgy natives. In July 2010, for instance, the *Wall Street Journal* reported that U.S. Special Operations forces were expanding their role in the Pakistani tribal borderlands by more regularly "venturing out with Pakistani forces on aid projects, deepening the American role in the effort to defeat Islamist militants in Pakistani territory that has been off limits to U.S. ground troops." The Pakistani government has not been eager to have American boots visibly on the ground in these areas, and so *Journal* reporter Julian Barnes wrote, "Because of Pakistan's sensitivities, the U.S. role has developed slowly."

Imagine how sensitive they might prove to be if those same forces began to land Russian helicopters in Pakistan as a way to "cloak" their operations and blend in? Or just what sort of hair-trigger the natives of Montana might be on if Pakistani special operations types were roaming Glacier National Park and landing old American helicopters outside Butte. Then consider the sensitivities of Pakistanis on learning that the head of the CIA's National Clandestine Service turned out to be a man of "impeccable credentials" (so said then-CIA director Leon Panetta). Among those credentials were his stint as the CIA station chief in Pakistan until sometime in 2009, his involvement in the exceedingly unpopular drone war in that country's tribal borderlands, and the way, as Panetta put it a tad vaguely, he "guided complex operations under some of the most difficult circumstances imaginable."

Here's the truth of the matter, as Whitlock's piece makes clear: we carry on in the most bizarre ways in far-off lands and think nothing of it. Historically, it has undoubtedly been the nature of imperial powers to consider every strange thing they do more or less the norm. For a waning imperial power, however, such an attitude has its own dangers. If we can't imagine the surpassing strangeness of our arrangements for making war in lands thousands of miles from the United States, then we can't begin to imagine how the world sees us, which means that we're blind to our own madness.

## Forever War

Sometimes it's the little things in the big stories that catch your eye. On September 27, 2010, the *Washington Post* ran the first of three pieces adapted from Bob Woodward's latest book *Obama's Wars*, a vivid account of the way the U.S. high command boxed the commander in chief into the smallest of Afghan corners. As an illustration, the *Post* included a graphic the military offered President Obama at a key November 2009 meeting called to review war policy. It caught in a nutshell the favored "solution" to the Afghan War of those in charge of fighting it—Admiral Mike Mullen, chairman of the Joint Chiefs of Staff, General David Petraeus, then Centcom commander, General Stanley McChrystal, then Afghan War commander, and Secretary of Defense Robert Gates, among others. Labeled "Alternative Mission in Afghanistan," it's a classic of visual wish fulfillment. Atop it is a soaring green line that was meant to represent the growing strength of the notoriously underwhelming "Afghan Forces," military and police, as they moved toward a theoretical goal of 400,000—an unlikely "end state" given present desertion rates. Underneath that green trajectory of putative success was a modest, herky-jerky blue curving line, representing the 40,000 U.S. troops Gates, Petraeus, Mullen, and company were pressuring the president to surge into Afghanistan.

The eye-catching detail, however, was the date on the chart. Sometime between 2013 and 2016, according to a hesitant dotted white line (that left plenty of room for error), those U.S. surge forces would be drawn down radically enough to dip somewhere below the 68,000 level. In other words, two to five years from that September, if all went as planned—a radical unlikelihood, given the Afghan War so far—the United States might be back to the force levels of early 2009, before the president's second surge was launched.

And when would those troops dwindle to near zero? 2019? 2025? The chart makers were far too politic to include anything beyond January 1, 2016, so we have no way of knowing what they were thinking. But look at that chart and ask yourself: Is there any doubt that our high command, civilian and military, was dreaming of and most forcefully recommending to the president a forever war, one which the Office of Management and Budget estimated would cost almost $900 billion?

Of course, as we now know, the military "lost" this battle. Instead of the 40,000 troops they desired, they "only" got 30,000 from a frustrated president, plus a few thousand support troops the Secretary of Defense was allowed to slip in, and some special operations forces that no one was putting much effort into counting, and don't forget those extra troops wrung out of NATO as well as small allies who, for a price, couldn't say no—all of which added up to a figure suspiciously close to the 10,000 the president had officially denied his war commanders.

When, on December 1, 2009, Barack Obama addressed the cadets of West Point and, through them, the rest of us to announce the second Afghan surge of his presidency, he was at least able to slip in a date to begin the drawdown of U.S. forces. ("But taken together, these additional American and international troops will allow us to accelerate handing over responsibility to Afghan forces, and allow us to begin the transfer of our forces out of Afghanistan in July of 2011.") Hardly a nanosecond passed before—first "on background" and soon enough in public—administration spokespeople rushed to reassure the rest of Washington that such a transfer would be "conditions based." Given conditions there since 2001, not exactly a reassuring statement.

## More, Never Less

Let's keep two things in mind here: just how narrow the options the president considered were, and just how large the surge he reluctantly launched was. By the end of fall 2009, it was common knowledge in Washington that the administration's fiercely debated Afghan War "review" never considered a "less" option, only ones involving "more." Thanks to Woodward, we can put definitive numbers to those options. The least of the "more" options was Vice President Biden's "counterterrorism-plus" strategy, focused on more trainers for the Afghan military and police plus more drone attacks and Special Forces operations. It involved a surge of 20,000 U.S. troops. According to Woodward, the military commanders, the chairman of the Joint Chiefs, and the secretary of defense more or less instantly ruled this out.

The military's chosen option was for those 40,000 troops and an emphasis on counterinsurgency. Between them lay a barely distinguishable 30,000 to 35,000 option. The only other option mentioned during the review process involved a surge of 85,000, and it, too, was ruled out by the military because troops in that quantity simply weren't available. This, then, was the full "range" of debate in Washington about the Afghan

War. No wonder the president, according to Woodward, exclaimed in anger, "So what's my option? You have given me one option."

It's also important to remember that this round of surgification involved a lot more than those 30,000 troops and various add-ons. Thanks to Woodward's book, for instance, we now know that, in 2002, the Bush administration allowed the CIA to organize a secret Afghan "paramilitary army," modeled after the U.S. Special Forces and divided into "counter-terrorist pursuit teams." Three thousand in all, these irregulars have been operating as proxy fighters and assassins in Afghanistan. And, in the Obama era, they have evidently also been venturing into the Pakistani tribal borderlands where CIA drone attacks are already part of everyday life. U.S. helicopters upped the ante in the first of two such incidents by venturing across the same border to attack retreating Taliban fighters in what U.S. military spokespeople termed "self-defense," but was known in the Vietnam era as "hot pursuit."

In addition, U.S. military commanders, the *New York Times* reports, have threatened worse. ("As evidence of the growing frustration of American officials, Gen. David H. Petraeus, the top American commander in Afghanistan . . . issued veiled warnings to top Pakistani commanders that the United States could launch unilateral ground operations in the tribal areas should Pakistan refuse to dismantle the militant networks in North Waziristan, according to American officials.")

All of this is part of the unspoken Pentagon doctrine of forever war. And lest you think that the 2016 date for an Afghan drawdown was a one-of-a-kind bit of planning, consider this line from a *New York Times* report by Michael Gordon and John Burns on Pentagon anxiety over the British government's desire to cut defense spending by up to 20 percent: "American and British officials said that they did not expect any cutbacks to curtail Britain's capabilities to fight in Afghanistan over the next five years." Let that sink in for a moment: "over the next five years." It obviously reflects the thinking of anonymous officials of some significance and, if you do the modest math, you once again find yourself more or less at January 1, 2016. In a just released *Rolling Stone* interview, even the president can be found saying, vaguely but ominously, of the Afghan War: "[I]t's going to take us several years to work through this issue."

Does this sound like a military getting ready to leave town any time soon?

And don't forget the $1.3 billion in funds pending in Congress that Pincus tells us the Pentagon has requested "for multiyear construction of military facilities in Afghanistan." We're obviously talking 2012 to 2015 here, too. Or how about the $6.2 billion a year that the Pentagon is projected to spend on the training of Afghan forces from 2012 through 2016? Or what about the Pentagon contract TomDispatch.com's Nick Turse dug up that was awarded to private contractor SOS International primarily for translators with an estimated completion date of September 2014? Or how about the gigantic embassy-cum-command-center-cum-citadel (modeled on the U.S. embassy in Baghdad, at present the largest in the world) which the Obama administration has decided to build in Islamabad, Pakistan?

And let's not leave out the army's incessant planning for the distant future embodied in a recently published report, "Operating Concept, 2016–2028," overseen by Brigadier General H. R. McMaster, a senior adviser to General Petraeus. It ditches the "Buck Rogers" visions of futuristic war, and instead describes counterinsurgency operations, grimly referred to as "wars of exhaustion," in one, two, many Afghanistans to the distant horizon.

Like an alcoholic on a bender, the present Pentagon and military cast of characters can't stop themselves. Forever war is in their blood, so much so that they're ready to face down the commander in chief, if necessary, to make it continue. This is really the definition of an addiction—not to victory, but to the state of war itself. Don't expect them to discipline themselves. They won't.

## The Stimulus Package in Kabul

You must have had a moment when you thought to yourself: It really isn't going to end, is it? Not ever.

For me, that moment came when the Associated Press covered U.S. ambassador to Afghanistan Karl Eikenberry's announcement that a $511 million contract had been awarded to Caddell Construction, one of America's "largest construction and engineering groups," for a massive expansion of the U.S. embassy in Kabul. According to the ambassador, that embassy is already "the largest . . . in the world with more than 1,100 brave and dedicated civilians . . . from 16 agencies and working next to their military counterparts in 30 provinces," and yet it seems it's still not large enough.

A few other things in his announcement caught my eye. Construction of the new "permanent offices and housing" for embassy personnel is not to be completed until sometime in 2014, and that $511 million is part of a $790 million bill to U.S. taxpayers that will include expansion work on consular facilities in the Afghan cities of Mazar-i-Sharif and Herat.

If the ambassador's announcement was meant to fly below the media radar screen in the United States, it was clearly supposed to be noticed in Afghanistan. After all, Eikenberry publicly insisted that the awarding of the contract should be considered "an indication . . . an action, a deed that you can take as a long-term commitment of the United States government to the government of Afghanistan."

Jo Comerford and the number-crunchers at the National Priorities Project have placed that $790 million outlay into an American context: "$790 million is more than ten times the money the federal government allotted for the State Energy Program in FY2011. It's nearly five times the total amount allocated for the National Endowment for the Arts . . . If that sum were applied instead to job creation in the United States, in new hires it would yield more than 22,000 teachers, 15,000 healthcare workers, and employ more than 13,000 in the burgeoning clean energy industry."

Still, to understand just why, among a flood of similar war reports, this one got under my skin, you need a bit of backstory.

### Singular Spawn or Forerunner Deluxe?

One night in May 2007, I was nattering on at the dinner table about reports of a monstrous new U.S. embassy being constructed in Baghdad, so big that it put former Iraqi dictator Saddam Hussein's grandiose Disneyesque palaces to shame. On 104 acres of land in the heart of the Iraqi capital (always referred to in news reports as almost the size of Vatican City), it was slated to cost $590 million. (Predictable cost overruns and delays would, in the end, bring that figure to at least $740 million, while the cost of running the place yearly is estimated at $1.5 billion.) Back then, more than half a billion dollars was impressive enough, even for a compound that was to have its own self-contained electricity-generation, water-purification, and sewage systems in a city lacking most of those things, not to speak of its own antimissile defense systems and twenty all-new blast-resistant buildings including restaurants, a recreation center, and other amenities. It was to be by far the largest, most heavily fortified embassy on the planet with a "diplomatic" staff of a thousand (a number that has only grown since).

My wife listened to my description of this future colossus, which bore no relation to anything ever previously called an "embassy," and then, out of the blue, said, "I wonder who the architect is?" Strangely, I hadn't even considered that such a mega-citadel might actually have an architect. So imagine my surprise on discovering that there was indeed a Kansas architect, BDY (Berger Devine Yaeger), previously responsible for the Sprint Corporation's world headquarters in Overland Park, Kansas, the Visitation Church in Kansas City, Missouri, and Harrah's Hotel and Casino in North Kansas City, Missouri. Better yet, BDY was so proud to have been taken on as architect to the wildest imperial dreamers and schemers of our era that it posted sketches at its website of what the future embassy, its "pool house," its tennis court, PX, retail and shopping areas, and other highlights were going to look like.

Somewhere between horrified and grimly amused, I wrote a piece at TomDispatch, entitled "The Mother Ship Lands in Baghdad" and, via a link to the BDY drawings, offered readers a little "blast-resistant spin" through Bush's colossus. From the beginning, I grasped that this wasn't an embassy in any normal sense and I understood as well something of what it was. Here's the way I put it at the time: "As an outpost, this vast compound reeks of one thing: imperial impunity. It was never meant to be an embassy from a democracy that had liberated an oppressed land. From the first thought, the first sketch, it was to be the sort of imperial control center suitable for the planet's sole 'hyperpower,' dropped into the middle of the oil heartlands of the globe. It was to be Washington's dream and Kansas City's idea of a palace fit for an embattled American proconsul—or a khan."

In other words, a U.S. control center at the heart of what Bush administration officials then liked to call "the Greater Middle East." To my surprise, the piece began racing around the Internet and other sites—TomDispatch did not then have the capacity to post images—started putting up BDY's crude drawings. The next thing I knew, the State Department had panicked, declared this a "security breach," and forced BDY to take down its site and remove the drawings. I was amazed, but—and here we come to the failure of my own imagination—I never doubted that BDY's bizarre imperial mother ship being prepared for landing in Baghdad was the singular spawn of the Bush administration. I saw it as essentially a vanity production sired by a particular set of fantasies about imposing a *Pax Americana* abroad and a *Pax Republicana* at home. It never crossed my mind that there would be two such "embassies."

So, on this, call me delusional. By May 2009, with Barack Obama in the White House, I knew as much. That was when two McClatchy reporters broke a story about a similar project for a new "embassy" in Islamabad, the capital of Pakistan, at the projected cost of $736 million.

### Simulating Ghosts

Now, with the news in from Kabul, we know that there are going to be three mother ships. All gigantic beyond belief. All (after the usual cost overruns) undoubtedly in the three-quarters-of-a-billion-dollar to billion-dollar range. All meant not to house modest numbers of diplomats acting as the face of the United States in a foreign land, but thousands of diplomats, spies, civilian personnel, military officials, agents, and operatives hunkering down long term for war and skullduggery.

Connect two points and you have a straight line. Connect three points and you have a pattern—in this case, simple and striking. The visionaries and fundamentalists of the Bush years may be gone and visionless managers of the tattered American imperium now directing the show. Nonetheless, they and the U.S. military in the region remain remarkably devoted to the control of the Greater Middle East. Even without a vision, there is still the war momentum and the money to support it.

While Americans fight bitterly over whether the stimulus package for the domestic economy was too large or too small, few in the United States even notice that the American stimulus package in Kabul, Islamabad, Baghdad, and elsewhere in our embattled Raj is going great guns. Embassies the size of pyramids are still being built, military bases to stagger the imagination continue to be constructed, and nowhere, not even in Iraq, is it clear that Washington is committed to packing up its tents, abandoning its billion-dollar monuments, and coming home.

In the United States, it's going to be paralysis and stagnation all the way, but in Peshawar and Mazar-i-sharif, not to speak of the greater Persian Gulf region, we remain the spendthrifts of war, perfectly willing, for instance, to ship fuel across staggering distances and unimaginably long supply lines to Afghanistan at $400 a gallon to further crank up an energy-heavy conflict. At home, it's peace all the way to the unemployment line, because peace, in our American world, increasingly seems to mean economic disaster. In the Greater Middle East, it's war to the horizon, all war all the time, and creeping escalation all the way around.

The folks who started us down this precipitous path and over an economic cliff are now in retirement and heading onto the memoir circuit. Our former president is chatting it up with Matt Lauer and Oprah. His vice president is nursing his heart while assumedly writing about "his service in four presidential administrations." His national security adviser, then secretary of state (for whom Chevron once named a double-hulled oil tanker) is already heading into her second and third memoir. But while they scribble and yak, their policy ghosts haunt us, as does their greatest edifice, that embassy in Baghdad, now being cloned elsewhere. Even without them or the neocons who pounded the drums for them, the U.S. military still pushes doggedly toward 2014 and beyond in Afghanistan, while officials "tweak" their drawdown non-schedules, narrow the president's non-options, and step in to fund and build yet more command-and-control centers in the Greater Middle East.

It looks and feels like the never-ending story, and yet, of course, the imperium is visibly fraying, while the burden of distant wars grows ever heavier. Those "embassies" are being built for the long haul, but a decade or two down the line, I wouldn't want to put my money on what exactly they will represent, or what they could possibly hope to control.

## How to Schedule a War

"Going, going, gone!" You can almost hear the announcer's voice throbbing with excitement, only we're not talking about home runs here, but about the disappearing date on which, for the United States and its military, the Afghan War will officially end.

Practically speaking, the answer to when it will be over is: just this side of never. If you take the word of our Afghan War commander, the secretary of defense, and top officials of the Obama administration and NATO, we're not leaving anytime soon. As with any clever time traveler, every date that's set always contains a verbal escape hatch into the future.

In my 1950s childhood, there was a cheesy (if thrilling) sci-fi flick, *The Incredible Shrinking Man*, about a fellow who passed through a radioactive cloud in the Pacific Ocean and soon noticed that his suits were too big for him. Next thing you knew, he was living in a doll house, holding off his pet cat, and fighting an ordinary spider transformed into a monster. Finally, he disappeared entirely, leaving behind only a sonorous voice to tell us that he had entered a universe where "the unbelievably small and the unbelievably vast eventually meet, like the closing of a gigantic circle."

The date for serious drawdowns of American troops in Afghanistan has followed a similar path toward the vanishing point and is now threatening to disappear "over the horizon" (a place where, we are regularly told, American troops will lurk once they have finally transferred their duties to the Afghan forces they are training). If you remember, back in December 2009, President Obama spoke of July 2011 as a firm date to "begin the transfer of our forces out of Afghanistan," the moment assumedly when the beginning of the end of the war would come into sight. In July 2010, Afghan president Hamid Karzai spoke of 2014 as the date when Afghan security forces "will be responsible for all military and law enforcement operations throughout our country." Administration officials, anxious about the effect that the 2011 date was having on an American public grown weary of an unpopular war and on an enemy waiting for us to depart, grabbed Karzai's date and ran with it (leaving many of his caveats about the war the Americans were fighting, particularly his desire to reduce the American presence, in the dust). Now, 2014 is the new 2011.

It has, in fact, been widely reported that Obama officials have been working in concert to "play down" the president's 2011 date, while refocusing attention on 2014. Top administration officials have been little short of voluble on the subject. Secretary of Defense Robert Gates ("We're not getting out. We're talking about probably a years-long process."), Secretary of State Hillary Clinton, and chairman of the Joint Chiefs admiral Mike Mullen, attending a security conference in Australia, all "cited 2014 . . . as the key date for handing over the defense of Afghanistan to the Afghans themselves." The *New York Times* headlined its report on the change in timing this way: "U.S. Tweaks Message on Troops in Afghanistan." Quite a tweak. Added *Times* reporter Elisabeth Bumiller, "The message shift is effectively a victory for the military, which has long said the July 2011 deadline undermined its mission by making Afghans reluctant to work with troops perceived to be leaving shortly."

### Inflection Points and Aspirational Goals

Barely had 2014 risen into the headlines before that date, too, began its vanishing act. As a start, it turned out that American planners weren't talking about just any old day in 2014, but its last one. As Lieutenant General William Caldwell, head of the NATO training program for Afghan security forces, put it while holding a Q&A with a group of bloggers, "They're talking about December 31st, 2014. It's the end of December in 2014 . . . that [Afghan] President Karzai has said they want Afghan security forces in the lead."

No one, officials rushed to say, was talking about 2014 as a date for *all* American troops to head for the exits, just combat troops—and maybe not even all of them. Possibly tens of thousands of trainers and other so-called noncombat forces would stay on to help with the "transition process." This follows the Iraq pattern where fifty thousand American troops remained after the departure of U.S. "combat" forces to great media fanfare.

In November 2010, behind "closed doors" at a NATO summit in Lisbon, Portugal, Afghan War commander Petraeus presented European leaders with a "phased four-year plan" to "wind down American and allied fighting in Afghanistan." Not surprisingly, it had the end of 2014 in its sights and the president quickly confirmed that "transition" date, even while opening plenty of post-2014 wiggle room. By then, as he described it, "our footprint" would only be "significantly reduced." (He also claimed that, post-2014, the United States would be maintaining a "counterterrorism capability" in Afghanistan—*and* Iraq—for which "platforms to . . . execute . . . counterterrorism operations," assumedly bases, would be needed.) Meanwhile, unnamed "senior U.S. officials" in Lisbon were clearly buttonholing reporters to "cast doubt on whether the United States, the dominant power in the 28-nation alliance, would end its own combat mission before 2015." As always, the usual qualifying phrases were profusely in evidence.

The "tweaking"—that is, the further chipping away at 2014 as a hard and fast date for anything—has only continued. Mark Sedwill, NATO's civilian counterpart to Petraeus, insisted that 2014 was nothing more than "an inflection point" in an ever more drawn-out drawdown process. That process would likely extend to "2015 and beyond," which, of course, put 2016 officially into play. And keep in mind that this is only for combat troops, not those assigned to "train and support" or keep "a strategic over watch" on Afghan forces. On the eve of NATO's Lisbon meeting, Pentagon spokesman Geoff Morrell declared 2014 nothing more than an "aspirational goal," rather than an actual deadline. As the conference began, NATO's secretary general Anders Fogh Rasmussen insisted that the alliance would be committed in Afghanistan "as long as it takes." And British Chief of the Defense Staff General Sir David Richards suggested that, given the difficulty of ever defeating the Taliban (or al-Qaeda) militarily, NATO should be preparing plans to maintain a role for its troops for the next thirty to forty years.

### On Ticking Clocks in Washington and Kabul

Up to now, only one of General Petraeus's two campaigns has been under discussion here: the one fought out not in Afghanistan, but in Washington and NATO capitals, over how to schedule a war. Think of it as the war for a free hand in determining how long the Afghan War is to be fought. It has been run from General Petraeus's headquarters in Kabul, the giant five-sided military headquarters on the Potomac presided over by Secretary of Defense Gates, and various think tanks filled with America's militarized intelligentsia scattered around Washington—and it has proven to be a classically successful "clear, hold, build" counterinsurgency operation. Pacification in Washington and a number of European capitals has occurred with remarkably few casualties. (Former Afghan War commander general Stanley McChrystal, axed by the president for insubordination, has been the exception, not the rule.)

With the ratification in Lisbon of that 2014 date "and beyond," the political clocks—an image General Petraeus loves—in Washington, European capitals, and American Kabul are now ticking more or less in unison.

Two other "clocks" are, however, ticking more like time bombs. If counterinsurgency is a hearts-and-minds campaign, then another target of General Petraeus's first COIN (counterinsurgency) campaign has been the restive hearts and minds of the American and European publics. In February 2010, the Dutch government fell over popular opposition to Afghanistan and, even as NATO met that weekend in November 2010, thousands of antiwar protestors were marching in London and Lisbon. Europeans generally want out and their governments know it, but (as has been true since 1945) the continent's leaders have no idea how to say no to Washington. In the United States, too, the Afghan War grows ever more unpopular, and while it was forgotten during the election season, no politician should count on that phenomenon lasting forever.

And then, of course, there's the other ticking bomb, the actual war in Afghanistan. In that campaign, despite a drumbeat of American/NATO publicity about "progress," the news has been grim. American and NATO casualties have been higher from 2010 to 2011 than at any other moment in the war. The Taliban seems, if anything, more entrenched in more parts of the country; the Afghan public, puzzled and unhappy with foreign troops and contractors traipsing across the land. And President Hamid Karzai, sensing a situation gone truly sour, has been regularly challenging the way General Petraeus is fighting the war in his country. (The nerve!)

No less unsettling, General Petraeus himself has seemed unnerved. He was reportedly "irked" by Karzai's comments and was said to have warned Afghan officials that their president's criticism might be making his "own position 'untenable,'" which was taken as a resignation threat. Meanwhile, the COIN-meister was in the process of imposing a new battle plan on Afghanistan that left counterinsurgency (at least as usually described) in a roadside ditch. No more was the byword "protect the people," but smash, kill, destroy. The war commander has loosed American firepower in a major way in the Taliban strongholds of southern Afghanistan.

In early 2010, then-commander McChrystal had significantly cut back on U.S. air strikes as a COIN-ish measure meant to lessen civilian casualties. In a striking reversal, air power was called in massively. In October 2010, U.S. planes launched missiles or bombs on a thousand separate Afghan missions, numbers seldom seen since the 2001 invasion. The army similarly loosed its massively powerful High Mobility Artillery Rocket System in the area around the southern city of Kandahar. Civilian deaths rose rapidly. Dreaded special operations night raids on Afghan homes by "capture/kill" teams tripled. With them, the body count also arrived. American officials eagerly began boasting to reporters about their efficiency in taking out midlevel Taliban leaders ("368 insurgent leaders killed or captured, and 968 lower-level insurgents killed and 2,477 captured, according to NATO statistics").

In the districts around Kandahar, a reported American tactic was simply to raze individual houses or even whole villages believed to be booby-trapped by the Taliban, as well as tree lines "where insurgents could hide." American troops were "blow[ing] up outbuildings, flatten[ing] agricultural walls, and carv[ing] new 'military roads,' because existing ones are so heavily mined . . . right through farms and compounds." The marines, reported Rajiv Chandrasekaran of the *Washington Post*, were also sending the first contingent of M1 Abrams tanks (with a "main gun that can destroy a house more than a mile away") into the south. Such tanks, previously held back for fear of reminding Afghans of their Russian occupiers, were, according to an unnamed U.S. officer he quotes, bringing "awe, shock, and firepower" to the south. None of this had anything to do with winning hearts and minds, just obliterating them. Not surprisingly, such tactics also generated villagers fleeing embattled farmlands, often for "squalid" refugee camps in overcrowded cities.

### Flip of the COIN

Suddenly, this war for which General Petraeus had won his counterinsurgency warriors at least a four- to six-year extension was being fought as if there were no tomorrow. Here, for instance, is a brief description from a *Guardian* reporter in Kandahar of the night war from a distance: "After the sun sets, the air becomes noisy with jets dropping bombs that bleach the dark out of the sky in their sudden eruptions; with the ripping sound of the miniguns of the Kiowa helicopter gunships and A-10 Warthogs hunting in the nearby desert. The night is also lit up by brilliant flares that fall as slow as floating snowflakes, a visible sign of the commando raids into the villages beyond. It is a conflict heard, but not often witnessed."

None of this qualifies as counterinsurgency, at least as described by the general and his followers. It does, however, resemble where counterinsurgencies have usually headed—directly into the charnel house of history.

Chandrasekaran quoted a civilian adviser to the NATO command in Kabul this way: "Because Petraeus is the author of the COIN [counterinsurgency] manual, he can do whatever he wants. He can manage the optics better than McChrystal could. If he wants to turn it up to 11, he feels he has the moral authority to do it." So Petraeus flipped a COIN and took a gamble. One thing is certain, however: Afghans will once again pay with their homes, farms, livelihoods, and lives, while Americans, Europeans, and Canadians will pay with lives and foot the bill for a war that couldn't be more bizarre, a war with no end in sight.

## CHAPTER 5

# Waist Deep in the Washington Quagmire

## Numbers to Die For

In my 1950s childhood, *Ripley's Believe It or Not* was part of everyday life, a syndicated comics page feature where you could stumble upon such mind-boggling facts as: "If all the Chinese in the world were to march four abreast past a given point, they would never finish passing though they marched forever and ever." Or if you were young and iconoclastic, you could chuckle over *Mad* magazine's parody, "Ripup's Believe It or Don't!"

With our Afghan and Iraq Wars on my mind, I've been wondering whether Ripley's moment hasn't returned. Here, for instance, are some figures offered in a March 30, 2010, *Washington Post* piece by Lieutenant General James H. Pillsbury, deputy commanding general of the U.S. Army Materiel Command, who is deeply involved in the "drawdown of the logistics operation in Iraq": "There are . . . more than 341 facilities; 263,000 soldiers, Defense Department civilians and contractor employees; 83,000 containers; 42,000 vehicles; 3 million equipment items; and roughly $54 billion in assets that will ultimately be removed from Iraq." Admittedly, that list lacks the "believe it or not" tagline, but otherwise Ripley's couldn't have put it more staggeringly. And here's Pillsbury's Ripley-esque kicker: the American drawdown will be the "equivalent, in personnel terms alone, of relocating the entire population of Buffalo, New York."

When it comes to that slo-mo drawdown, all the numbers turn out to be staggering. They are also a reminder of just how the Pentagon has been fighting its wars in these last years—like a compulsive shopper without a twelve-step recovery program in sight. Whether it's 3.1 million items of equipment, 2.8 million, or 1.5 million (all numbers cited in one media account or another), whether 341 "facilities" (not including perhaps ten megabases which are still operating with tens of thousands of American soldiers, civilians, and private contractors working and living on them) or 290 bases are to be shut down, the numbers from Iraq are simply out of this world.

Where armies once had baggage trains and camp followers, our camp followers now help plant our military in foreign soil, build its housing and defenses, and then supply it with vast quantities of food, water, fuel, and god knows what else. In this way, our troops carry not just packs on their backs, but a total, transplantable society right down to the PXs, massage parlors, food courts, and miniature golf courses.

In Ripley's terms, if you were to put all the vehicles, equipment, and other materiel we managed to transport to Iraq and Afghanistan "four abreast," they, too, might stretch on close to forever. And wouldn't that be an illustration worthy of the old Ripley's cartoon—all those coffeemakers and porta-potties and Internet cafés, even imported sand that, if more widely known about, might change the phrase "taking coals to Newcastle" to "bringing sand to Iraq"?

You see, for all the sand Iraq did have, from the point of view of the U.S. military it didn't have the perfect type for making the miles of protective "blast walls" that became a common feature of the post-invasion landscape. So, according to Stephen Farrell of the *New York Times*, U.S. taxpayer dollars shipped in boatloads of sand from the United Arab Emirates and Qatar to create those 15-ton blast walls at $3,500 a pop. U.S. planners are now evidently wondering whether to ship some of the leftover walls thousands of miles by staggeringly roundabout routes to Afghanistan at a transportation cost of $15,000 each.

When it comes to the U.S. drawdown in Iraq and the buildup in Afghanistan, in fact, the numbers, any numbers, are little short of unbelievable.

• *Believe it or not*, U.S. commanders in our war zones have more than one billion congressionally mandated dollars a year at their disposal to spend on making "friends with local citizens and help[ing] struggling economies." It's all socked away in the Commander's Emergency Response Program. Think of it as a local community-bribery account that, best of all, seems not to require the slightest accountability to Congress for where or how the money is spent.

• *Believe it or not* (small change department), the Pentagon is planning to spend an initial $50 million from a "$350 million Pentagon program designed to improve the counterterrorism operations of U.S. allies" on Croatia, Georgia, Hungary, Latvia, Lithuania, and Estonia, all of whom, in the latest version of the Coalition of the Billing, just happen to have small numbers of troops deployed in Afghanistan.

• *Believe it or not*, the Defense Logistics Agency shipped 1.1 million hamburger patties to Afghanistan in the month of March 2010 (nearly doubling the March 2009 figure).

• *Believe it or not*, the State Department has paid private contractors Triple Canopy $438 million since mid-2005 simply to guard the massive U.S. Embassy in Baghdad. That's more than half the price tag to build the embassy. Triple Canopy now has 1,800 employees dedicated to embassy protection in the Iraqi capital, mainly Ugandan and Peruvian security guards. At $736 million to build, the embassy itself is a numbers wonder, and has even had its sizeable playing field astroturfed—"the first artificial turf sports field in Iraq"—also assumedly at taxpayer expense.

• *Believe it or not*, according to Nick Turse, nearly four hundred bases for U.S. troops, CIA operatives, special operations forces, NATO allies, and civilian contractors have already been constructed in Afghanistan, topping the base-building figures for Iraq by about one hundred in a situation where almost every bit of material has to be transported into the country. The base-building spree has yet to end.

• *Believe it or not*, according to the *Washington Post*, the Defense Department has awarded a contract worth up to $360 million to the son of an Afghan cabinet minister to transport U.S. military supplies through some of the most dangerous parts of Afghanistan—and his company has no trucks. (He hires subcontractors who evidently pay off the Taliban as part of a large-scale protection racket that allows the supplies through unharmed.) This contract is, in turn, part of a $2.1 billion Host Nation Trucking contract whose recipients may be deeply involved in extortion and smuggling rackets, and over which the Pentagon reportedly exercises little oversight.

• *Believe it or not*, the staggering logistics effort involved in transporting part of the American way of war from Iraq to Afghanistan is now being compared by those involved to Hannibal (not Lecter) crossing the Alps with his cohort of battle elephants, or to that ancient conqueror of conquerors, Alexander the Great ("the largest building boom in Afghanistan since Alexander built Kandahar").

If war were really a *Believe It or Not* matter, or victory lay in the number of hamburgers transported, the U.S. military would have been the winner long ago. After all, it may be the most product-profligate military with the heaviest "footprint" in history. Though it's seldom thought strange and rarely commented upon in the United States, the Pentagon practices war as a form of mass consumption and so, not surprisingly, bears a striking resemblance to the society from which it comes. Like the Taliban, it carries its way of life to war on its back.

It's striking, of course, that all this is happening at a moment when, domestically, small businesses can't get loans and close to 10 percent of the population is officially out of work, while state governments are desperately scrabbling for every available dollar even as they cut what would once have been considered basic services. In contrast, the Pentagon is fighting its distant wars as if American pockets had no bottoms, the national treasury had no limits, and there was no tomorrow.

And there's one more small contrast to be made when it comes to the finest military in the history of the world: for all the private security guards, mountains of burgers, lakes of gasoline, miles of blast walls, and satchels of cash to pass out to the locals, it's been remarkably unsuccessful in its pacification campaigns against some of the motliest forces of our time. The U.S. military has been fought to something like a draw by relatively modest-sized, relatively lightly armed minority insurgencies that don't even pass muster when it comes to shooting straight.

Vast piles of money and vast quantities of materiel have been squandered; equipment by the boatload has been used up; lives have been wasted in profusion; and yet the winners of our wars might turn out to be Iran and China. The American way of war, unfortunately, has the numbers to die for, just not to live by.

## A Reluctance to Leave

Yes, we could. No kidding. We really *could* withdraw our massive armies, now close to two hundred thousand troops combined, from Afghanistan and Iraq (and that's not even counting our similarly large stealth army of private contractors, which helps keep the true size of our double occupations in the shadows). We could undoubtedly withdraw them all reasonably quickly and reasonably painlessly.

Not that you would know it from listening to the debates in Washington or catching the mainstream news. There, withdrawal, when discussed at all, seems like an undertaking beyond the waking imagination. In Iraq alone, all those bases to dismantle and millions of pieces of equipment to send home in a drawdown operation worthy of years of intensive effort, the sort of thing that makes the desperate British evacuation from Dunkirk in World War II look like a Sunday stroll in the park. And that's only the technical side of the matter.

There's also the conviction that anything but a withdrawal that would make molasses in January look like the hare of Aesopian fable—at least two years in Iraq, five to ten in Afghanistan—would endanger the planet itself, or at least its most important country: ours. Without our eternally steadying hand, the Iraqis and Afghans, it's taken for granted, would be lost.

It's accepted in Washington that, if we were to leave Afghanistan precipitously, the Taliban would take over, al-Qaeda would be back big time in no time, and then more of our giant buildings would obviously bite the dust. And yet, the longer we've stayed and the more we've surged, the more resurgent the Taliban has become, the more territory this minority insurgency has spread into. If we stay long enough, we may, in fact, create the majority insurgency we claim to fear.

It's common wisdom in the United States that, before we pull our military out, Afghanistan, like Iraq, must be secured as a stable enough ally, as well as at least a fragile junior democracy, which consigns real departure to some distant horizon. And that sense of time may help explain the desire of U.S. officials to hinder Afghan president Hamid Karzai's attempts to negotiate with the Taliban and other rebel factions now. Washington, it seems, favors a "reconciliation process" that will last years and only begin after the U.S. military seizes the high ground on the battlefield.

The reality that dare not speak its name in Washington is this: no matter what might happen in an Afghanistan that lacked us—whether (as in the 1990s) the various factions there leaped for each other's throats or the Taliban established significant control, though (as in the 1990s) not over the whole country—the stakes for Americans would be minor in nature. Not that anyone of significance here would say such a thing.

Tell me, what kind of a stake could Americans really have in one of the most impoverished lands on the planet, about as distant from us as could be imagined, geographically, culturally, and religiously? Yet, as if to defy commonsense, we've been fighting there—by proxy and directly—on and off for thirty years and with no end in sight.

Most Americans evidently remain convinced that an Afghan "safe haven" there was the key to al-Qaeda's success, and that Afghanistan was the only place in which that organization could conceivably have planned 9/11, even though perfectly real planning also took place in Hamburg, Germany, which we neither bombed nor invaded.

In a future in which our surging armies actually succeeded in controlling Afghanistan and denying it to al-Qaeda, what about Somalia, Yemen, or, for that matter, England? It's now conveniently forgotten that the first, nearly successful attempt to take down one of the World Trade Center towers in 1993 was planned in the wilds of New Jersey. Had the Bush administration been paying the slightest attention, or had reasonable precautions been taken, including locking the doors of airplane cockpits, 9/11 and so the invasion of Afghanistan would have been relegated to the far-fetched plot of some Tom Clancy novel.

## Vietnam and Afghanistan

The annals of history are well stocked with countries that invaded and occupied other lands and then left, often ingloriously and under intense pressure. But they did it.

It's worth remembering that, in 1975, when the South Vietnamese Army collapsed and we essentially fled the country, we abandoned staggering amounts of equipment there. Helicopters were pushed over the sides of aircraft carriers to make space, barrels of money were burned at the U.S. Embassy in Saigon, military bases as large as anything we've built in Iraq or Afghanistan fell into North Vietnamese hands, and South Vietnamese allies were deserted in the panic of the moment. Nonetheless, when there was no choice, we got out. Not elegantly, not nicely, not thoughtfully, not helpfully, but out.

Keep in mind that then, too, disaster was predicted for the planet, should we withdraw precipitously—including rolling Communist takeovers of country after country, the loss of "credibility" for the American superpower, and a murderous bloodbath in Vietnam itself. All were not only predicted by Washington's Cassandras, but endlessly cited in the war years as reasons not to leave. And yet here was the shock that somehow never registered among all the so-called lessons of Vietnam: nothing of that sort happened afterwards. Today, Vietnam is a reasonably prosperous land that maintains friendly relations with its former enemy, the United States. After Vietnam, no other "dominos" fell and there was no bloodbath in that country. Of course, it could have been different—and elsewhere, sometimes, it has been. But even when local skies darken, the world doesn't end.

And here's the truth of the matter: the world won't end, not in Iraq, not in Afghanistan, not in the United States, if we end our wars and withdraw. The sky won't fall, even if the United States gets out reasonably quickly, even if subsequently blood is spilled and things don't go well in either country. We got our troops there remarkably quickly. We're quite capable of removing them at a similar pace. We could, that is, leave. There are, undoubtedly, better and worse ways of doing this, ways that would further penalize the societies we've invaded, and ways that might be of some use to them, but either way we could go.

### A Brief History of American Withdrawal

Of course, there's a small problem here. All evidence indicates that Washington doesn't want to withdraw—not really, not from either region. It has no interest in divesting itself of the global control-and-influence business, or of the military-power racket. That's hardly surprising since we're talking about a great imperial power and control (or at least imagined control) over the planet's strategic oil lands.

And then there's another factor to consider: habit. Over the decades, Washington has gotten used to staying. The United States has long been big on arriving, but not much for departure. After all, sixty-five years later, striking numbers of American forces are still garrisoning the two major defeated nations of World War II, Germany and Japan. We still have about three dozen military bases on the modest-sized Japanese island of Okinawa, and are at this very moment fighting tooth and nail, diplomatically speaking, not to be forced to abandon one of them. The Korean War was suspended in an armistice more than fifty years ago and, again, striking numbers of American troops still garrison South Korea.

Similarly, to skip a few decades, after the Serbian air campaign of the late 1990s, the U.S. built up the enormous Camp Bondsteel in Kosovo with its 7-mile perimeter, and we're still there. After Gulf War I, the United States either built or built up military bases and other facilities in Saudi Arabia, Kuwait, Qatar, Oman, and Bahrain in the Persian Gulf, as well as the British island of Diego Garcia in the Indian Ocean. And it's never stopped building up its facilities throughout the Gulf region. In this sense, leaving Iraq, to the extent that we do, is not quite as significant a matter as sometimes imagined, strategically speaking. It's not as if the U.S. military were taking off for Dubuque.

A history of American withdrawal would prove a brief book indeed. Other than Vietnam, the U.S. military withdrew from the Philippines under the pressure of "people power" (and a local volcano) in the early 1990s, and from Saudi Arabia, in part under the pressure of Osama bin Laden. In both countries, however, it has retained or regained a foothold in recent years. President Ronald Reagan pulled American troops out of Lebanon after a devastating 1983 suicide truck bombing of a marine barracks there, and the president of Ecuador, Rafael Correa, functionally expelled the U.S. from Manta Air Base in 2008 when he refused to renew its lease. ("We'll renew the base on one condition: that they let us put a base in Miami—an Ecuadorian base," he said slyly.) And there were a few places like the island of Grenada, invaded in 1983, that simply mattered too little to Washington to stay.

Unfortunately, whatever the administration, the urge to stay has seemed a constant. It's evidently written into Washington's DNA and embedded deep in domestic politics where sure-to-come "cut and run" charges and blame for "losing" Iraq or Afghanistan would cow any administration. Not surprisingly, when you look behind the main news stories in both Iraq and Afghanistan, you can see signs of the urge to stay everywhere.

Perhaps it's historically accurate to say that great powers generally leave home, head elsewhere armed to the teeth, and then experience the urge to stay. With our trillion-dollar-plus wars and trillion-dollar-plus annual national security budget, there's a lot at stake in staying, and undoubtedly in fighting two, three, many Afghanistans (and Iraqs) in the years to come.

Sooner or later, we will leave both Iraq and Afghanistan. It's too late in the history of this planet to occupy them forever and a day. Better sooner.

## Will Our Generals Ever Shut Up?

There's a history still to be written about how our highest military commanders came to never shut up. There should be, but no longer is, something startling about all this. Generals and admirals now mouth off regularly on a wide range of policy issues, appealing to the American public both directly and via deferential (sometimes fawning) reporters, pundits, and commentators. They and their underlings clearly leak news repeatedly for tactical advantage in policymaking situations. They organize what are essentially political-style barnstorming campaigns for what once would have been "foreign policy" positions. Increasingly this is just the way the game is played.

Certainly, in 1990, as Gulf War I was approaching, Americans experienced the first full flowering of a new form of militarized "journalism" in which, among other things, retired high-ranking military officers, like so many play-by-play analysts on *Monday Night Football*, became regular TV news consultants. They were called upon to narrate and analyze the upcoming battle ("showdown in the Gulf"), the brief offensive that followed, and the aftermath in something close to real time. Amid nifty logos, dazzling *Star Wars*–style graphics, theme music, and instant-replay nose-cone snuff films of "precision" weapons wiping out the enemy, they offered a running commentary on the progress of battle as well as on the work of commanders in the field, some of whom they might once have served with.

And that was just the beginning of the way, after years of post–Vietnam War planning, the Pentagon took control of the media battlefield and so the popular portrayal of American-style war. In the past, the reporting of war had often been successfully controlled by governments, while generals had polished their images with the press or—like Omar Bradley and Douglas MacArthur—even employed public-relations staffs to do it for them. But never had generals and war planners gone before the public as actors, supported by all the means a studio could muster on their behalf and determined to produce a program that would fill the day across the dial for the duration of a war. The military even had a version of a network standards and practices department with its guidelines for on-air acceptability. Military handlers made decisions—like refusing to clear for publication the fact that Stealth pilots viewed X-rated movies before missions—reminiscent of network show-vetting practices.

When it came time for Gulf War II, the invasion of Iraq in 2003, the military had added the practice of putting reporters through weeklong prewar "boot camps" and then "embedding" them with the troops (a Stockholm Syndrome–type experience that many American reporters grew to love). It also built itself a quarter-million-dollar stage set for nonstop war briefings at Centcom headquarters in Doha, Qatar. All of this was still remarkably new in the history of relations between the Pentagon and the media, but it meant that the military could address the public more or less directly both through those embedded reporters and over the shoulders of that assembled gaggle of media types in Doha.

As long as war took its traditional form, this approach worked well, but once it turned into a protracted and inchoate guerrilla struggle, and "war" and "wartime" became the endless (often dismal) norm, something new was needed. In the Bush years, the Pentagon responded to endless war in part by sending out an endless stream of well-coached, well-choreographed retired military "experts" to fill the gaping maw of cable news. In the meantime, something quite new had developed.

You no longer needed to be a retired military officer to offer play-by-play commentary on and analysis of our wars. Now, at certain moments, the main narrators of those wars turned out to be none other than the generals running, or overseeing, them. They regularly got major airtime to explain to the American public how their wars were going, as well as to expound on their views on more general issues. This was something new. Among the American commanders of World War II and the Korean War, only Douglas MacArthur did anything faintly like this, which made him an outlier (or perhaps an omen) and in a sense that's why President Harry Truman fired him. Generals Eisenhower, Patton, Ridgeway, and others, did not think to go on media tours touting their own political lines while in uniform.

Admittedly, Vietnam War commander general William Westmoreland was an early pioneer of the form. He had, however, been pushed onto the stage to put a public face on the American war effort by President Lyndon Johnson, who was desperate to buck up public opinion. Westmoreland returned from Vietnam in 1968 just before the disastrous Tet Offensive for a "whirlwind tour" of the country and uplifting testimony before Congress. In a speech at the National Press Club, he spoke of reaching "an important point where the end begins to come into view," and later in a televised press conference, even more infamously used the phrase "the light at the end of tunnel." Events would soon discredit his optimism.

Still, we've reached quite a different level of military/media confluence today. Take the two generals fighting our Afghan and Iraq Wars in mid-August 2010: General Petraeus and General Ray Odierno.

Having spent six weeks assessing the Afghan situation and convinced that he needed to buy more time for his war from the American public, Petraeus launched a full-blown, well-organized media tour from his headquarters in Kabul. In it, he touted "progress" in Afghanistan, offered comments subtly but visibly at odds with the president's original July 2011 drawdown date, and generally evangelized for his war. He began with an hour-long interview with Dexter Filkins of the *New York Times* and another with Rajiv Chandrasekaran, national editor of the *Washington Post*.

These were timed to be released on August 15, the morning he appeared on NBC's Sunday political show *Meet the Press*. (Moderator David Gregory traveled to the Afghan capital to toss softball questions at Washington's greatest general and watch him do push-ups in a "special edition" of the show.) Petraeus then followed up with a Katie Couric interview on *CBS Evening News*, as part of an all-fronts "media blitz" that would include Fox News, AP, *Wired* magazine's *Danger Room* blog, and in a bow to the allies, the BBC and even NATO TV, among others.

At almost the same moment, General Odierno was ending his tour of duty as Iraq War commander by launching a goodbye media blitz of his own from Baghdad, which included interviews with Christiane Amanpour of ABC's *This Week*, Bob Schieffer of CBS's *Face the Nation*, MSNBC's Andrea Mitchell, CNN's *State of the Union*, *PBS Newshour*, and the *New York Times*, among others. He, too, had a policy line to promote and he, too, expressed himself in ways subtly but visibly at odds with an official Obama position, emphasizing the possibility that some number of U.S. troops might need to stay in Iraq beyond the 2011 departure deadline.

As he said to Schieffer, "If [the Iraqis] ask us that they might want us to stay longer, we certainly would consider that." Offering another scenario as well, he also suggested that, as Reuters put it, "U.S. troops . . . could move back to a combat role if there was 'a complete failure of the security forces' or if political divisions split Iraqi security forces." (He then covered his flanks by adding, "but we don't see that happening.")

In February 2009, less than a month after Obama took office, Odierno was already broadcasting his desire to have up to 35,000 troops remain in Iraq after 2011, and at the end of 2009, Secretary of Defense Gates was already suggesting that a new round of negotiations with a future Iraqi government might extend our stay for years. All this, of course, could qualify as part of a more general campaign to maintain the Pentagon's 800-pound status, the military's clout, and a global military presence.

### A Chorus of Military Intellectuals

Pentagon foreign policy is regularly seconded by a growing cadre of what might be called military intellectuals at think tanks scattered around Washington. Such figures, many of them qualifying as "warrior pundits" and "warrior journalists," include: Michael O'Hanlon, senior fellow at the Brookings Institution; retired Lieutenant Colonel John Nagl, president of the Center for a New American Security and Petraeus adviser; former U.S. Army officer Andrew Exum, fellow at the Center for a New American Security, founder of the Abu Muqawama website, and a McChrystal adviser; former Australian infantry officer and Petraeus adviser David Kilcullen, non-resident senior fellow at the Center for a New American Security; Thomas Ricks, formerly of the *Washington Post*, author of the bestselling Iraq War books *Fiasco* and *The Gamble*, Petraeus admirer, and senior fellow at the same center; Frederick Kagan of the American Enterprise Institute, the man Gates credited with turning around his thinking on Afghanistan and a Petraeus hiree in Afghanistan; Kimberley Kagan of the Institute for the Study of War, an adviser to both Petraeus and McChrystal; Kenneth Pollack, director of the Saban Center for Middle East Policy at the Brookings Institution; and Stephen Biddle, senior fellow for defense policy at the Council on Foreign Relations and another Petraeus as well as McChrystal adviser.

These figures, and numerous others like them, have repeatedly been invited to U.S. war zones by the military, flattered, toured, given face time with commanders, sometimes hired by them, and sometimes even given the sense that they are the ones planning our wars. They then return to Washington to offer sophisticated, "objective" versions of the military line.

Toss into this mix the former neocons who caused so much of the damage in the early Bush years and who regularly return at key moments as esteemed media "experts" (not the fools and knaves they were), including former deputy secretary of defense Paul Wolfowitz, former head of the Coalition Provisional Authority (CPA) L. Paul Bremer III, and former senior adviser to the CPA Noah Feldman, among others. For them, being wrong means never having to say you're sorry. And, of course, they and their thoughts are dealt with remarkably respectfully, while those who were against the Iraq War from the beginning remain the rarest of commodities on op-ed pages, as sources in news articles, and on the national radio and TV news.

This combined crew of former warriors, war-zone bureaucrats, and warrior pundits have been, like Odierno, stumping for a sizeable residual U.S. military force to stay in Iraq until hell freezes over. They regularly compare Iraq to postwar South Korea, where U.S. troops are still garrisoned nearly sixty years after the Korean War and which, after decades of U.S.-supported dictators, now has a flourishing democracy.

Combine the military intellectuals, the former neocons, the war commanders, the retired military-officer-commentators, the secretary of defense, and other Pentagon civilians, and you have an impressive array of firepower of a sort that no Eisenhower, Ridgeway, or even MacArthur could have imagined. They may disagree fiercely with each other on tactical matters when it comes to pursuing American-style war, and they certainly don't represent the views of a monolithic military. There are undoubtedly generals who have quite a different view of what the defense of the United States entails. As a group, though, civilian and military, in and out of uniform, in the Pentagon or in a war zone, they agree forcefully on the need to maintain an American global military presence over the long term.

## Producing War

Other than Robert Gates, the key figure of the moment has clearly been David Petraeus, who might be thought of as our Teflon general. He could represent a genuine challenge to the fading tradition of civilian control of the military. Treated as a demigod and genius of battle on both sides of the aisle in Washington, he would have been hard for any president, especially this one, to remove from command. (Obama, of course, finally "removed" him in 2011 by appointing him CIA director.) As a four-star who would have to throw a punch at Michelle Obama on national television to get fired, he had significant latitude to pursue the war policies of his choice in Afghanistan. He also has—should he care to exercise it someday—the potential and the opening to pursue much more. It's not completely farfetched to imagine him as the first mini-Caesar-in-waiting of our American times.

As yet, he and other top figures may plan their individual media blitzes, but they are not consciously planning a media strategy for a coherent Pentagon foreign policy. The result is all the more chilling for not being fully coordinated, and for being so little noticed or attended to by the media that play such a role in promoting it. What's at stake here goes well beyond the specific issue of military insubordination that usually comes up when military-civilian relations are discussed. After all, we could be seeing, in however inchoate form, the beginning of a genuine Pentagon/military production in support of Pentagon timing, our global military presence, and the global mission that goes with it.

In Iraq, Afghanistan, and elsewhere, you can see that Pentagon version of an American foreign policy straining to be born. In the end, of course, it could be stillborn, but it could also become an all-enveloping system offering Americans a strange, skewed vision of a world constantly at war and of the importance of planning for more of the same. To the extent that it now exists, it is dominated by the vision of figures who have been deeply immersed in the imperial mayhem that our wars created, have left us armed to the teeth and flailing at ghosts and demons, and are still enmeshed in the process by which American money has been squandered to worse than no purpose in distant lands.

Nothing in the record indicates that anyone should listen to what these men have to say. Yet nothing in the record indicates that Washington won't be all ears and the media won't remain an enthusiastic conduit for whatever they say we must do, no matter how steep the price.

## Cutting $100 Billion—Easy,
## If Only Washington Had a Brain

In 2011, we were treated to a "debate" in Washington in which only one question was on the table: how much of the federal budget do we cut?

The Republican leadership of the House of Representatives originally picked $40 billion as its target figure for cuts to the as-yet-not-enacted 2011 budget. That was the gauntlet it threw down to the Obama administration, only to find its own proposal slashed to bits by the freshman class of that body's conservative majority. The upstarts insisted on adhering to a Republican Pledge to America vow to cut $100 billion from the budget. With that figure on the table, pundits were predicting widespread pain in the land, including the possible loss of at least seventy thousand jobs "as government aid to cops, teachers, and research is slashed."

In the meantime, the Obama administration offered its own entry in the cut-and-burn sweepstakes. Its plan called for ending or trimming more than two hundred federal programs in 2012. It also reportedly offered cuts adding up to $1.1 trillion over a decade and put in place a "five-year freeze on domestic programs [that] would reduce spending in that category to the lowest level, measured against the economy, since President Dwight D. Eisenhower left office in 1961."

It all sounded daunting, and the muttering was only beginning about "entitlement" programs—Social Security, Medicare, and Medicaid—that had yet to be touched.

Which reminds me: Didn't I mention Afghanistan?

If so, how fortunate, because there's a perfectly obvious path toward that Republican goal of $100 billion. If we were to embark on it, there would be even more cuts to follow and—believe it or not—they wouldn't be all that painful, provided we did one small thing: change our thinking about making war.

After all, according to the Pentagon, the cost of the Afghan War in 2012 will be almost $300 million a day or, for all 365 of them, $107.3 billion. Like anything having to do with American war-fighting, however, such figures regularly turn out to be undercounts. Other estimates for our yearly war costs there go as high as $120 to $160 billion.

And let's face it, it's a war worth ending fast. Almost a decade after the Bush administration invaded Afghanistan, the U.S. military is still fruitlessly engaged in possibly the stupidest frontier war in our history. It's just the sort of conflict that has historically tended to drive declining imperial powers around the bend.

There's genuine money to be slashed simply by bringing the troops home, but okay, I hear you. You live in Washington and you can't bear to give up that war, lock, stock, and barrel. I understand. Really, I do. So let's just pretend that we're part of that "moderate" and beleaguered House leadership and really only want to go after $40 billion in the federal budget.

In that case, here's an idea, We've been training the Afghan military and police forces for almost a decade now, dumping an estimated $29 billion plus into the endeavor, only to find that, unlike the Taliban, our Afghans generally prefer not to fight and love to desert. What if the Obama administration were simply to stop the training program? What if we weren't to spend the $11.6 billion slated for 2011, or the up to $12.8 billion being discussed for next year, or the $6 billion or more annually thereafter to create a security force of nearly four hundred thousand Afghans that we'll have to pay for into eternity, since the Afghan government is essentially broke?

What if, instead, we went cold turkey on our obsession with training Afghans? For one thing, you'd promptly wipe out more than a quarter of that $40 billion the House leadership wants cut and many more billions for years to come. (And that doesn't even take into account all the savable American dollars going down the tubes in Afghanistan—a recent report from the U.S. special inspector general for Afghanistan reconstruction suggested it adds up to $12 billion for the Afghan army alone—in graft, corruption, and pure incompetence.)

Are we actually safer if we get rid of police, firefighters, and teachers here in the United States, while essentially hiring hordes of police and military personnel to secure Afghanistan? I suspect you know how most Americans would answer that question.

## Dumb Intelligence Runs Rampant

Here's another way to approach both those $40 billion and $100 billion targets. Start with the budget for the labyrinthine U.S. Intelligence Community, which is officially $80.1 billion. That, of course, is sure to prove an undercount. So, just for the heck of it, let's take a wild guess and assume that the real figure probably edges closer to $100 billion. I know, the Republican House majority will never agree to get rid of all seventeen U.S. intelligence agencies, and neither will the Democrats. They'll claim that Washington would be blinded by such an act—although it's no less reasonable to argue that, without the blinders of what we call "intelligence," which is largely a morass of dead thinking about our world, our leaders might finally be able to see again.

Nonetheless, in the spirit of compromise with a crew that hates the "federal bureaucracy" (until the words "national security" come up), how about cutting back from seventeen intelligence outfits to maybe three? Let's say, the Central Intelligence Agency, the Defense Intelligence Agency, and the National Security Agency. I'll bet you're talking an easy $40 to $50 billion dollars in savings right there, and the cost of the job-retraining programs for the out-of-work intelligence analysts and operatives would be minimal by comparison.

According to a *Washington Post* series, "Top Secret America," here are just a few of the things that taxpayers have helped our intelligence bureaucracy do: Produce fifty thousand intelligence reports annually, create the redundancy of "51 federal organizations and military commands, operating in 15 U.S. cities, [to] track the flow of money to and from terrorist networks," and, in the category of the monumental (as well as monumentally useless), construct "33 building complexes for top-secret intelligence work . . . since September 2001. Together they occupy the equivalent of almost three Pentagons or 22 U.S. Capitol buildings—about 17 million square feet of space."

Take just one example: the National Geospatial-Intelligence Agency, which has sixteen thousand employees and a "black budget thought to be at least $5 billion per year." Until now, you may not have known that such an outfit was protecting your security, but you're paying through the nose for its construction spree anyway. Believe it or not, as Gregg Easterbrook has pointed out, it now has a gleaming new, nearly Pentagon-sized headquarters complex rising in Virginia at the cost of $1.8 billion—almost as expensive, that is, as the Freedom Tower now going up at Ground Zero in Manhattan.

Or let's check out some smaller, distinctly chopable potatoes. Officially, America's Iraq War is ending (even if in a Shiite-dominated state allied with Iran). All American military personnel are, at least theoretically, to leave the country by year's end. Whether that happens or not, the Obama administration evidently remains convinced that it's in our interest to prolong our effort to control that country. As a result, the planned "civilian" presence left behind to staff the three-quarters-of-a-billion-dollar citadel of an "embassy" the United States built in downtown Baghdad as well as various consular outposts will look uncomfortably like a mini-army.

As *Wired*'s *Danger Room* blog put it, the U.S. ambassador to Iraq "will become a de facto general of a huge, for-hire army." We're talking about 5,100 mercenaries paid to guard the 12,000 "civilians," representing various U.S. government agencies and the State Department there. To guard the Baghdad embassy alone—really a regional command headquarters—there will be 3,650 hired guns under contract for almost $1 billion. The full complement of heavily armed mercenaries will operate out of "15 different sites . . . including 3 air hubs, 3 police training centers . . . and 5 Office of Security Cooperation sites."

In 2010, *USA Today* estimated that the cost of operating just the monstrous Baghdad embassy was more than $1.5 billion a year. God knows what it is now.

What if the cost-cutters in Washington were to conclude that it was a fruitless task to try to manage the unmanageable (i.e., Iraq) and that, instead of militarizing the State Department, the United States should return to the business of diplomacy with a modest embassy and a consulate or two to negotiate deals, discuss matters of common interest, and hand out the odd visa. That would represent a cost-cutting extravaganza on a small scale. The same could be said for the near billion-dollar "embassy" being built in Islamabad, Pakistan, and the $790 million going into another such embassy and consulates in Afghanistan.

## Deep in the Big Muddy

It's important to note that none of the potential cost-cutting measures I've mentioned touch the big palooka. I'm talking about the Pentagon budget, a very distinctive "entitlement" program on the American landscape. Given the news reports on "Pentagon cuts" lately, you might think that the Obama administration is taking a hatchet to the Defense Department's funds, but no such luck. Defense analyst Miriam Pemberton has written, "The Pentagon is following the familiar tradition of planning ambitious increases, paring them back, and calling this a cut." In fact, the proposed Pentagon budget for 2012 actually represents an increase over the already stunningly bloated 2011 version of the same.

Keep in mind that U.S. military spending equals that of the next fifteen countries combined (most of them allies) and represents 47 percent of total global military spending. If Washington's mindset were different, it wouldn't be hard to find that $100 billion the Republican House freshmen are looking for in the Pentagon budget alone—quite aside from cuts in supplemental war-fighting funds—and still be the most heavily armed nation on the planet.

And here's my question to you: Don't you find it odd that cuts of this potential size are so obviously available and yet, with all the raging and groaning about deficits and budget-cutting, no one who matters seems to focus on such possibilities at all? To head down this path, Washington would need to make only the smallest of changes: it would have to begin thinking outside the war box for about a minute and thirty seconds.

Our leaders would have to conclude the obvious: that, in these last years, war hasn't proved the best way to advance American interests. We would have to decide that real security does not involve fighting permanently in distant lands, pursuing a "war on terror" in seventy-five countries, or enlarging the Pentagon (and the weapons-makers that go with it) year after year.

Americans would have to begin to think anew. That's all. The minute we did, our financial situation would look different and for all we know, something like non-war, if not peace, might begin to break out.

Forty years ago, Americans regularly spoke about a war 7,500 miles away in Vietnam as a "quagmire." We were, as one protest song of that era went, "waist deep in the Big Muddy." Today, Afghanistan, too, looks like a quagmire, but don't be fooled. The real quagmire isn't there; it's right here in Washington, D.C., that capital mythically built on a swamp.

# CHAPTER 6

# Living with War

## Ballot Box Blues

Voting in the 2010 election was the single most reflexive political act of my life, in the single most dispiriting election I can remember. As I haven't missed a midterm or presidential election since my first vote in 1968, that says something. Certainly, my version of election politics started long before I could vote. I remember collecting campaign buttons in the 1950s and also—for the 1956 presidential campaign in which Dwight Eisenhower (and his vice president, Richard Nixon) faced off against Democratic Party candidate Adlai Stevenson—singing this ditty:

> *Whistle while you work*
> *Nixon is a jerk*
> *Eisenhower has no power*
> *Stevenson will work!*

Even in the world of kids, even then, politics could be gloves-off stuff. Little good my singing did, though: Stevenson was trounced, thus beginning my political education. My father and mother were dyed-in-the-wool Depression Democrats, and my mother was a political caricaturist for the then-liberal (now Murdoch-owned) tabloid the *New York Post.* I still remember the fierce drawings she penned for that paper's front page of red-baiting senator Joe McCarthy. She also came away from those years filled with political fears, reflected in her admonition to me throughout the 1960s: "It's the whale that spouts that gets caught."

Still, I was sold on the American system. It was a sign of the times that I simply couldn't wait to vote. The first election rally I ever attended, in 1962, was for John F. Kennedy, already president. I remember his face, a postage-stamp-sized blur of pink, glimpsed through a sea of heads and shoulders. Even today, I can feel a remnant of the excitement and hope of that moment. In those years before our government had become "the bureaucracy" in young minds, I was imbued with a powerful sense of civic duty that, I suspect, was commonplace. I daydreamed relentlessly about becoming an American diplomat and so representing my country to the world.

The first presidential campaign I followed with a passion was in 1964, after Kennedy's assassination. In memory, I feel as if I voted in it, though I couldn't have since the voting age was then twenty-one, and I was only twenty. Nonetheless, I all but put my X beside the "peace candidate" of that moment, Lyndon B. Johnson, who had, in such an untimely manner, inherited the Oval Office and a war in Vietnam. What other vote was there, since he was running against a Republican extremist and warmonger, an Arizona senator named Barry Goldwater?

Not long after his inauguration, however, Johnson launched Operation Rolling Thunder, the bombing of North Vietnam. It had been planned before the election, but was kept suitably under wraps while Goldwater was being portrayed as a man intent on getting American boys killed in Asia and maybe nuking the planet as well.

Four years later, with half a million U.S. troops in South Vietnam and the war reaching conflagration status, I was "mad as hell and not going to take this anymore"—and that was years before Paddy Chayefsky penned those words for the film *Network*. I was at least as mad as any present-day Tea Partier and a heck of a lot younger. By 1968, I had been betrayed by my not-quite-vote for Johnson and learned my lesson—they were all warmongers—and so, deeply involved in antiwar activities, I rejected both Vice President Hubert Humphrey, who had barely peeped about the war, and his opponent Richard Nixon (that "jerk" of my 1956 ditty), who was promising "peace with honor," but as I understood quite well, preparing to blast any Vietnamese, Cambodian, or Laotian within reach. I voted instead, with some pride, for Black Panther Eldridge Cleaver.

Nor was it exactly thrilling in 1972 when "tricky Dick," running for reelection, swamped Senator George McGovern, who actually wanted to bring American troops home and end the war, just before the Watergate scandal fully broke. And don't forget the 1980 election in which Jimmy Carter was hung out to dry by the Iran hostage crisis. As I remember it, I voted late and Democratic that Tuesday in November, came home, made a bowl of popcorn, and sat down in front of the TV just in time to watch Carter concede to Ronald Reagan. Don't think I didn't find that dispiriting.

And none of this could, of course, compare to campaign 2000 with its "elected by the Supreme Court" tag or election night 2004, when early exit polls seemed to indicate that Senator John Kerry, himself an admittedly dispiriting figure, might be headed for the White House. My wife and I threw a party that night, which started in the highest of spirits, only to end, after a long, dismal night, in the reelection of George W. Bush. On the morning of November 3, I wrote at TomDispatch.com that I had "the election hangover of a lifetime," as I contemplated the way American voters had re-upped for "the rashest presidency in our history (short perhaps of that of Jefferson Davis)."

"They have," I added, "signed on to a disastrous crime of a war in Iraq, and a losing war at that, which will only get worse; they have signed on to whatever dangerous schemes these schemers can come up with. They have signed on to their own impoverishment. This is the political version of the volunteer army. Now they have to live with it. Unfortunately, so do we."

## Hermetic Systems and Mad Elephants

Years later, we are indeed poorer in all the obvious ways, and some not so obvious ones as well. How, then, could the 2010 midterms have been the *most* dispiriting elections of my life, especially when Brian Williams of NBC *Nightly News* assured us, in the days leading up to the event, that it would have "the power to reshape our nation's politics." Okay, you and I know that's BS, part of the endless, breathless handicapping of the midterms that went on nonstop for weeks on the TV news.

Still, the most dispiriting? After all, I'm the guy who penned a piece eight days after the 2008 election entitled "Don't Let Barack Obama Break Your Heart." In what was, for most people I knew, a decidedly upbeat moment, I then wrote, for instance: "So, after January 20th, expect Obama to take possession of George Bush's disastrous Afghan War; and unless he is far more skilled than Alexander the Great, British Empire builders, and the Russians, his war, too, will continue to rage without ever becoming a raging success."

And take my word for it, when I say dispiriting I'm not even referring to just how dismal my actual voting experience was for the 2010 election in New York City. I mean, two senators and a governor I don't give a whit about and not a breath of fresh air anywhere—not unless you count the Republican gubernatorial and "Tea Party" candidate, a beyond-mad-as-hell businessman who made a fortune partially thanks to state government favors and breaks of every sort and then couldn't wait to take out that government. (And when Carl Paladino talks about taking something out, you instinctively know that he's not a man of metaphor.) Okay, that *is* dispiriting, just not in a lifetime award kind of way.

No, it's the whole airless shebang we call elections that's gotten to me, the bizarrely hermetic, self-financing, self-praising, self-promoting system we still manage to think of as "democratic." That includes, of course, the media echo chamber that ginned up a nationally nondescript political season into an epochal life-changer via a powerfully mad—as in mad elephant—populace ready to run amok.

### What Goes Up . . .

I'm no expert on elections, but sometimes all you need is a little common sense. So let's start with a simple principle: what goes up must come down.

For at least thirty years now, what's gone up is income disparity in this country. Paul Krugman called this period "the Great Divergence." After all, between 1980 and 2005, "more than 80 percent of total increase in Americans' income went to the top 1 percent" of Americans in terms of wealth, and today that 1 percent controls 24 percent of the nation's income. Or put another way, after three decades of "trickle-down" economics, what's gone up are the bank accounts of the rich. In 2009, for instance, as Americans generally scrambled and suffered, lost jobs, watched pensions, IRAs, or savings shrink and houses go into foreclosure, the number of millionaires actually increased. The combined wealth of the four hundred richest Americans (all billionaires) rose by 8 percent in 2010, even as, in the second quarter of the year, the net worth of American households fell by 2.8 percent.

Up at the top, individually and corporately, ever more money is on hand to "invest" in protecting what one already possesses or might still acquire. Hence, the 2010 elections had a price tag that obliterates all previous midterm records, estimated at $4 billion to $4.2 billion, mostly from what is politely called "fundraising" or from "outside interest groups"—from that 1 percent and some of the wealthiest corporations, mainly for media and influence campaigns. In other words, the already superrich and the giant corporations that sucked up so much dough over the last thirty years now have tons of it to "invest" in our system in order to reap yet more favors—to invest, that is, in Sharron Angle *and* Harry Reid. If that isn't dispiriting, what is?

The right-wing version of this story is that a thunderstorm of money is being invested in a newly aroused, mad-as-hell collection of Americans ready to storm to power in the name of small government, radically reduced federal deficits, and, of course, lower taxes. This is a fantasy concoction, though, even if you hear it on the news 24-7. First of all, those right-wing billionaires and corporate types are *not* for small government. They regularly and happily back, and sometimes profit from, the ever-increasing power of the national security state to pry, peep, suppress, and oppress, abridge liberties and make war endlessly abroad. They are Pentagon lovers. They adore the locked-down "homeland."

In addition, they are *for* the government giving *them* every sort of break, any sort of hand—just not for that government laying its hands on them. They are, in this sense, America's real welfare queens. They want a powerful, protective state, but one that benefits them, not us. All of those dollars that scaled the heights in these last decades are now helping to fund their program. For what they need, they only have to throw repeated monkey wrenches into the works and the Tea Party, which really isn't a party at all, is just the latest of those wrenches.

Faced with all our national woes, are we really a mad-as-hell nation? On that, the jury is out, despite the fact that you've heard how "angry" we are a trillion times in the news. Maybe we're a depressed-as-hell nation. What we do know, however, is that the rich-as-hell crew are making good use of the mad-as-hell one.

In October 2010, Amy Gardner of the *Washington Post* offered a revealing report on the Tea Party landscape. Of the 1,400 Tea Party groups nationwide that the *Post* tried to contact, it reached 647. Many of the rest may have ceased to exist or may never have existed at all. ("The findings suggest that the breadth of the tea party may be inflated.") What the *Post* researchers found bore little relationship to the angry, Obama-as-Hitler-sign-carrying bunch supposedly ready to storm the gates of power. They discovered instead a generally quiescent movement in which "70 percent of the grass-roots groups said they have not participated in any political campaigning this year." Most of them were small, not directly involved in electoral politics, and meant to offer places to talk and exchange ideas. Not exactly the stuff of rebellion in the streets.

On the other hand, the funding machines like Tea Party Express (run by Sal Russo, longtime Republican operative, aide to Ronald Reagan, and fundraiser/media strategist for former New York governor George Pataki), FreedomWorks (run by Dick Armey, former Republican House majority leader), and Americans for Prosperity (started by oil billionaire David Koch) had appropriated the Tea Party name nationally and were pouring money into "Tea Party candidates." And don't forget the Tea-Partyish funding groups set up by Karl Rove, George W. Bush's bosom buddy and close adviser. That these influential "tea partiers" turn out to be familiar right-wing insiders—"longtime political players," as the *Post* put it, who since the 1980s "have used their resources and know-how to help elect a number of candidates"—shouldn't be much of a shock. Nor can it be so surprising that familiar right-wing political operatives are intent on creating a kind of political mayhem under the Tea Party label.

As for the TV set that filled your living room with the sound and fury of an "epochal" election, isn't it curious how little attention all the commentators, pundits, and talking heads on that screen paid to where so much of that money was actually landing? I mean, of course, in the hands of their bosses. Vast amounts of it have come down on the media itself, particularly television. I'm talking about all those screaming "attack ads," including the ones sponsored by the unnamed outside interest groups that the talking heads just love to analyze, rebroadcast, and discuss endlessly? These are the very ads enriching the media outfits that employ them in a moment when the news world is in financial turmoil. It was estimated that, for election 2010, the TV ad bill would reach $3 billion (up from $2.7 billion in the 2008 presidential campaign year, and $2.4 billion in the 2006 midterms that brought the Democrats back to power in Congress). For the companies behind the screen, in other words, those ads are manna from heaven.

If, in another context, someone was selling you on the importance of a phenomenon and was at the same time directly benefiting from that phenomenon, it would be considered a self-evident conflict of interest. In this particular case, all those ad dollars are visibly to the benefit of the very media promoting the world-shaking importance of each new election season. But remind me, when was the last time you saw anyone on television, or really just about anywhere, even suggest that this might represent a conflict of interest?

The media aren't just reporting on a particular election season, they're also filling every space they can imagine with boosterism for just the kinds of elections we now experience. They are, in a sense, modern-day carnies, offering endless election spiels to usher you inside the tent. Whatever they themselves may individually think about it, they are working to boost the profitability of their companies just as surely as any of those right-wing funders are boosting their corporate (or personal) profits. They are not outsiders looking in, but a basic part of the hermetic, noisy, profitable system we think of as an election campaign.

As for the election itself, none of us really had to wait for the results of midterm 2010, the Anger Extravaganza, to know that it wouldn't be transformative. This isn't rocket science. We already knew what the Democrats were capable of (or, more exactly, not capable of) with sixty votes in the Senate and a humongous advantage in the House of Representatives, as well as the presidency. So you should have a perfectly realistic assessment of how much less of "the people's business" is likely to be done in a more divided Congress, in which the Republicans control the House.

After the election, whatever the results, we already knew that Obama would move even more toward "the center," even if for decades the so-called center has been drifting rightward without ever settling on a home; that he would try to "work with" the Republicans; that this would prove the usual jokes; and that the election, however breathlessly reported as a Republican triumph or Tea Party miracle (or anything else), would essentially be a gum-it-up-more event. Though none of the voluble prognosticators and interpreters you'll listen to or read are likely to say so, those right-wing fundraisers and outside interest groups pouring money into Tea Party candidates, angry maniacs, dopes, and whoever else is on the landscape undoubtedly could care less. Yes, a Congress that gave them everything they wanted on a proverbial silver platter would be a wonder, but gum-it-up works pretty darn well, too. For most Americans, a Washington in gridlock in a moment of roiling national crisis may be nothing to write home about, but for those fundraisers and outside interest groups, it only guarantees more manna from heaven.

And the good news, as far as they are concerned, is that the state that matters, the national security, war-making one, hardly needs Congress at all, or rather knows that no Congress will ever vote "no" to moneys for such matters. Meanwhile, the media will begin cranking up for an even more expensive Election 2012. Long before this election season came to a close, my hometown paper was already sporting its first pieces with headlines like "Looking Ahead to the 2012 Race" and beginning to handicap the presidential run to come. ("Although [President Obama] will not say so, there is at least a plausible argument that he might be better off if [the Democrats] lose . . . [I]f Republicans capture Congress, Mr. Obama will finally have a foil heading toward his own re-election battle in 2012.")

Whether the country I once wanted to represent was ever there in the form I imagined is a question I'll leave to the historians. What I can say is that it's sure not there now.

## The Nuclear Story That Refuses to Go Away

Even though we promptly dubbed the site of the 9/11 attacks in New York City "Ground Zero"—once a term reserved for an atomic blast— Americans have never really come to grips either with the atomic bombings of Hiroshima and Nagasaki or with the nuclear age that they ushered in. There can be no question that, as the big bang that might end it all, the atomic bomb haunted Cold War America. In those years, while the young (myself included) watched endless versions of nuclear disaster transmuted into B-horror films, the grown-ups who ran our world went on a vast shopping spree for world-ending weaponry, building nuclear arsenals that came to number in the tens of thousands.

When the Cold War finally ended with the Soviet Union's quite peaceful collapse, however, a nuclear "peace dividend" never quite arrived. The arsenals of the former superpower adversaries remained quietly in place, drawn down but strangely untouched, awaiting a new mission, while just beyond sight, the knowledge of the making of such weapons spread to other countries ready to launch their own threatening mini–Cold Wars.

Even fifty years after that first bomb went off over the Aioi Bridge in Hiroshima, it still proved impossible in the United States to agree upon a nuclear creation tale. Was August 6, 1945, the heroic ending to a global war or the horrific beginning of a new age? The *Enola Gay*, the plane that dropped the Hiroshima bomb, and a shattered schoolchild's lunchbox from Hiroshima could not yet, it turned out, inhabit the same exhibit space at the Smithsonian's National Air and Space Museum in Washington, D.C.

Still, for people of a certain age like me, Hiroshima is where it all began. So I would like to try, once again, to lay out the pieces of a nuclear story that none of us, it seems, can yet quite tell.

In my story, there are three characters and no dialogue. There is my father, who volunteered at age thirty-five for the Army Air Corps, immediately after the Japanese attack on Pearl Harbor. He fought in Burma, was painfully silent on his wartime experiences, and died on Pearl Harbor Day in 1983. Then there's me, growing up in a world in which my father's war was glorified everywhere, in which my play fantasies in any park included mowing down Japanese soldiers—but whose nightmares were of nuclear destruction. Finally, there is a Japanese boy whose name and fate are unknown to me.

This is a story of multiple silences. The first of those, the silence of my father, was once no barrier to the stories I told myself. If anything, his silence enhanced them, since in the 1950s male silence seemed a heroic attribute (and perhaps it was, though hardly in the way I imagined at the time). Sitting in the dark with him then at any World War II movie was enough for me.

As it turned out though, the only part of his war I possessed was its final act, and around this too, there grew a puzzling silence. The very idea of nuclear destruction seemed not to touch him. Like other schoolchildren, I went through nuclear-attack drills with sirens howling outside, while—I had no doubt—he continued to work unfazed in his office. It was I who watched the irradiated ants and nuclearized monsters of our teen-screen life stomp the Earth. It was I who went to the French film *Hiroshima Mon Amour*, where I was shocked by my first sight of the human casualties of the A-bombing, and to *On the Beach* to catch a glimpse of how the world might actually end. It was I who saw the mushroom cloud rise in my dreams, felt its heat sear my arm before I awoke. Of all this I said not a word to him, nor he to me.

On his erstwhile enemies, however, my father was not silent. He hated the Japanese with a war-bred passion. They had, he told me, "done things" that could not be discussed to "boys" he had known. Subsequent history—the amicable American occupation of Japan or the emergence of that defeated land as an ally—did not seem to touch him. His hatred of all things Japanese was not a ruling passion of my childhood only because Japan was so absent from our lives. There was nothing Japanese in our house (one did not buy their products), we avoided the only Japanese restaurant in our part of town, and no Japanese ever came to visit. Even the evil Japanese I saw in war movies, who might sneeringly hiss, "I was educated in your University of Southern California" before they met their suicidal fates were, I now know, regularly played by non-Japanese actors.

In the end, I followed my own path to Hiroshima, drawn perhaps to the world my father so vehemently rejected. In 1979, as an editor, I published *Unforgettable Fire*, the drawings of Hiroshima residents who had lived through that day, the first time any sizable number of images of the human damage there made it into mainstream American culture. I visited Japan in 1982, thanks to the book's Japanese editor who took me to Hiroshima, an experience I found myself unable to talk about on return. This, too, became part of the silences my father and I shared.

To make a story thus far would seem relatively simple. Two generations face each other across the chasm of a war and an act that divided them. It is the story we all know. And yet, there is my third character and third silence—the Japanese boy who drifted into my consciousness after an absence of almost four decades only a few years ago. I no longer remember how he and I were put in contact sometime in the mid-1950s. Like me, my Japanese pen pal must have been eleven or twelve years old. If we exchanged photos, I have no memory of his face, nor does a name come to mind. If I can remember half-jokingly writing my own address at that age ("New York City, New York, USA, Planet Earth, the Solar System, the Galaxy, the Universe"), I can't remember writing his. I already knew by then that a place called Albany was the capital of New York State, but New York City still seemed to me the center of the world. In many ways, I wasn't wrong.

Even if he lived in Tokyo, my Japanese pen pal could have had no such illusions. Like me, he had undoubtedly been born during World War II. Perhaps in his first year of life he had been evacuated from one of Japan's charred cities. For him, that disastrous war would not have been a memory. If he had gone to the movies with his father in the 1950s, he might have seen *Godzilla* (not the U.S. Air Force) dismantle Tokyo and he might have hardly remembered those economically difficult first years of American occupation. But he could not at that time have imagined himself at the center of the universe.

I have a faint memory of the feel of his letters; a crinkly thinness undoubtedly meant to save infinitesimal amounts of weight (and so, money). We wrote, of course, in English, for much of the planet, if not the solar-system-galaxy-universe, was beginning to operate in that universal language that seemed to radiate from my home city to the world like the rays of the sun. But what I most remember are the exotic-looking stamps that arrived on (or in) his letters. For I was, with my father, an avid stamp collector. On Sunday afternoons, my father and I prepared and mounted our stamps, consulted our *Scott's Catalog*, and pasted them in. In this way, the Japanese section of our album was filled with that boy's offerings, without comment, but also without protest from my father.

We exchanged letters—none of which remain—for a year or two, and then who knows what interest of mine or his overcame us. Perhaps only the resistance boys can have to writing letters. In any case, he, too, entered a realm of silence. Only now, remembering those quiet moments of closeness when my father and I worked on our albums, do I note that he existed briefly and without discussion in our lives. He existed for both of us, perhaps, in the ambiguous space that silence can create. And now I wonder sometimes what kinds of nuclear dreams my father may have had.

For all of us, in a sense, the Earth was knocked off its axis on August 6, 1945. In that one moment, my father's war ended and my war—the Cold War—began. But in my terms it seems so much messier than that. For we and that boy continued to live in the same world together for a long time, accepting and embroidering each other's silences. When I think of him now, when I realize that he, my father, and I still can't inhabit the same story except in silence, a strange kind of emotion rushes up in me, which is hard to explain.

The bomb still runs like a fissure, but also like an attracting current— a secret unity—through our lives. The rent it tore in history was deep and the generational divide, given the experiences of those growing up on either side of it, profound. But any story would also have to hold the ways, even deeper and harder to fathom, in which we lived through it all together in pain, hatred, love, and, most of all, silence.

## Defining an American State of War

With at least six wars cooking (in Iraq, Afghanistan, Pakistan, Libya, Yemen, and more generally, the Global War on Terror), Americans find themselves in a new world of war.

War has a way of turning almost anything upside down, including language. This undoubtedly means that you're using a set of antediluvian war words or definitions from your father's day. It's time to catch up. So here's the latest word in war words: what's in, what's out, what's inside out. What follows are nine common terms associated with our present wars that probably don't mean what you think they mean.

**Victory:** *Like defeat, it's a loaded word and rather than define it, Americans should simply avoid it.*

In his final press conference before retirement, Secretary of Defense Robert Gates was asked whether the United States was "winning in Afghanistan." He replied, "I have learned a few things in four and a half years, and one of them is to try and stay away from loaded words like 'winning' and 'losing.' What I will say is that I believe we are being successful in implementing the president's strategy, and I believe that our military operations are being successful in denying the Taliban control of populated areas, degrading their capabilities, and improving the capabilities of the Afghan national security forces."

In 2005, George W. Bush, whom Gates also served, used the word *victory* fifteen times in a single speech ("National Strategy for Victory in Iraq"). Keep in mind, though, that our previous president learned about war in the movie theaters of his childhood where the marines always advanced and Americans actually won. Think of his victory obsession as the equivalent of a mid–twentieth-century hangover.

In 2011, despite the complaints of a few leftover neocons dreaming of past glory, you can search Washington high and low for "victory." You won't find it. It's the verbal equivalent of a Yeti. Admittedly, the assassination of Osama bin Laden was treated as if it were VJ Day ending World War II, but actually win a war? Don't make Gates laugh!

Maybe, if everything comes up roses, in some year soon we'll be celebrating DE (Degrade the Enemy) Day.

**Enemy**: *Any super-evil pipsqueak on whose back you can raise at least $1.2 trillion a year for the National Security Complex.*

"I actually consider al-Qaeda in the Arabian Peninsula with Al-Awlaki as a leader within that organization probably the most significant risk to the U.S. homeland." So said Michael Leiter, presidential adviser and the director of the National Counterterrorism Center, in February 2011, months before Osama bin Laden was killed (and Leiter himself resigned). Since bin Laden's death, Leiter's assessment has been heartily seconded in word and deed in Washington. For example, in June 2011, *New York Times* reporter Mark Mazzetti wrote, "Al-Qaeda's affiliate in Yemen is believed by the C.I.A. to pose the greatest immediate threat to the United States, more so than even al-Qaeda's senior leadership believed to be hiding in Pakistan."

Now, here's the odd thing. Once upon a time, statements like these might have been tantamount to announcements of victory: That's all they've got left? Of course, once upon a time, if you asked an American who was the most dangerous man on the planet, you might have been told Adolf Hitler, Joseph Stalin, or Mao Zedong. These days, don't think enemy at all. Think comic book–style arch villain like Lex Luthor or Doctor Doom—anyone, in fact, capable of standing in for globe-encompassing Evil.

Post–bin Laden, America's super-villain of choice is Anwar al-Awlaki, an enemy with seemingly near superhuman powers to disturb Washington, but no army, no state, and no significant finances. The U.S.-born "radical cleric" lives as a semi-fugitive in Yemen, a poverty-stricken land of which, until recently, few Americans had heard. Al-Awlaki is considered at least partially responsible for two high-profile plots against the United States: the underwear bomber and package bombs sent by plane to Chicago synagogues. Both failed dismally, even though neither Superman nor the Fantastic Four rushed to the rescue.

As an Evil One, al-Awlaki is a voodoo enemy, a YouTube warrior ("the bin Laden of the Internet") with little but his wits and whatever superpowers he can muster to help him. He was reputedly responsible for helping to poison the mind of army psychiatrist major Nidal Hasan before he blew away thirteen people at Fort Hood, Texas. There's no question of one thing: he's gotten inside Washington's war-on-terror head in a big way. As a result, the Obama administration is significantly intensifying its war against him and the ragtag crew of tribesmen he hangs out with who go by the name of Al-Qaeda in the Arabian Peninsula.

*Covert war: It used to mean secret war, a war "in the shadows" and so beyond the public's gaze. Now, it means a conflict in the full glare of publicity that everybody knows about, but no one can do anything about. Think: in the news, but off the books.*

Go figure: today, our "covert" wars are front-page news. And America's most secretive covert warriors, elite SEAL Team 6, caused "SEAL-mania" to break out nationwide after Osama bin Laden was killed. Moreover, no minor drone strike in the "covert" CIA-run air war in the Pakistani tribal borderlands goes unreported. In fact, future plans for the launching or intensification of Pakistani-style covert wars are now openly discussed, debated, and praised in Washington, as well as widely reported on.

Think of covert war today as the equivalent of a heat-seeking missile aimed directly at the mainstream media newshole. The "shadows" that once covered whole operations now only cover accountability for them.

*Permanent bases: In the American way of war, military bases built on foreign soil are the equivalent of heroin. The Pentagon can't help building them and can't live without them, but "permanent bases" don't exist, not for Americans. Never.*

That's simple enough, but let me be absolutely clear anyway: Americans may have at least 865 bases around the world (not including those in war zones), but we have no desire to occupy other countries. And wherever we garrison, we don't want to stay, not permanently anyway.

In the grand scheme of things, for a planet more than four billion years old, our ninety bases in Japan, a mere sixty-odd years in existence, or our 227 bases in Germany, some also around for sixty-odd years, or those in Korea, fifty-odd years, count as little. Moreover, we have it on good word that permanent bases are un-American. Secretary of Defense Donald Rumsfeld said as much in 2003 when the first of the Pentagon's planned Iraqi megabases were already on the drawing boards. Hillary Clinton said so again in June 2011 about Afghanistan, and an anonymous American official added for clarification: "There are U.S. troops in various countries for some considerable lengths of time which are not there permanently." Korea anyone? So get it straight, Americans don't want permanent bases. Period.

And that's amazing when you think about it, since globally Americans are constantly building and upgrading military bases. The Pentagon is hooked. In Afghanistan, it's gone totally wild—more than four hundred of them and still building! Not only that, Washington is now deep into negotiations with the Afghan government to transform some of them into "joint bases" and stay on them if not until hell freezes over, then at least until Afghan soldiers can be whipped into an American-style army. Latest best guesstimate for that? 2017 without even getting close. Fortunately, we plan to turn those many bases we built to the tune of billions of dollars, including the gigantic establishments at Bagram and Kandahar, over to the Afghans and just hang around, possibly "for decades," as—and the word couldn't be more delicate or thoughtful—"tenants."

And by the way, accompanying reports that the CIA is preparing to lend the U.S. military a major covert hand, drone-style, in its Yemen campaign, was news that the agency is building a base of its own on a rushed schedule in an unnamed Persian Gulf country. Just one base. But don't expect that to be the end of it. After all, that's like eating one potato chip.

**Withdrawal**: *We're going, we're going . . . just not quite yet, and stop pushing!*

If our bases are shots of heroin, then for the U.S. military leaving anyplace represents a form of "withdrawal," which means the shakes. Like drugs, it just feel so darn good to go in that Washington keeps doing it again and again. Getting out's the bear. Who can blame them if they don't want to leave?

In Iraq, for instance, Washington has been in the grips of withdrawal fever since the Bush administration agreed in 2008 that all U.S. troops would leave by the end of 2011. You can still hear those combat boots dragging in the sand with top administration and military officials practically begging the Iraqis to let us remain on a few of our monster bases, like the ill-named Camp Victory or Balad Air Base. But here's the thing: even if the U.S. military officially departs, lock, stock, and (gun) barrel, Washington's still not really planning on leaving. Instead, the Obama administration is planning to militarize the State Department, turning its embassy in Baghdad and its consulates into a little archipelago of bases defended by 5,100 hire-a-guns and a small mercenary air force.

In sum, "So Long, It's Been Good to Know Ya" is not a song that Washington likes to sing.

**Drone War** *(see also covert war): A permanent air campaign using missile-armed pilotless planes that banishes both withdrawal and victory to the slagheap of history.*

Is it even a "war" if only one side ever appears in person and only one side ever suffers damage? In this sense, America's drones are something new in the history of warfare. Drones are, of course, the weaponry of choice in our covert wars, which means that the military just can't wait to usher chosen reporters into its secret labs and experimental testing grounds to reveal dazzling visions of future robotic destruction.

To make sense of drones, we probably have to stop thinking about "war" and start envisaging other models—for example, that of the executioner who carries out a death sentence on another human being at no danger to himself. If a pilotless drone is actually an executioner's weapon, a modern airborne version of the guillotine, the hangman's noose, or the electric chair, the death sentence it carries with it is not decreed by a judge and certainly not by a jury of peers.

It's assembled by intelligence agents based on fragmentary (and often self-interested) evidence, organized by targeters, and given the thumbs-up by military or CIA lawyers. All of them are scores, hundreds, thousands of miles away from their victims, people they don't know and may not faintly understand or share a culture with. In addition, the capital offenses are often not established, still to be carried out, never to be carried out, or nonexistent. The fact that drones, despite their "precision" weaponry, regularly take out innocent civilians as well as prospective or actual terrorists reminds us that, if this is our model, Washington is a drunken executioner.

In a sense, Bush's Global War on Terror called drones up from the depths of its unconscious to fulfill its most basic urges: to be endless and to reach anywhere on Earth with an Old Testament–style sense of vengeance. The drone makes mincemeat of victory (which involves an endpoint), withdrawal (for which you have to be there in the first place), and national sovereignty (see below).

*Corruption: Something inherent in the nature of war-torn Iraqis and Afghans from which only Americans, in and out of uniform, can save them.*

Don't be distracted by the $6.6 billion that, in the form of shrink-wrapped $100 bills, the Bush administration loaded onto C-130 transport planes, flew to liberated Iraq in 2003 for "reconstruction" purposes, and somehow mislaid. The U.S. special inspector general for Iraq reconstruction did suggest that it might prove to be "the largest theft of funds in national history." On the other hand, accidents happen.

Iraq's parliamentary speaker claims that up to $18.7 billion in Iraqi oil funds have gone missing in action, but Iraqis, as you know, are corrupt and unreliable. So pay no attention. Anyway, not to worry, it wasn't our money. All those crisp Benjamins came from Iraqi oil revenues that just happened to be held by U.S. banks. And in war zones, what can you do? Sometimes bad things happen to good $100 bills!

In any case, corruption is endemic to the societies of the Greater Middle East, which lack the institutional foundations of democratic societies. Not surprisingly then, in impoverished, narcotized Afghanistan, it's run wild. Fortunately, Washington has fought nobly against its ravages for years. Time and again, top American officials have cajoled, threatened, even browbeat Afghan president Hamid Karzai and his compatriots to get them to crack down on corrupt practices and hold honest elections to build support for the American-backed government in Kabul.

Here's the funny thing though: a report on Afghan reconstruction released by the Senate Foreign Relations Committee's Democratic majority staff in June 2011 suggested that the military and foreign "developmental" funds that have poured into the country, and which account for 97 percent of its gross domestic product, have played a major role in encouraging corruption. To find a peacetime equivalent, imagine firemen rushing to a blaze only to pour gasoline on it and then lash out at the building's dwellers as arsonists.

*National sovereignty: 1. Something Americans cherish and wouldn't let any other country violate; 2. Something foreigners irrationally cling to, a sign of unreliability or mental instability.*

Here's the credo of the American war state in the twenty-first century. Please memorize it. The world is our oyster. We shall not weep. We may missile (bomb, assassinate, night raid, invade) whom we please, when we please, where we please. This is to be called "American safety."

Those elsewhere, with a misplaced reverence for their own safety or security, or an overblown sense of pride and self-worth, who put themselves in harm's way—watch out. After all, in a phrase: Sovereignty 'R' Us.

Note: As we still live on a one-way imperial planet, don't try reversing any of the above, not even as a thought experiment. Don't imagine Iranian drones hunting terrorists over Southern California or Pakistani special operations forces launching night raids on small Midwestern towns. Not if you know what's good for you.

*War: A totally malleable concept that is purely in the eye of the beholder.*

Which is undoubtedly why the Obama administration decided not to ask Congress for approval of its Libyan intervention as required by the War Powers Resolution of 1973. The administration instead issued a report essentially declaring Libya not to be a "war" at all, and so not to fall under the provisions of that resolution. As that report explained: "U.S. operations [in Libya] do not involve [1] sustained fighting or [2] active exchanges of fire with hostile forces, nor do they involve [3] the presence of U.S. ground troops, U.S. casualties, or a serious threat thereof, or [4] any significant chance of escalation into a conflict characterized by those factors."

This, of course, opens up the possibility of quite a new and sunny American future, one in which it will no longer be wildly utopian to imagine war becoming extinct. After all, the Obama administration is already moving to intensify and expand its (fill in the blank) in Yemen, which will meet all of the above criteria, as its (fill in the blank) in the Pakistani tribal borderlands already does. Someday, Washington could be making America safe all over the globe in what would, miraculously, be a thoroughly warless world.

## CHAPTER 7

# Imperial Decline

## Living in the Fifty-First State (of Denial)

I graduated from college in 1966 on a gloriously sunny day. Then again, it was a sunnier moment in this country. We were, after all, still surfing the crest of post–World War II American wealth and productivity. The first oil crisis of 1973 wasn't even on the horizon. I never gave a thought to the gas I put in the tank of the used Volkswagen "bug" I bought with a friend my last year in college. In those days, the oil for that gas had probably been pumped out of an American well on land (and not dumped in the Gulf of Mexico). Gas, in any case, was dirt cheap. *No one* thought about it—or Saudi Arabia (unless they were working for an oil company or the State Department).

Back in 1966, the world was in debt to us. We were the high-tech brand you wanted to own—unless, of course, you were a guerrilla in the jungles of Southeast Asia who held some quaint notion about having a nation of your own.

Here's what I didn't doubt then: that I would get a job. I didn't spend much time thinking about my working future, because American affluence and the global dominance that went with it left me unshakably confident that, when I was ready, I would land somewhere effortlessly. The road trips of that era, the fabled counterculture, so much of daily life

161

would be predicated on, and tied to, the country's economic power, cheap oil, staggering productivity, and an ability to act imperially on a global stage without seeming (to us Americans at least) like an imperial entity.

I was living in denial then about the nature of our government, our military, and our country, but it was an understandable state. After all, we—the sixties generation—grew up so much closer to a tale of American democracy and responsive government. We had faith, however unexamined, that the government should hear us, that if we raised our voices loudly enough, our leaders *would* listen. We had, in other words, a powerful, deeply ingrained sense of agency, now absent in this country.

That, I suspect, is why we took to the streets in protest—not just because we despaired of American war policy, which we did, but because under that despair we still held on tightly to a hope, which the next decades would strip from our world and later generations. And we had hopeful models as well. The great civil rights movement of the 1950s and 1960s was still a force to be reckoned with—and the assassinations of Martin Luther King, Jr., the riots of 1968, the shock of American troops occupying American inner cities, as yet had no reality for us.

Even in protest, there was a sense of . . . well, the only word I can think of is "abundance." At the time, everything seemed abundant. President Lyndon Johnson's Great Society program was expansively under way in the midst of war—and even guns and butter seemed (for a while) a plausible enough combination for a country like ours. The Peace Corps, that creation of the Kennedy presidency—which my future wife joined in 1964—was still new and it, too, encapsulated that sense of American abundance and the hubris that went with it. It was based, after all, on the idea that you could take a bunch of American kids, just out of college, with no particular skills, and ship them off with minimal training to needy nations around the world to improve life, all as part of a great Cold War publicity face-off with the Soviet Union. And those kids, who turned out in droves to experience something bigger and better than themselves, did often enough find ingenious ways to offer limited amounts of help. The Peace Corps was but one small measure of a pervasive sense—about to be shattered—of our country's status as the globe's preeminent can-do nation. There was nothing we couldn't do. (Hadn't we, after all, singlehandedly rebuilt devastated Europe and Japan after World War II?)

Then, of course, there was "the war." Vietnam, that is. It was the oozing oil spill of that moment, regularly referred to as "an American tragedy," never a Vietnamese one. The tragic aspect of it, above all, seemed to be that victory would not come, that, as Henry Kissinger would later put it, speaking of Communist North Vietnam, "I can't believe a fourth-rate power doesn't have a breaking point." The very idea of defeat—hardly mentionable in those years but ever-present—was corrosive to what, in a book of mine, I once called America's "victory culture." Because the Vietnamese refused to give way in that "meat grinder" of a war in which millions of them and tens of thousands of American soldiers would die, doubt oozed into the crevices of American life, and began to eat away at confidence.

Even the nightmare of war, however, had a positive side—and you can thank the draft for that. The United States then had a civilian, rather than a professional (verging on mercenary) army. It was, in a sense, still faintly in the tradition of the "people's armies" that began with the French Revolution's *levée en masse*. For young men nationwide and those who knew them, the draft—the possibility that you, or your son, husband, lover, friend, might actually end up fighting America's misbegotten war in Southeast Asia—ensured, strangely enough, a deeper connection both to war and country, something now absent in most people's lives.

With rare exceptions, we live today unconnected to the wars our government has been fighting for the past decade. As a result, most of us also live in a state of denial about the damage our country is doing to itself and others in distant lands. That kind of denial is a luxury in a country now known far less for its affluence and still squandering what wealth it has on wars and armaments. Today, it's guns, not butter, and that fateful choice, regularly renewed, seems totally divorced from our lives, though we will, in the end, pay a price for it.

### Can't-Do America

Who can deny that our world is in trouble? Or that our troubles, like our wars, have a momentum of their own against which we generally no longer raise our voices in protest? That we have, in a sense, been disarmed as citizens?

If, however, we are caught in a system, so are our leaders. In recent years, we've had two presidents, George W. Bush and Barack Obama. In most obvious ways—style, thinking, personality, sensibility, impulses—they couldn't be more different, as have been the ways they have approached problems. One was a true believer in the glories of American military and executive power, the other is a manager of a declining power and what passes for a political "pragmatist" in our world. Yet, more times than is faintly comfortable, the two of them have ended up in approximately the same policy places—whether on the abridgement of liberties, the expansion of the secret activities of military special operations forces across the Greater Middle East, the CIA drone war in the Pakistani borderlands and elsewhere, our expanding wars, Pentagon budgets, offshore oil drilling and nuclear power, or other policies that matter in our lives.

This should be more startling than it evidently is for most Americans. If the policies of these two disparate figures often have a Tweedledum-and-Tweedledee-ish look to them, then what we face is not specific party politics or individual style, but a system with its own steamroller force, and its own set of narrow, repetitive "solutions" to our problems. We also face an increasingly militarized, privatized government, its wheels greased by the funds of giant corporations, that now regularly seems to go about the business of creating new Katrinas.

Compared to the long-gone world I graduated into, the world of today's graduates seems to me little short of dystopian, even if, on the surface, it still has something of the look of American abundance. If nothing changes in this equation, our collective experience, as far as I can tell, will be of less available, less decent jobs and of less wealth less well distributed, as well as of a federal government that has everything to do with giant corporations, their lobbyists and publicists, and the military-industrial complex—and little to do with the needs of most people.

Our lives are also encased in what I would call a grid of exterminationism. It was in my youth, of course, that the world became exterminable, thanks to nuclear weapons. Today—with other threats, especially global warming and resource scarcity, joining those doomsday weapons in what feels like a fatal brew—how could the young not feel despair, whether fully recognized or not? How could they not have the urge to avoid looking toward the horizon, toward a future too grim to think about? If you can't imagine a future, however, you probably can't form a movement to change anything.

In short, it seems we are living in our nation's fifty-first state, a state of American denial, in a land that is being hollowed out. As we now know, America's aging infrastructure is quite literally hollowing out, as well as springing leaks, and not just a mile under the waters of the Gulf of Mexico either. The hollowing out, however, goes deeper—right down to the feeling that, with disaster in the air, little can be done and nothing reversed. The can-do nation of my youth has given way to a can't-do nation with a busted government.

When the first deep-water oil spill happened in Santa Barbara, California, in 1969, Americans were shocked and there were actual protests. In the streets. Shock, that is, was followed by the urge to act. But more recently, as parts of the Gulf of Mexico were being turned into a dead sea, there may have been shock and even complaint, but there was next to no protest. One Associated Press headline from May 29, 2010, captured the moment perfectly: "A Nation Mesmerized: Can BP Plug the Gulf Gusher?" Mesmerized is a good word for it. The whole world is watching—and nothing more.

## One and a Half Cheers for American Decline

Here's a simple reality: the United States is an imperial power in decline—and not just the sort of decline that is going to affect your children or grandchildren someday. We're talking about massive unemployment that's going nowhere and an economy that shows no sign of ever returning good jobs to this country on a significant scale, even if "good times" do come back sooner or later. We're talking about an aging, fraying infrastructure—with its collapsing bridges and exploding gas pipelines—that a little cosmetic surgery isn't going to help.

The problem in all this isn't the American people. They already know the score. The problem is all those sober official types, military and civilian, who pass for "realists," and are now managing "America's global military presence," its vast garrisons, its wars and alarums. All of them are living in Cloud Cuckoo Land.

Ordinary Americans aren't. They know what's going down, and to judge by the polls, they have a perfectly realistic assessment of what needs to be done. Jim Lobe of Inter Press Service reported on the release of a major biennial survey, "Constrained Internationalism: Adapting to New

Realities," by the Chicago Council on Global Affairs (CCGA). Here's the heart of it, as Lobe describes it:

> The survey's main message . . . [is] that the U.S. public is looking increasingly toward reducing Washington's role in world affairs, especially in conflicts that do not directly concern it. While two-thirds of citizens believe Washington should take an "active part in world affairs," 49 percent—by far the highest percentage since the CCGA first started asking the question in the mid-1970s—agreed with the proposition that the U.S. should "mind its own business internationally and let other countries get along the best they can on their own."
>
> Moreover, 91 percent of respondents agreed that it was "more important at this time for the [U.S.] to fix problems at home" than to address challenges to the (U.S.) abroad—up from 82 percent who responded to that question in CCGA's last survey in 2008.

That striking 49 percent figure is no isolated outlier. As Charles Kupchan and Peter Trubowitz point out in an article in the journal *International Security*, a December 2009 Pew poll got the same 49 percent response to the same "mind its own business" question. It was, they comment, "the highest response ever recorded, far surpassing the 32 percent expressing that attitude in 1972, during the height of opposition to the Vietnam War."

Along the same lines, the CCGA survey found significant majorities expressing an urge for their government to cooperate with China, but not actively work to limit the growth of its power, and not to support Israel if it were to attack Iran. Similarly, they opted for a "lighter military footprint" and a lessening of the U.S. role as "world policeman." When it comes to the Afghan War specifically, a number of polls indicate that skepticism about it continues to rise. All of this adds up not to traditional "isolationism," but to a realistic foreign policy, one appropriate to a nation not garrisoning the planet or dreaming of global hegemony.

This may simply reflect a visceral sense of imperial decline under the pressure of two unpopular wars. Explain it as you will, it's exactly what Washington is incapable of facing. A CCGA survey of elite, inside-the-Beltway opinion would undoubtedly find much of America's leadership class still trapped inside an older global paradigm and so willing to continue pouring hundreds of billions of dollars into Afghanistan and elsewhere rather than consider altering the American posture on the planet.

## Imperial Denial Won't Stop Decline

Despite much planning during and after World War II for a future role as the planet's preeminent power, Washington used to act as if its "responsibilities" as the "leader of the Free World" had been thrust upon it. That, of course, was before the Soviet Union collapsed. After 1991, it became commonplace for pundits and officials alike to refer to the United States as the only "sheriff" in town, the "global policeman," or the planet's "sole superpower."

Whatever the American people might then have thought a post–Cold War "peace dividend" would mean, elites in Washington already knew, and acted accordingly. As in any casino when you're on a roll, they doubled down their bets, investing the fruits of victory in more of the same—especially in the garrisoning and control of the oil-rich Persian Gulf region. And when the good fortune only seemed to continue and the sole enemies left in military terms proved to be a few regional "rogue states" of no great importance and small non-state groups, it went to their heads in a big way.

In the wake of 9/11, the new crew in Washington and the pundits and think-tankers surrounding them saw a planet ripe for the taking. They were convinced that a *Pax Americana* in the Greater Middle East was within their grasp if only they acted boldly, and they didn't doubt for a moment that they could roll back Russia—they were, after all, former Cold Warriors—and put China in its place at the same time. Their language was memorable. They spoke of "cakewalks" and "shock and awe" aerial blitzes and missions accomplished.

And they meant it. They were ready to walk the walk—or so they thought. This was the remarkably brief period when the idea of "empire" or "empire lite" was proudly embraced and friendly pundits started comparing the United States to the Roman or British Empires. It's hard to believe how recently that was and how relatively silent the present group in Washington has fallen when it comes to the glories of American power. Now they just hope to get by, in itself a sign of decline. That's why we've entered a period when, except for inanely repetitious, overblown references to the threat of al-Qaeda, no one in Washington cares to offer Americans an explanation—any explanation—of why we're fighting globally. They prefer to manage the pain while holding the line.

It's not that they don't see decline at all, but that they prefer to think of it as a mild, decades-long process, the sort of thing that might lead to a diminution of American power by 2025. At the edges, however, you can feel other assessments creeping up—in, for instance, former Bush-era National Security Council deputy Robert Blackwill's call for the United States to pull back its troops to northern Afghanistan, ceding the Pashtun south to the Taliban.

Sooner or later—and I doubt it will take as long as many imagine—you'll hear far more voices, ever closer to the heartlands of American power, rising in anxiety or even fear. Don't think nine or ten years either. This won't be a matter of choice. Our leadership may be delusional, but there will be nothing more to double down with, and so "America's global military presence" will begin to crumble. And whether they want it or not, whether there's even an antiwar movement or not, those troops will start coming home, not to a happy nation or to an upbeat situation, but home in any case.

It may sound terrible, and in Afghanistan and elsewhere, terrible things will indeed happen in the interim, while at home the economy will, at best, limp along, the infrastructure will continue to deteriorate, more jobs will march south, and American finances will worsen. If we're not quite heading for what Arianna Huffington calls "Third World America," we're not heading for further fame and fortune either.

But cheer up. The news isn't all bad. Truly. We've just gotten way too used to the idea that the United States must be the planet's preeminent nation, the global hegemon, the sole superpower, *numero uno*. We've convinced ourselves that neither we nor the world can exist without our special management.

So here's the good news: it's actually going to feel better to be just another nation, one more country, even if a large and powerful one, on this overcrowded planet, rather than *the* nation. It's going to feel better to only arm ourselves to defend our actual borders, rather than constantly fighting distant wars or skirmishes and endlessly preparing for more of the same. It's going to feel better not to be constantly engaged in an arms race of one or playing the role of the globe's major arms dealer. It's going to feel better to focus on American problems, maybe experiment a little at home, and offer the world some real models for a difficult future, instead of talking incessantly about what a model we are while we bomb and torture and assassinate abroad with impunity.

So take some pleasure in this: our troops *are* coming home and you're going to see it happen. And in the not so very distant future it won't be our job to "police" the world or be the "global sheriff." And won't that be a relief? We can form actual coalitions of equals to do things worth doing globally and never have to organize another "coalition of the billing," twisting arms and bribing others to do our military bidding.

Since by the time we get anywhere near such a world our leaders will have run this country into the ground, it's hard to offer the traditional three cheers for such a future. But how about at least one-and-a-half prospective cheers for the possible return of perspective to our American world, for a significant lessening, even if not the decisive ending, of an American imperial role and of the massive military "footprint" that goes with it?

## Life in the Echo Chamber

The Arab Spring in 2011 represents a global moment unlike any in memory, perhaps in history. Yes, comparisons can be made to the wave of people power that swept Eastern Europe as the Soviet Union collapsed. For those with longer memories, perhaps 1968 might come to mind, that abortive moment when, in the United States, France, Germany, Japan, Mexico, Brazil, and elsewhere, including Eastern Europe, masses of people mysteriously inspired by each other took to the streets of global cities to proclaim that change was on the way. For those searching the history books, perhaps you've focused on the year 1848, when, in a time that also mixed economic gloom with novel means of disseminating the news, the winds of freedom seemed briefly to sweep across Europe. And, of course, if enough regimes fall and the turmoil goes deep enough, there's always 1776, the American Revolution, or 1789, the French one, to consider. Both shook up the world for decades after.

But here's the truth of it: you have to strain to fit the Arab Spring into any previous paradigm, even as—from Wisconsin to China—it already threatens to break out of the Arab world and spread like a fever across the planet. Never in memory have so many unjust or simply despicable rulers felt quite so nervous—or possibly quite so helpless, despite being armed to the teeth—in the presence of unarmed humanity. There has to be joy and hope in that alone.

Watching staggering numbers of people, many young and dissatisfied, take to the streets in Algeria, Djibouti, Iran, Iraq, Jordan, Libya, Mauritania, Morocco, Oman, Sudan, Syria, and Yemen, not to mention Bahrain, Egypt, and Tunisia, is inspirational. Watching them face security forces using batons, tear gas, rubber bullets, and in all too many cases, real bullets (in Libya, even helicopters, and planes) and somehow grow stronger is little short of unbelievable. Seeing Arabs demanding something we were convinced was the birthright and property of the West, of the United States in particular, has to send a shiver down anyone's spine.

The nature of this potentially world-shaking phenomenon remains uncertain. Are freedom and democracy about to break out all over? And if so, what will that turn out to mean? If not, what exactly are we seeing? I doubt those who are protesting, and in some cases dying, know themselves. And that's good news. That the future remains—always—the land of the unknown should offer us hope, not least because that's the bane of ruling elites who want to, but never can, take possession of it.

Nonetheless, you would expect that a ruling elite, observing such earth-shaking developments, might rethink its situation, as should the rest of us. After all, if humanity can suddenly rouse itself this way in the face of the armed power of state after state, then what's really possible on this planet of ours?

Seeing such scenes repeatedly, who wouldn't rethink the basics? Who wouldn't feel the urge to reimagine our world?

## Five Ways to Be Tone Deaf in Washington

So much of what Washington did imagine in these last years proved laughable, even before this moment swept it away. Just take any old phrase from the Bush years. How about "You're either with us or against us"? What's striking is how little it means today. Looking back on Washington's desperately mistaken assumptions about how our world works, this might seem like the perfect moment to show some humility in the face of what nobody could have predicted.

It would seem like a good moment for Washington—which, since September 12, 2001, has been remarkably clueless about real developments on this planet—to step back and recalibrate. As it happens, there's no evidence it's doing so. In fact, that may be beyond Washington's present capabilities, no matter how many billions of dollars it pours into "intelligence." And by "Washington," I mean not just the Obama administration, or the Pentagon, or our military commanders, or the vast intelligence bureaucracy, but those pundits and think-tankers who swarm the capital, and the media that reports on them all. It's as if the cast of characters that makes up "Washington" now lives in some kind of echo chamber in which it can only hear itself talking.

As a result, Washington still seems remarkably determined to play out the string on an era that is all too swiftly passing into the history books. While many have noticed the Obama administration's hapless struggle with catch up with events in the Middle East, even as it clings to a familiar coterie of grim autocrats and oil sheiks, let me illustrate this point in another area entirely—the largely forgotten war in Afghanistan. After all, hardly noticed, buried beneath 24-7 news from Egypt, Bahrain, Libya, and elsewhere in the Middle East, that war continues on its destructive, costly course with nary a blink.

You might think that, as vast swathes of the Greater Middle East are set ablaze, someone in Washington would take a new look at our Af-Pak War and wonder whether it isn't simply beside the point. No such luck, as the following five tiny but telling examples that caught my attention indicate. Consider them proof of the well-being of the American echo chamber and evidence of the way Washington is proving incapable of rethinking its longest, most futile, and most bizarre war.

1. Let's start with a February 20, 2011, *New York Times* op-ed, "The 'Long War' May Be Getting Shorter," an upbeat account of Afghan War commander general David Petraeus's counterinsurgency operations in southern Afghanistan. Its authors, Nathaniel Fick and John Nagl, members of an increasingly militarized Washington intelligentsia, jointly head the Center for a New American Security in Washington. Nagl was part of the team that wrote the 2006 revised army counterinsurgency manual

for which Petraeus is given credit and was an adviser to the general in Iraq. Fick, a former marine officer who led troops in Afghanistan and Iraq and then was a civilian instructor at the Afghanistan Counterinsurgency Academy in Kabul, had recently paid a visit to the country (under whose auspices we do not know). The two of them are typical of many of Washington's war experts who tend to develop incestuous relationships with the military, moonlighting as enablers or cheerleaders for our war commanders, and still remain go-to sources for the media.

In another society, their op-ed would simply have been considered propaganda. Here's its money paragraph: "It is hard to tell when momentum shifts in a counterinsurgency campaign, but there is increasing evidence that Afghanistan is moving in a more positive direction than many analysts think. It now seems more likely than not that the country can achieve the modest level of stability and self-reliance necessary to allow the United States to responsibly draw down its forces from 100,000 to twenty-five troops over the next four years." This is a classic Washington example of moving the goalposts. What our two experts are really announcing is that, even if all goes well in our Afghan War, 2014 will not be its end date. Not by a long shot.

Of course, this is a position that Petraeus has supported. Four years from now our "withdrawal" plans, according to Nagl and Fick, will leave 25,000 troops in place. If truth-telling or accuracy were the point of their exercise, their piece would have been titled, "The 'Long War' Grows *Longer*."

Even as the Middle East explodes and the United States plunges into a budget "debate" significantly powered by our stunningly expensive wars that won't end, these two experts implicitly propose that General Petraeus and his successors fight on in Afghanistan at more than $100 billion a year into the distant reaches of time, as if nothing in the world were changing. This already seems like the definition of obliviousness and one day will undoubtedly look delusional, but it's the business-as-usual mentality with which Washington faces a new world.

2. Or consider two striking comments General Petraeus himself made that bracket our new historical moment. At a morning briefing on January 19, 2011, according to *New York Times* reporter Rod Nordland, the general was in an exultant, even triumphalist, mood about his war. It was just days before the first Egyptian demonstrators would take to the

streets, and only days after Tunisian autocrat Zine Ben Ali had met the massed power of nonviolent demonstrators and fled his country. And here's what Petraeus so exuberantly told his staff: "We've got our teeth in the enemy's jugular now, and we're not going to let go."

It's true that the general had, for months, been generally intensifying the war in the Taliban's home territory. Still, under the best of circumstances, his was an exultantly odd image. It obviously called up the idea of a predator sinking its teeth into the throat of its prey, but surely somewhere in the military unconscious lurked a more classic American pop-cultural image—the werewolf or vampire. Evidently, the general's idea of an American future involves an extended blood feast in the Afghan version of Transylvania, for like Nagl and Fick he clearly plans to have those teeth in that jugular for a long time to come.

A month later, on February 19, just as all hell was breaking loose in Bahrain and Libya, the general visited the Afghan presidential palace in Kabul and, in dismissing Afghan claims that recent American air raids in the country's northeast had killed scores of civilians, including children, he made a comment that shocked President Hamid Karzai's aides. We don't have it verbatim, but the *Washington Post* reports that, according to "participants," Petraeus suggested "Afghans caught up in a coalition attack in northeastern Afghanistan might have burned their own children to exaggerate claims of civilian casualties." One Afghan at the meeting responded: "I was dizzy. My head was spinning. This was shocking. Would any father do this to his children? This is really absurd."

In the American echo chamber, the general's comments may sound, if not reasonable, then understandably exuberant and emphatic: We've got the enemy by the throat. We didn't create Afghan casualties; they did it to themselves. Elsewhere, they surely sound obtusely tone deaf or simply vampiric, evidence that those inside the echo chamber have no sense of how they look in a shape-shifting world.

3. Now let's step across the ill-defined border between Afghanistan and Pakistan into another world of American obtuseness. On February 15, just four days after Hosni Mubarak stepped down as president of Egypt, Barack Obama decided to address a growing problem in Pakistan. Raymond Davis, a former U.S. Special Forces soldier armed with a Glock semiautomatic pistol and alone in a vehicle cruising a poor neighborhood

of Pakistan's second largest city, Lahore, shot and killed two Pakistanis he claimed had menaced him at gunpoint. (One was evidently shot in the back.) Davis reportedly got out of the vehicle firing his pistol, then photographed the dead bodies and called for backup. The responding vehicle, racing to the scene the wrong way in traffic, ran over a motorcyclist, killing him before fleeing. (Subsequently, the wife of one of the Pakistanis Davis killed committed suicide by ingesting rat poison.)

The Pakistani police took Davis into custody with a carful of strange equipment. No one should be surprised that this was not a set of circumstances likely to endear an already alienated population to its supposed American allies. In fact, it created a popular furor as Pakistanis reacted to what seemed like the definition of imperial impunity, especially when the U.S. government, claiming Davis was an "administrative and technical official" attached to its Lahore consulate, demanded his release on grounds of diplomatic immunity and promptly began pressuring an already weak, unpopular government with loss of aid and support.

Senator John Kerry paid a hasty visit, calls were made, and threats to cut off U.S. funds were raised in the halls of Congress. Despite what was happening elsewhere and in tumultuous Pakistan, American officials found it hard to imagine that beholden Pakistanis wouldn't buckle. On February 15, with the Middle East in flames, President Obama weighed in, undoubtedly making matters worse: "With respect to Mr. Davis, our diplomat in Pakistan," he said, "we've got a very simple principle here that every country in the world that is party to the Vienna Convention on Diplomatic Relations has upheld in the past and should uphold in the future, and that is if our diplomats are in another country, then they are not subject to that country's local prosecution."

The Pakistanis refused to give way to that "very simple principle" and not long after, "our diplomat in Pakistan" was identified by the British *Guardian* as a former Blackwater employee and present employee of the CIA. He was, the publication reported, involved in the agency's secret war in Pakistan. That war, especially much-ballyhooed "covert" drone attacks in the Pakistani tribal borderlands whose returns have been overhyped in Washington, continues to generate blowback in ways that Americans prefer not to grasp. Of course, the president knew that Davis was a CIA agent, even when he called him "our diplomat." As it turned

out, so did the *New York Times* and other U.S. publications, which re-
frained from writing about his real position at the request of the Obama
administration, even as they continued to report (evasively, if not simply
untruthfully) on the case.

Given what's happening in the region, this represents neither reasonable policy-making nor reasonable journalism. If the late Chalmers
Johnson, who made the word "blowback" part of our everyday language,
happens to be looking down on American policy from some niche in
heaven, he must be grimly amused by the brain-dead way our top officials
blithely continue to try to bulldoze the Pakistanis.

4. Meanwhile, on February 18, back in Afghanistan, the U.S. Treasury
Department imposed sanctions on one of that country's "largest money
exchange houses," charging "that it used billions of dollars transferred in
and out of the country to help hide proceeds from illegal drug sales." Here's
how Ginger Thompson and Alissa J. Rubin of the *New York Times* contex-
tualized that act: "The move is part of a delicate balancing act by the Obama
administration, which aims to crack down on the corruption that reaches
the highest levels of the Afghan government without derailing the counterinsurgency efforts that are dependent on Mr. Karzai's cooperation."

In a world in which Washington's word seems to travel ever less far
with ever less authority, the response to this echo-chamber-style description, and especially its central image—"a delicate balancing act"—would
be: no, not by a long shot. In relation to a country that's the prime narco-
state on the planet, what could really be "delicate"? If you wanted to describe the Obama administration's bizarre, pretzled relationship with
President Karzai and his people, words like "contorted," "confused," and
"hypocritical" would have to be trotted out. If realism prevailed, the
phrase "indelicate imbalance" might be a more appropriate one to use.

5. Finally, journalist Dexter Filkins wrote a striking piece, "The Afghan
Bank Heist," which appeared in the February 14, 2011, *New Yorker* maga-
zine, on the shenanigans that brought Kabul Bank, one of Afghanistan's
top financial institutions, to the brink of collapse. While bankrolling
Hamid Karzai and his cronies by slipping them staggering sums of cash,
the bank's officials essentially ran off with the deposits of its customers.
(Think of Kabul Bank as the institutional Bernie Madoff of Afghanistan.)
In his piece, Filkins quotes an anonymous American official this way on

the crooked goings-on he observed: "If this were America, fifty people would have been arrested by now."

Consider that line the echo-chamber version of stand-up comedy as well as a reminder that only mad dogs and Americans stay out in the Afghan sun. Like a lot of Americans now in Afghanistan, that poor diplomat needs to be brought home—and soon. He's lost touch with the changing nature of his own country. While we claim it as our duty to bring "nation-building" and "good governance" to the benighted Afghans, at home the United States is being unbuilt, democracy is essentially gone with the wind, the oligarchs are having a field day, the Supreme Court has insured that massive influxes of money will rule any future elections, and the biggest crooks of all get to play their get-out-of-jail-free cards whenever they want. In fact, the Kabul Bank racket—a big deal in an utterly impoverished society—is a minor sideshow compared to what American banks, brokerages, mortgage and insurance companies, and other financial institutions did via their "Ponzi schemes of securitization" when, in 2008, they drove the U.S. and global economies into meltdown mode.

And none of the individuals responsible went to prison, just old-fashioned Ponzi schemers like Madoff. Not one of them was even put on trial. Indeed, in February 2011, federal prosecutors dropped one of the last possible cases from the 2008 meltdown. Angelo R. Mozilo, the former chairman of Countrywide Financial Corporation, once the nation's top mortgage company, did have to settle a civil suit focused on his "ill-gotten gains" in the subprime mortgage debacle for $67.5 million, but as with his peers, no criminal charges were filed.

### We're Not the Good Guys

Imagine this: for the first time in history, a movement of Arabs is inspiring Americans in Wisconsin and possibly elsewhere. Right now, in other words, there *is* something new under the sun, and we didn't invent it. It's not ours. We're not—catch your breath here—even the good guys. They were the ones calling for freedom and democracy in the streets of Middle Eastern cities, while the United States performed another of those indelicate imbalances in favor of the thugs we've long supported in the Middle East.

History is now being reshaped in such a way that the previously major events of the latter years of the foreshortened American century—the Vietnam War, the end of the Cold War, even 9/11—may all be dwarfed by this new moment. And yet, inside the Washington echo chamber, new thoughts about such developments dawn slowly. Meanwhile, our beleaguered, confused, disturbed country is ever less the model for anyone anywhere, though again you wouldn't know that here.

Oblivious to events, Washington clearly intends to fight its perpetual wars and garrison its perpetual bases, creating yet more blowback and destabilizing yet more places, until it eats itself alive. This is the definition of all-American decline in an unexpectedly new world.

## Signs of the Great American Unraveling

It's already gone, having barely outlasted its moment—just long enough for the media to suggest that no one thought it added up to much.

Okay, it was a little more than the military wanted, something less than Joe Biden would have liked, not enough for the growing group of antiwar congressional types, but way too much for John McCain, Lindsey Graham, & Co.

I'm talking about the thirteen minutes of "remarks" on "the way forward in Afghanistan" that President Obama delivered in the East Room of the White House in June 2011.

Billed as the beginning of the end of the Afghan War, it should have been big and it couldn't have been smaller. The patented Obama words were meant to soar, starting with a George W. Bush–style invocation of 9/11 and ending with the usual copious blessings upon this country and our military. But on the evidence, they couldn't have fallen flatter. I doubt I was alone in thinking that it was like seeing Ronald Reagan on an unimaginably bad day in an ad captioned "It's never going to be morning again in America."

### Idolater President

If you let the event slide instantly into your mental trash can, I don't blame you. Still, the president's Afghan remarks shouldn't be sent down the memory hole quite so quickly.

For one thing, while the mainstream media's pundits and talking heads are always raring to discuss his policy remarks, the words that frame them are generally ignored—and yet the discomfort of the moment can't be separated from them. So start with this: whether by inclination, political calculation, or some mix of the two, our president has become a rhetorical idolater.

These days he can barely open his mouth without also bowing down before the U.S. military in ways that once would have struck Americans as embarrassing, if not incomprehensible. In addition, he regularly prostrates himself before this country's special mission to the world and never ceases to emphasize that the United States is indeed an exception among nations. Finally, in a way once alien to American presidents, he invokes God's blessing upon the military and the country as regularly as you brush your teeth.

Think of these as the triumvirate without which no Obama foreign-policy moment would be complete: greatest military, greatest nation, our God. And in this he follows directly, if awkwardly, in Bush's footsteps.

I wouldn't claim that Americans had never had such thoughts before, only that presidents didn't feel required to say them in a mantra-like way just about every time they appeared in public. Sometimes, of course, when you feel a compulsion to say the same things ad nauseam, you display weakness, not strength; you reveal the most fantastic of fantasy worlds, not a deeper reality.

The president's recent Afghan remarks were, in this sense, par for the course. As he plugged his plan to bring America's "long wars" to what he called "a responsible end," he insisted that "[l]ike generations before, we must embrace America's singular role in the course of human events." He then painted this flattering word portrait of us: "We're a nation that brings our enemies to justice while adhering to the rule of law, and respecting the rights of all our citizens. We protect our own freedom and prosperity by extending it to others. We stand not for empire, but for self-determination . . . and when our union is strong no hill is too steep, no horizon is beyond our reach . . . we are bound together by the creed that is written into our founding documents, and a conviction that the United States of America is a country that can achieve whatever it sets out to accomplish."

I know, I know. You're wondering whether you just mainlined into a Sarah Palin speech and your eyes are glazing over. But hang in there, because that's just a start. For example, in an Obama speech of any sort, what America's soldiers never lack is the extra adjective. They aren't *just* soldiers, but "our extraordinary men and women in uniform." They aren't *just* Americans, but "patriotic Americans." (Since when did an American president have to describe American soldiers as, of all things, "patriotic"?) And in case you missed the point that, in their extraordinariness and their outsized patriotism they are better than other Americans, he made sure to acknowledge them as the ones we "draw inspiration from."

In a country that now "supports the troops" with bumper-sticker fervor but pays next to no attention to the wars they fight, perhaps Obama is simply striving to be the premier American of the twenty-first century. Still, you have to wonder what such presidential fawning, omnipresent enough to be boilerplate, really represents. The strange thing is we hear this sort of thing all the time. And yet no one comments on it. And let's not forget that no significant White House moment ends these days without the president bestowing God's blessing on the globe's most extraordinary nation and its extraordinary fighters, or as he put it in his Afghan remarks: "May God bless our troops. And may God bless the United States of America."

The day after he revealed his drawdown plan to the nation, the president traveled to Fort Drum in New York State to thank soldiers from the army's 10th Mountain Division for their multiple deployments to Afghanistan. Before those extraordinary and patriotic Americans, he quite naturally doubled down.

Summoning another tic of this presidential moment (and of the Bush one before it), he told them that they were part of "the finest fighting force in the world." Even that evidently seemed inadequate, so he upped the hyperbole. "I have no greater job," he told them, "nothing gives me more honor than serving as your commander in chief. To all of you who are potentially going to be redeployed, just know that your commander in chief has your back. . . . God bless you, God bless the United States of America, climb to glory."

As ever, all of this was overlooked. Nowhere did a single commentator wonder, for instance, whether an American president was *really* supposed to feel that being commander in chief offered greater "honor" than being president of a nation of citizens. In another age, such a statement would have registered as, at best, bizarre. These days, no one even blinks.

And yet who living in this riven, confused, semi-paralyzed country of ours truly believes that, in 2011, Americans can achieve whatever we set out to accomplish? Who thinks that, not having won a war in memory, the U.S. military is incontestably the finest fighting force now or ever, or that this country is at present specially blessed by God, or that ours is a mission of selfless kindheartedness on planet Earth?

Obama's remarks have no wings these days because they are ever more divorced from reality. Perhaps because this president in fawning mode is such an uncomfortable sight, and because Americans generally feel so ill-at-ease about their relationship to our wars, however, such remarks are neither attacked nor defended, discussed nor debated, but as if by some unspoken agreement simply ignored.

Here, in any case, is what they aren't: effective rallying cries for a nation in need of unity. Here's what they may be: strange, defensive artifacts of an imperial power in visible decline, part of what might be imagined as the Great American Unraveling. But hold that thought a moment. After all, the topic of the president's remarks *was* Afghanistan.

### The Unreal War

If Obama framed his Afghan remarks in a rhetoric of militarized supernational surrealism, then what he had to say about the future of the war itself was deceptive in the extreme—not lies perhaps, but full falsehoods half told. Consider just the two most important items: that his "surge" consisted only of 33,000 American troops and that "by next summer," Americans are going to be on the road to leaving Afghanistan.

Unfortunately, it just ain't so. First of all, the real Obama surge was minimally almost 55,000 and possibly 66,000 troops, depending on how you count them. When he came into office in January 2009, there were about 32,000 American troops in Afghanistan. Another 11,000 had been designated to go in the last days of the Bush administration, but only departed in the first Obama months. In March 2009, the president announced his own "new strategy for Afghanistan and Pakistan" and dispatched 21,700 more troops. Then, in December 2009 in a televised speech to the nation from West Point, he announced that another 30,000 would be going. (With "support troops," it turned out to be 33,000.)

In other words, in September 2012, if indeed he withdraws those 33,000 troops, only about half the actual troop surge of the Obama years will have left Afghanistan. In addition, though seldom discussed, the Obama "surge" was hardly restricted to troops. There was a much bally-hooed "civilian surge" of State Department and aid types that more than tripled the "civilian" effort in Afghanistan. Their drawdown was addressed by Secretary of State Hillary Clinton in the wake of the president's remarks, but only in the vaguest of terms.

Then there was a major surge of CIA personnel (along with U.S. Special Operations forces), and there's no indication whatsoever that anyone in Washington intends reductions there, or in the drone surge that went with it. As a troop drawdown begins, CIA agents, those special ops forces, and the drones are clearly slated to remain at or beyond a surge peak.

Finally, there was a surge in private contractors—hired foreign guns and hired Afghans—tens of thousands of them. It goes unmentioned, as does the surge in base building, which has yet to end.

All of this makes mincemeat of the idea that we are in the process of ending the Afghan War. The president did say, "Our mission will change from combat to support. By 2014, this process of transition will be complete, and the Afghan people will be responsible for their own security." And that was a foggy enough formulation that you might be forgiven for imagining more or less everything will be over "by 2014"—which, by the way, means not January 1, but December 31 of that year.

If what we know of U.S. plans in Afghanistan plays out, however, December 31, 2014, will be the date for the departure of the last of the full Obama surge of 64,000 troops, at best. In other words, almost five years after Obama entered office, more than thirteen years after the Bush administration launched its invasion, we could find ourselves back to or just below something close to Bush-era troop levels. Tens of thousands of U.S. forces would still be in Afghanistan, some of them "combat troops" officially relabeled (as in Iraq) for less warlike activity. All would be part of an American "support" mission that would include huge numbers of "trainers" for the Afghan security forces and also U.S. Special Forces operatives and CIA types engaged in "counterterror" activities in the country and region.

The U.S. general in charge of training the Afghan military has suggested that his mission wouldn't be done until 2017 (and no one who knows anything about the country believes that an effective Afghan army will be in place then either). In addition, although the president didn't directly mention this in his speech, the Obama administration has been involved in quiet talks with the government of Afghan president Hamid Karzai to nail down a "strategic partnership" agreement that would allow American troops, spies, and air power to hunker down as "tenants" on some of the giant bases we've built. There they would evidently remain for years, if not decades (as some reports have it).

In other words, on December 31, 2014, if all goes as planned, the United States will be girding for years more of wildly expensive war, even if in a slimmed-down form. This is the reality, as American planners imagine it, behind the president's speech.

### Overstretched Empire

Of course, it's not for nothing that we regularly speak of best-laid plans going awry, something that applies doubly, as in Afghanistan, to the worst-laid plans. It's increasingly apparent that our disastrous wars are, as Chairman of the Senate Foreign Relations Committee John Kerry admitted, "unsustainable." After all, just the cost of providing air conditioning to U.S. personnel in Iraq and Afghanistan—$20 billion a year—is more than NASA's entire budget.

Yes, despite Washington's long-lost dreams of a *Pax Americana* in the Greater Middle East, some of its wars there are still being planned as if for a near-eternity, while others are being intensified. Those wars are still fueled by overblown fears of terrorism, encouraged by a remarkably well-funded National Security Complex in an atmosphere of permanent armed crisis, and run by a military that, after a decade of not-so-creative destruction, can't stop doing what it knows how to do best (which isn't winning a war).

Although Obama claims that the United States is no empire, all of this gives modern meaning to the term "overstretched empire." And it's not really much of a mystery what happens to overextended imperial powers that find themselves fighting "little" wars they can't win, while their treasuries head south.

The growing unease in Washington about America's wars reflects a dawning sense of genuine crisis, a sneaking suspicion even among hawkish

Republicans that they preside ineffectually over a great power in precipitous decline.

If you want to take the temperature of the present crisis, you can do
it through Obama's words. The less they ring true, the more discordant
they seem in the face of reality, the more he fawns and repeats his various
mantras, the more uncomfortable he makes you feel, the more you have
the urge to look away, the deeper the crisis.

What will he say when the Great American Unraveling truly begins?

## Sleepwalking into the Imperial Dark

This can't end well.

But then, how often do empires end well, really? They live vampiri-
cally by feeding off others until, sooner or later, they begin to feed on
themselves, to suck their own blood, to hollow themselves out. Sooner
or later, they find themselves, as in our case, economically stressed and
militarily extended in wars they can't afford to win or lose.

Historians have certainly written about the dangers of overextended
empires and of endless war as a way of life, but there's something distant
and abstract about the patterns of history. It's quite another thing to take
it in when you're a part of it; when, as they used to say in the overheated
1960s, you're in the belly of the beast.

I don't know what it felt like to be inside the Roman Empire in the
long decades, even centuries, before it collapsed, or to experience the waning years of the Spanish Empire, or the twilight of the Qing Dynasty, or of
Imperial Britain as the sun first began to set, or even of the Soviet Empire
before the troops came slinking home from Afghanistan, but at some point
it must have seemed at least a little like this—truly strange, like watching
a machine losing its parts. It must have seemed as odd and unnerving as
it does now to see a formerly mighty power enter a state of semi-paralysis
at home even as it staggers on blindly with its war-making abroad.

The United States is, of course, an imperial power, however much we
might prefer not to utter the word. We still have our globe-spanning array
of semi-client states. Our military continues to garrison much of the
planet. And we are waging war abroad more continuously than at any
time in memory. Yet who doesn't sense that the sun is now setting on us?

## A Country in Need of Prozac

Have you noticed how repetitiously our president, various presidential candidates, and others now insist that we are "the greatest nation on Earth" (as they speak of the U.S. military being "the finest fighting force in the history of the world")? And yet, doesn't that phrase leave ash in your mouth? Look at this country and its frustrations today and tell me: Does anyone honestly believe that anymore?

It wasn't a mistake that the fantasy avenger figure of Rambo became immensely popular in the wake of defeat in Vietnam or that, unlike American heroes of earlier decades, he had such a visibly, almost risibly overblown musculature. As eye-candy, it was pure overcompensation for the obvious. Similarly, when the United States was actually "the greatest" on this planet, no one needed to say it over and over again.

Can there be any question that something big is happening here, even if we don't quite know what it is because, unlike the peoples of past empires, we never took pride in or were even able to think of ourselves as imperial? And if you were indeed in denial that you lived in the belly of a great imperial power, if like most Americans you managed to ignore the fact that we were pouring our treasure into the military or setting up bases in countries that few could have found on a map, then you would naturally experience the empire going down as if through a glass darkly.

Nonetheless, the feelings that should accompany the experience of an imperial power running off the rails aren't likely to disappear just because analysis is lacking. Disillusionment, depression, and dismay flow ever more strongly through the American bloodstream. Just look at any polling data on whether this country, once the quintessential land of optimists, is heading in "the right direction" or on "the wrong track," and you'll find that the "wrong track" numbers are staggering, and growing by the month. On the rare occasions when Americans have been asked by pollsters whether they think the country is "in decline," the figures have been similarly over the top.

It's not hard to see why. A loss of faith in the American political system is palpable. For many Americans, it's no longer "our government" but "the bureaucracy." Washington is visibly incapable of doing much of significance, while state governments, facing the "steepest decline in state tax receipts on record," are, along with local governments, staggering under massive deficits and cutting back in areas—education, policing, firefighting—that are crucial to daily life.

Years ago, in the George W. Bush era, I wanted to put a new word in our domestic political vocabulary: "Republican'ts." It was my way of expressing the feeling that something basic to this country—a "can do" spirit—was seeping away. I failed, of course, and since then that "can't do" spirit has visibly spread far beyond the Republican Party. Simply put, we're a country in need of Prozac.

Facing the challenges of a world on edge—from Japan to the Greater Middle East, from a shaky global economic system to weather that has become anything but entertainment—the United States looks increasingly incapable of coping. It no longer invests in its young, or plans effectively for the future, or sets off on new paths. It literally *can't do*. And this is not just a domestic crisis, but part of imperial decline.

We just don't treat it as such, tending instead to deal with the foreign and domestic as essentially separate spheres, when the connections between them are so obvious. If you doubt this, just pull into your nearest gas station and fill up the tank. Of course, who doesn't know that this country, once such a generator of wealth, is now living with unemployment figures not seen since the Great Depression, as well as unheard of levels of debt, that it's hooked on foreign energy (and like most addicts has next to no capacity for planning how to get off that drug), or that it's living through the worst period of income inequality in modern history? And who doesn't know that a crew of financial fabulists, corporate honchos, lobbyists, and politicians have been fattening themselves off the faltering body politic?

And if you don't think any of this has anything to do with imperial power in decline, ask yourself why the options for our country so often seem to have shrunk to what our military is capable of; or why the only significant part of the government whose budget is still on the rise is the Pentagon; or why, when something is needed, this administration, like its predecessor, regularly turns to that same military.

Once upon a time, helping other nations in terrible times would have been an obvious duty of the civil sector of the U.S. government. Today, from Haiti to Japan, in such moments it's the U.S. military that acts. In response to the Japanese triple disaster of earthquake, tsunami, and nuclear meltdown, for instance, the Pentagon mounted a large-scale recovery effort, involving eighteen thousand people, twenty U.S. Navy ships, and even fuel barges bringing fresh water for reactor-cooling efforts at the Fukushima Daiichi nuclear complex. The effort was given a military code name, Operation Tomodachi (Japanese for "friend"), and is, among other things, an obvious propaganda campaign meant to promote the usefulness of America's archipelago of bases in that country.

Similarly, when the administration needs something done in the Middle East, these days it's as likely to send the secretary of defense as the secretary of state to visit. And of course, as is typical, when a grim situation in Libya worsened and something "humanitarian" was called for, the Obama administration (along with NATO) threw air power at it.

Predictably, as in Afghanistan and the Pakistani borderlands, air power failed to bring about speedy success. What's most striking is not that Libyan ruler Muammar Gaddafi didn't instantly fall, or that the Libyan military didn't collapse when significant parts of its tank and artillery forces were taken out, or that the swift strikes meant to turn the tide soon stretched into months of no-fly-zone NATO squabbling and military stalemate (as the no-fly-zone version of war against Saddam Hussein's Iraq stretched to twelve years without ultimate success).

Imperially speaking, two things are memorable about the American military effort in Libya. First, Washington doesn't seem to have the conviction of what's left of its power, as its strange military dance in (and half-out of) the air over that country indicates. Second, even in the military realm, Washington is increasingly incapable of drawing lessons from its past actions. As a result, its arsenal of potential tactics is made up largely of those that have failed in the recent past. Innovation is no longer part of empire.

### The Uses of Fear

From time to time, the U.S. government's "Intelligence Community" musters its collective savvy and plants its flag in the future in periodic reports that go under the generic rubric of "global trends." The last of these, *Global Trends 2025*, was prepared for a new administration taking office in January 2009, and it was typical. In a field once left to utopian or dystopian thinkers, pulp-fiction writers, oddballs, visionaries, and even outright cranks, these compromise-minded bureaucratic documents break little ground and rock no boats, nor do they predict global tsunamis. Better to forecast what the people you brief already believe, and skip the oddballs with their strange hunches, the sorts who might actually have a knack for recognizing the shock of the future lurking in the present.

As group efforts, then, these reports tend to project the trends of the present moment relatively seamlessly and reasonably reassuringly into the future. For example, the last time around they daringly predicted a gradual, fifteen-year soft landing for a modestly declining America: "Although the United States is likely to remain the single most powerful actor, [the country's] relative strength—even in the military realm—will decline and U.S. leverage will become more constrained."

Even though it was being finished amid the global meltdown of 2008, nothing in it would have kept you up at night, sleepless and fretting. More than fifteen years into the future, our IC could imagine no wheels falling off the American juggernaut, nothing that would make you wonder if this country could someday topple off the nearest cliff. Twists, unpleasant surprises, unhappy endings? Not for this empire, according to its corps of intelligence analysts.

And the future being what it is, if you read that document now, you'd find none of the more stunning events that have disrupted and radically altered our world since late 2008: no Arab lands boiling with revolt, no Hosni Mubarak under arrest with his sons in jail, no mass demonstrations in Syria, no economies of peripheral European countries imploding one by one, nor a cluster of nuclear plants in Japan melting down. You won't find once subservient semi-client states thumbing their noses at Washington, not even in 2025.

You won't, for example, find the Saudis in, say 2011, openly exploring deeper relations with Russia and China as a screw-you response to Washington's belated decision that Egyptian autocrat Hosni Mubarak should leave office, or Pakistani demands that the CIA and American Special Operations forces start scaling back activities on their turf, or American officials practically pleading with an Iraqi government it once helped put in power (and now moving ever closer to Iran) to please, please let U.S. troops stay past an agreed-upon withdrawal deadline of December 31, 2011, or Afghan president Hamid Karzai publicly blaming the Americans for the near collapse of his country's major bank in a cesspool of corruption (in which his own administration was, of course, deeply implicated).

Only two-plus years after *Global Trends 2025* appeared, it doesn't take the combined powers of the IC to know that American decline looks an awful lot more precipitous and bumpier than imagined. But let's not just blame our intelligence functionaries for not divining the future we're already in. After all, they, too, were in the goldfish bowl, and when you're there, it's always hard to describe the nearest cats.

Nor should we be surprised that, like so many other Americans, they were in denial. After all, our leaders spent years organizing their version of the world around a Global War on Terror, when (despite the 9/11 attacks) terror was hardly America's most obvious challenge. It proved largely a "war" against phantoms and fantasies, or against modest-sized ragtag bands of enemies.

The spasms of fear that coursed through our society in the near-decade after September 11, 2001, and the enemy, "Islamic terrorism," to which those spasms were attached are likely to look far different to us in retrospect. Yes, many factors—including the terrifyingly apocalyptic look of 9/11 in New York City—contributed to what happened. There was fear's usefulness in prosecuting wars in the Greater Middle East that President Bush and his top officials found appealing. There was the way it ensured soaring budgets for the Pentagon and the national security state. There was the way it helped the politicians, lobbyists, and corporations hooked into a developing homeland-security complex. There was the handy-dandy way it glued eyeballs to a one-event-fits-all version of the world that made the media happy, and there was the way it justified increasing powers for our national security managers and dwindling liberties for Americans.

But think of all that as only the icing on the cake. Looking back, those terror fears coursing through the body politic will undoubtedly seem like Rambo's muscles: a deflection from the country's deepest fears. They were, in that sense, consoling. They allowed us to go on with our lives, to visit Disney World, as George W. Bush urged in the wake of 9/11, in order to prove our all-American steadfastness.

Above all, even as our imperial wars in the oil heartlands of the planet went desperately wrong, they allowed us not to think about empire or, until the economy melted down in 2008, decline. They allowed us to focus our fears on "them," not us. They ensured that, like the other great imperial power of the Cold War era, when things began to spiral out of control we would indeed sleepwalk right into the imperial darkness.

Now that we're so obviously there, the confusion is greater than ever. Theoretically, none of this should necessarily be considered bad news, not if you don't love empires and what they do. A post-imperial United States could, of course, be open to all sorts of possibilities for change that might be exciting indeed.

Right now, though, it doesn't feel that way, does it? It makes me wonder: Could this be how it's always felt inside a great imperial power on the downhill slide? Could this be what it's like to watch, paralyzed, as a country on autopilot begins to come apart at the seams while still proclaiming itself "the greatest nation on Earth"?

I don't know. But I do know one thing: this can't end well.

## China as Number One?

Tired of Afghanistan and all those messy, oil-ish wars in the Greater Middle East that just don't seem to pan out? Count on one thing: part of the U.S. military feels just the way you do, especially a largely sidelined navy—and that's undoubtedly one of the reasons why the specter of China as this country's future enemy has once again reared its ugly head.

Back before 9/11, China was the favored future uber-enemy of Secretary of Defense Donald Rumsfeld and all those neocons who signed onto the Project for the New American Century and later staffed George W. Bush's administration. After all, if you wanted to build a military beyond compare to enforce a long-term *Pax Americana* on the planet, you needed a nightmare enemy large enough to justify all the advanced weapons systems in which you planned to invest. As late as June 2005, neocon journalist Robert Kaplan was still writing in the *Atlantic* about "How We Would Fight China," an article with this provocative tagline: "The Middle East is just a blip. The American military contest with China in the Pacific will define the twenty-first century. And China will be a more formidable adversary than Russia ever was."

As everyone knows, however, that "blip" proved far too much for the Bush administration. Finding itself hopelessly bogged down in two ground wars with ragtag insurgency movements on either end of the Greater Middle Eastern "mainland," it let China-as-Monster-Enemy slip beneath the waves. In the process, the navy and, to some extent, the air force became adjunct services to the army (and the marines). In Iraq and Afghanistan, for instance, U.S. Navy personnel far from any body of water found themselves driving trucks and staffing prisons.

It was the worst of times for the admirals, and probably not so great for the flyboys either, particularly after Secretary of Defense Robert Gates began pushing pilotless drones as the true force of the future. Naturally, a no-dogfight world in which the U.S. military eternally engages enemies without significant air forces is a problematic basis for proposing future air force budgets.

There's no reason to be surprised then that, as the war in Iraq began to wind down in 2009–2010, the "Chinese naval threat" began to quietly reemerge. China was, after all, immensely economically successful and beginning to flex its muscles in local territorial waters. The alarms sounded by military types or pundits associated with them grew stronger in the early months of 2011 (as did news of weapons systems being developed to deal with future Chinese air and sea power).

"Beware America, time is running out!" warned retired air force lieutenant general and Fox News contributor Thomas G. McInerney while describing China's first experimental stealth jet fighter. Others focused on China's "string of pearls": a potential set of military bases in the Indian Ocean that might someday (particularly if you have a vivid imagination) give that country control of the oil lanes. Meanwhile, Kaplan, whose book about rivalries in that ocean came out in 2010, was back in the saddle, warning: "Now the United States faces a new challenge and potential threat from a rising China which seeks eventually to push the U.S. military's area of operations back to Hawaii and exercise hegemony over the world's most rapidly growing economies."

Behind the overheated warnings lay a deeper, if often unstated, calculation, shared by far more than budget-anxious military types and those who wrote about them: that the United States was heading toward the status of late, great superpower and that, one of these years not so far down the line, China would challenge us for the number one spot on the seas—and on the planet.

## The Usefulness of a Major Enemy

You know the background here: the victor in the Cold War, the self-proclaimed "sole superpower" ready to accept no other nation or bloc of nations that might challenge it (ever), the towering land that was to be the Roman Empire, the British Empire, and the Vulcans all rolled into one. Well, those dreams are already in history's dustbin. These days, Washington appears capable of doing little with its still-staggering military might but fight Pashtun guerrillas to a draw in distant Afghanistan and throw its air power and missile-armed drones at another fifth-rate power in a "humanitarian" gesture with the usual destruction and predictable non-results.

Toss in the obvious—rotting infrastructure, fiscal gridlock in Washington, high unemployment, cutbacks in crucial local services, and a general mood of paralysis, depression, and confusion—and even if the Chinese are only refurbishing a mothballed 1992 Ukrainian aircraft carrier as their first move into the imperial big time, is it really so illogical to imagine them as the next "sole superpower"? After all, China passed Japan in 2010 as the world's number two economy, the same year it officially leaped over the United States to become the world's number one emitter of greenhouse gases. Its growth rate came in at something close to 10 percent right through the great financial meltdown of 2008, making it the world's fastest expanding major economy.

By mid-2010, it had 477,000 millionaires and sixty-four billionaires (second only to the United States), and what's always being touted as a burgeoning middle class with an urge for the better things in life. It also had the world's largest car market (again, the United States came in second), and staggering traffic jams to prove it, not to speak of a willingness to start threatening neighbors over control of the seas. In short, all the signs of classic future imperial success.

And those around the U.S. military aren't alone in sounding the alarm. On April 25, 2011, the International Monetary Fund (IMF) quietly posted a report at its website indicating that by 2016, the "age of America" would be over and, by one measure at least, the Chinese economy would take over first place from the American one.

With growing fears in the military-industrial complex of future cuts in the Pentagon budget, there will undoubtedly be increased jockeying among the armed services for slices of the military pie. This means a heightened need for the sort of enemies and looming challenges that would justify the weapons systems and force levels each service so desperately wants. And there's nothing like having a rising power of impressive proportions sink some money into its own military (even if the sums are still embarrassingly small compared to the United States) to keep those fires burning.

In the Chinese case, it also helps when that country uses its control over rare earth metals to threaten Japan in a dispute over territorial waters in the East China Sea, begins to muscle neighbors on the high seas, and—so rumor has it—is preparing to name its refurbished aircraft carrier after the Qing Dynasty admiral who conquered the island of Taiwan.

### The Unpredictability of China

Still, for all those naval- and air-power types who would like to remove American power from a quicksand planet and put it offshore, for those who would like to return to an age of superpower enmity, in fact, for all those pundits and analysts of whatever stripe picking China as the globe's next superstar or super evildoer, I have a small suggestion: take a deep breath. Then remember: we've already been through this once. Might it not be worth approaching that number-one prediction with more humility the second time around?

Back in 1979, Ezra Vogel, Harvard professor and Asia specialist, put out a book that was distinctly ahead of its time in capturing the rise to wealth and glory of a new global power. He entitled it *Japan as Number One: Lessons for America*, and in praising the ways Japanese industry operated and the resulting "Japanese miracle," the title lacked only an exclamation point. Vogel certainly caught the temper of the times, and his scholarly analysis was followed, in the 1980s, by a flood of ever more shrill articles and books predicting (in fascination or horror) that this would indeed someday be a Japanese world. The only problem, as we now know: 'tweren't so. The Japanese economic bubble burst around 1990 and a "lost decade" followed, which has never quite ended. Then, of course, there was the 2011 earthquake-cum-tsunami-cum-nuclear-disaster that further crippled the country.

So how about *China as Number One: Lessons for America*? After all, the Chinese economy is threatening to leave Japan in the dust; if you were one of its neighbors, you might indeed be fretting about your offshore claims to the mineral wealth under various local seas; and everyone knows that Shanghai is now *Blade Runner* without the noir, just forty-story towers as far as the eye can see. So what could go wrong?

As a specialty line, our intelligence services offer new administrations predictions on the world to come by projecting present trends into a recognizably similar future. And why shouldn't that be the logical way to proceed? So if you project Chinese growth rates into the future, as the IMF has recently done, you end up with a monster of success (and a military with a global reach). It's not that hard, in other words, to end up with the U.S. Navy's nightmare enemy.

But so much on our present planet suggests that we're not in a world of steady, evolutionary development but of what the evolutionary biologist Stephen Jay Gould called "punctuated equilibrium," of sudden leaps and discontinuous change. Imagine then another perfectly logical scenario: What if, like Japan, China hits some major speed bumps on the highway to number one?

As you think about that, keep something else in mind. China's story over the last century-plus already represents one of the great discontinuous bursts of energy of our modern moment. To predict most of the twists and turns along the way would have been next to impossible. In 1972, in the wake of the Cultural Revolution that Mao Zedong had set in motion six years earlier, to take but one example, no intelligence service, no set of seers, no American would have predicted today's China or, for that matter, a three-and-a-half-decade burst of Communist Party–controlled capitalist industrial expansionism. The pundit who offered such a prediction then would have been drummed out of the corps of analysts.

No one at the time could have foreseen that the giant, independent-but-impoverished Communist land would become the expansive number two capitalist economy it is today. In fact, from the turn of the previous century, when China was the basket case of Asia and a combined Japanese/Western force marched on Beijing, when various great powers took parts of the country as their own property or "concessions," followed by ensuing waves of warlordism, nationalism, revolutionary ferment, war with Japan, civil war, and finally the triumph of a Communist regime that united the country: the essence of China's story has been unpredictability.

So what confidence should we now have in projections about China that assume more of the same, especially since, looking toward the future, that country seems like something of a one-trick pony? After all, the ruling Communist Party threw the dice definitively for state capitalism and untrammeled growth decades ago and now sits atop a potential volcano. As the country's leaders undoubtedly know, only one thing may keep the present system safely in place: ever more growth.

The minute China's economy falters, the minute some bubble bursts, whether through an overheating economy or for other reasons, the country's rulers have a problem on their hands that could potentially make the Arab Spring look mild by comparison. What many here call China's growing "middle class" remains anything but—and there are literally hundreds of millions of forgotten peasants and migrant workers who have found the Chinese success story less than a joy.

## A Revolutionary Tradition for the Ages

It might take only a significant economic downturn, a period that offered little promise to Chinese workers and consumers, to unsettle that country in major ways. After all, despite its striking growth rates, it remains in some fashion a poor land. And one more factor should be taken into consideration that few of our seers ever consider. It's no exaggeration to say that China has a revolutionary tradition unlike that of any other nation or even region on the planet.

Since at least the time of the Yellow Turban Rebellion in 184 CE, led by three brothers associated with a Taoist sect, the country has repeatedly experienced millenarian peasant movements bursting out of its interior with ferocious energy. There is no other record like it. The last of these was undoubtedly Mao Zedong's Communist revolution. Others would certainly include the peasant uprising at the end of the Ming Dynasty in the seventeenth century and, around the time of the American Civil War, the Taiping Rebellion. That was led by a man we would today call a cultist who had created a syncretic mix of Chinese religions and Christianity— and who considered himself the younger brother of Jesus Christ. Before Qing Dynasty forces finally suppressed it and a series of other rebellions, an estimated twenty million people died.

When Chinese leaders banned and then tried to stamp out the fast-spreading Falun Gong movement, they were not—as reported here—simply "repressing religion," they were suppressing what they undoubtedly feared could be the next Taiping Rebellion. Even if few intelligence analysts in the West are thinking about any of this, rest assured that the Communist rulers of China know their own history. That's one reason why they have been so quick to crack down on any Arab Spring–like demonstrations.

In addition, though I'm no economist, when I look around this planet I continue to wonder (as the Chinese must) about the limits of growth for all of us, but especially for such a vast country that is desperate for energy and other raw materials, with an aging population and an environment already heavily polluted by the last forty years of unchecked industrial expansion. There is no question that China has invested in its military, put together a powerful (if largely defensive) navy, elbowed its neighbors on questions of undersea mineral rights, and gone on a global search to lock up future energy resources and key raw materials.

Nonetheless, if predictions were to be made and trends projected, it might be far more reasonable to predict a cautious Chinese government, focused on keeping its populace under control and solving confounding domestic problems, than an expansively imperial one. It's almost inconceivable that China could or would ever play the role the United States played in 1945 as the British Empire went down. It's hard even to imagine China as another Soviet Union in a great global struggle with the United States.

And speaking of the conjunctures of history, here's another thought for the U.S. Navy: What if this isn't an imperial planet anymore? What if, from resource scarcity to global warming, humanity is nudging up against previously unimagined limits on unbridled growth? From at least the seventeenth century on, successive great powers have struggled to control vast realms of a globe in which expansion eternally seemed the name of the game. For centuries, one or more great powers were always on hand when the previous great imperial power or set of powers faltered.

In the wake of World War II, with the collapse of the Japanese and German Empires, only two powers worthy of the name were left, each so mighty that together they would be called "superpowers." After 1991, only one remained, so seemingly powerful that it was sometimes termed a "hyperpower" and many believed it had inherited the Earth.

What if, in fact, the United States is indeed the last empire? What if a world of rivalries, on a planet heading into resource scarcity, turned out to be less than imperial in nature? Or what if—and think of me as a devil's advocate here—this turned out not to be an imperial world of bitter rivalries at all, but in the face of unexpectedly tough times, a partnership planet?

Unlikely? Sure, but who knows? That's the great charm of the future. In any case, just to be safe, you might not want to start preparing for the Chinese century quite so fast or bet your bottom dollar on China as number one. Not just yet anyway.

# On Being a Critic

## All the World's a Stage (for Us)

In March 2010, I wrote about a crew of pundits and warrior-journalists eager not to see the U.S. military leave Iraq. That piece appeared on the op-ed page of the *Los Angeles Times* (and in a longer version at TomDispatch.com) and then began wandering the media world. One of its stops was the military newspaper *Stars and Stripes*.

From a military man came this emailed response: "Read your article in *Stars and Stripes*. When was the last time you visited Iraq?" A critique in fifteen well-chosen words. So much more effective than a long, angry email, and his point was interesting. At least, it interested me. After all, as I wrote back, I was then a sixty-five-year-old guy who had never been anywhere near Iraq and undoubtedly never would be. I have to assume that my emailer had spent time there, possibly more than once, and disagreed with my assessments.

Firsthand experience is not to be taken lightly. What, after all, *do* I know about Iraq? Only the reporting I've been able to read from thousands of miles away or analysis found on the blogs of experts like Juan Cole. On the other hand, even from thousands of miles away, I was one of many who could see enough, by early 2003, to go into the streets and demonstrate against an onrushing disaster of an invasion that a lot of people, theoretically far more knowledgeable on Iraq than any of us, considered just the cat's meow, the "cakewalk" of the new century.

It's true that I've never strolled down a street in Baghdad or Ramadi or Basra, armed or not, and that's a deficit if you want to write about the American experience in Iraq. It's also true that I haven't spent hours sipping tea with Iraqi tribal leaders, or been inside the Green Zone, or set foot on even one of the vast American bases that the Pentagon's private contractors have built in that country. (Nor did that stop me from writing regularly about "America's ziggurats" when most of the people who visited those bases didn't consider places with 20-mile perimeters, multiple bus lines, PXs, familiar fast-food franchises, Ugandan mercenary guards, and who knows what else, to be particularly noteworthy structures on the Iraqi landscape and so, with rare exceptions, worth commenting on.)

I'm certainly no expert on Shiites and Sunnis. I'm probably a little foggy on my Iraqi geography. And I've never seen the Tigris and Euphrates Rivers. On the other hand, it does occur to me that a whole raft of American pundits, government officials, and military types who have done all of the above, who have spent time up close and personal in Iraq (or, at least, in the American version of the same), couldn't have arrived at dumber conclusions over these last many years.

So, firsthand experience, valuable as it may be for great reporters like, say, Anthony Shadid of the *Washington Post* and now the *New York Times,* or Patrick Cockburn of the British *Independent,* can't be the be-all and end-all either. Sometimes being far away, not just from Iraq, but from Washington and all the cloistered thinking that goes on there, from the visibly claustrophobic world of American global policymaking, has its advantages. Sometimes, being out of it, experientially speaking, allows you to open your eyes and take in the larger shape of things, which is often the obvious (even if little noted).

I can't help thinking about a friend of mine whose up-close and personal take on U.S. military commanders in Afghanistan was that they were trapped in an American-made box, incapable of seeing beyond its boundaries—of, that is, seeing Afghanistan.

I have no doubt that *being there* is generally something to be desired. But if you take your personal blinders with you, it often hardly matters where you are. Thinking about my *Stars and Stripes* reader's question, the conclusion I've provisionally come to is this: It's not just where you go, it's also how you see what's there, and no less important *who* you see, that matters—which means that sometimes you can actually see more by going nowhere at all.

## An Iraqi Tragedy

When American officials, civilian or military, open their eyes and check out the local landscape, no matter where they've landed, all evidence indicates that the first thing they tend to see is themselves. That is, they see the world as an American stage and those native actors in countries we've invaded and occupied or where (as in Pakistan, Somalia, and Yemen) we conduct what might be called semi-war as so many bit players in an American drama. This is why, in both Iraq and Afghanistan, military commanders and top officials like Secretary of Defense Robert Gates or National Security Adviser James Jones continued to call so unself-consciously for putting an Iraqi or Afghan "face" on whichever war was being discussed, that is, to follow the image to its logical conclusion, putting an Iraqi or Afghan mask over a face that they recognize, however inconveniently or embarrassingly, as American.

This is why American officials regularly say that "Afghans are in the lead," when they aren't. This is why, when you read newspaper descriptions of how the United States is giving Afghan president Hamid Karzai the "leading role" in deciding about the latest military offensive or pushing such-and-such an official (with his U.S. or Western "mentors" in the wings) to take the lead in some action that seems to have been largely planned by Americans, the Afghans sound like so many puppets (which doesn't mean that they are)—and this doesn't embarrass Americans in the least.

Generally speaking, the American post-9/11 language of power ostensibly aimed at building up the forces Washington supports in Muslim lands invariably sounds condescending. *They* are always peripheral to *us*, even when they are being urged or prodded to be at the center of the action. This is why their civilians who come in harm's way are referred to as "collateral damage," an inconceivable way to describe American civilians in harm's way. This is why, from the Vietnam era to today, in the movies that are made about our wars, even the antiwar ones, Americans invariably hog center stage, while you usually have to keep a careful watch to find passing evidence of those we are fighting against—or for. This was why, forty years ago, the Vietnam War was regularly referred to here, whether by hawks or doves, as an "American tragedy," not a Vietnamese one—and why the same thinking applies to Afghanistan and Iraq today.

This is why, using imagery that might have come out of the mouths of nineteenth-century colonialists, American officials long talked patronizingly about teaching the Iraqi "child" to pedal the "bike" of democracy (with us, as global parents, holding onto the bike's seat). This is the context within which even a president wondered when to take off "the training wheels." This is evidently why, today, the introduction of "democracy" to Iraq is considered an American gift so precious that it somehow makes up for anything that's happened in the past eight years. This is why, for instance, pundit Tom Friedman could write this sentence about the "U.S. project in Iraq": "Former president George W. Bush's gut instinct that this region craved and needed democracy was always right."

Like Afghanistan before it, Iraq is now largely the "forgotten" war, and here's a little of what's been forgotten in the process, of what Friedman suggests he'd prefer to leave future historians to sort out: that the American invasion led to possibly hundreds of thousands of Iraqi deaths; that literally millions of Iraqis had to flee into exile abroad and millions more were turned into refugees in their own country; that the capital, Baghdad, was significantly ethnically cleansed in a brutal Shiite-Sunni civil conflict; that the country was littered with new "killing fields"; that a devastating insurgency roiled the land and still brings enough death and terror to Baghdad to make it one of the more dangerous places on the planet; that a soaring unemployment rate and the lack of delivery of the most basic services, including reliable electricity and potable water, created nightmarish conditions for a vast class of impoverished Iraqis; that the U.S. government, for all its nation-building boasts, proved remarkably incapable of "reconstructing" the country or its oil industry, even though American private contractors profited enormously from work on both; that a full-scale foreign military occupation left Americans on almost three hundred bases nationwide and in the largest embassy on the planet; that American advisers remain attached to, and deeply embedded in, an

Iraqi military that still lacks a credible air force and is unlikely to be able to operate and resupply itself on its own for years to come.

## The Pride of Us

In other words, as bad as Saddam Hussein was (and he was a megalomaniacal monster), what followed him was a staggering catastrophe for Iraq, even if Americans no longer care to give it much thought. Against the charnel house that Friedman would prefer to leave to history, however, stands one counterbalancing factor, the gift of "democracy." Even many who never supported George W. Bush's "democracy agenda" now seem to take some pride in this.

Let's leave aside for a moment the fact that the Bush administration arrived in Iraq with remarkably undemocratic plans for the country and was thwarted only by the unwavering insistence of the revered Shiite cleric Ali Sistani on a one-person, one-vote election. In all of this, there are staggering levels of hypocrisy—in the fact that we were for Saddam before we were against him. In the fact, as well, that the U.S. government has, in instance after instance, regularly fostered and supported military juntas, strongmen, and dictators, while holding off or overthrowing democracies not to our taste or not in what Washington defined as our interests.

Perhaps stranger yet, the democracy that we actually have in the United States—and so can offer as our ultimate apology for invading and occupying other countries—is rarely subjected to analysis in the context of the glorious urge to export the same. So let's just stop for a moment and think a little about the American urge to be thrilled that, despite every disaster, against all odds, our grand accomplishment lies in bringing American democracy to Iraq.

## The Rectification of Names

Democracy, like terrorism, is a method, a means to an end, not an end in itself. Nobody is ruled by elections any more than any organization is run by terror or has terror as its ultimate goal. If this obvious point had been accepted in the wake of the 9/11 attacks, the absurdity of the idea of a Global War on Terror would have been self-evident, as would a global war to deliver "democracy" to faraway peoples.

Democracy, after all, is a way to determine and then express the majoritarian will of a people, a way to deliver power to "the people" or, more important, for those people to take possession of it themselves. It's the sort of thing that, by its nature, is hard to import from great distances, especially when, as in our case, the delivery system to be exported seems strikingly deficient. And keep in mind that the "people" exporting that system to Iraq were largely incapable of seeing Iraqis as actors in their own democratic drama. They were incapable, that is, of imagining the nature of the lives they wanted to shape and change.

In a sense, that was hardly less true when they looked homeward. After all, the glorious democracy they trumpeted to the world bore little relation to the *Pax Republicana* headed by an imperial presidency (complete with a cult of executive power) that they dreamed of installing in Washington for generations to come. Given the nature of American democracy today—the first billion-dollar presidential election, the staggering levels of lobbying and influence-peddling that go with it, the stunning barrages of bizarre advertising, the difficulty of displacing incumbents in Congress, the increasingly corporate-owned and financed campaigns, a half-broken congressional system, a national security state with unparalleled powers and money, and so on— why all the effort to take it to Iraq? Why measure Iraqis against it and find them lacking? After all, in 2000, our presidential election went to the non-majoritarian candidate, thanks to decisions made by Supreme Court justices appointed by his father. If this had happened in Nigeria, Afghanistan, or perhaps Iraq, we would know just what we were dealing with.

The fact is we have no word to adequately describe what, at the national level, we still persist in calling "democracy," what we regularly ask others to admire to the skies or bow down before. Writing for the website Talking Points Memo Café, Todd Gitlin termed our system a "semi-democracy." That, at least, represents an honest start.

In imperial China, when a new dynasty arrived on the scene, the emperor performed a ritual called the "rectification of names" in the belief that the previous dynasty had fallen in part because reality and the names we have for it had ceased to correspond. We in the United States undoubtedly now need such a ceremony. We certainly need a new term for our own "democracy" before we're so quick to hold it up as the paragon for others to match.

We also need to rethink our language when it comes to the U.S. military undertaking "nation building" in distant lands—as if countries could be constructed to our taste in just the way that KBR or DynCorp construct military bases in them. We need to stop our commanders from bragging about our skill in creating a "government in a box" for our Afghan friends, when our government at home is largely boxed-in and strikingly dysfunctional.

So, no, I have never been to Iraq, but yes, I've been here for years, watching, and I can see, among other things, that the American mirror on the wall, which shows us ourselves in such beautiful, Disneyesque detail, has a few cracks in it. It looks fragile. I'd think twice about sending it abroad too often.

# A Note on the Text

Thirty-two of the thirty-three pieces that make up this book were written between April 2010 and mid-2011, thirty-one for my website TomDispatch.com. Barely more than a year on the calendar, but given our exploding world, it seemed like years, not months. Has there ever been a time—not in my life anyway—when so much seemed to happen all at once? So consider this my small record of a period when, for all the fear-suffused attempts to lock America down, the world came pouring in anyway. It's important, however, to note that the essays included here are not the originals I wrote. They were edited, trimmed or cut down, modestly updated, and woven into book form. The tell-tale signs of the immediate moment—all the *recently*s and *next week*s, along with examples that were gripping then but are forgotten today—have been removed; as have most of the thematic repetitions that are bound to pop up in any set of weekly responses to ongoing events. Nothing basic or significant about them has, however, been changed; for better or worse, nothing had to be, which tells you something about our present world.

Though this book generally moves chronologically within its chapters, for the sake of whatever flow it may have, I decided not to include in the text the original date on which each piece was posted. For the record, and in case readers should wish to check out any of the essays in their original form at TomDispatch.com, below is a list of them with the dates they were posted (and their original titles, if changed). Note that the second piece in the book was written for, and published in a slightly different form by, *Harper's Magazine*. "The Nuclear Story That Refuses to Go Away" is the sole other intruder. I wrote it in 2004 on a subject that's haunted me from childhood and feels hardly less relevant now.

*American Warscapes*—October 17, 2010
*How the Movies Saved My Life* (*Harper's Magazine*—October 2011)
*The United States of Fear*—November 30, 2010
*Welcome to Post-Legal America*—May 30, 2010
*The 100 Percent Doctrine in Washington*—June 9, 2011
*Obama's Bush-League World*—July 12, 2011
*Washington Drunk on War*—June 15, 2010
*The Urge to Surge*—January 4, 2011
*Osama bin Laden's American Legacy*—May 5, 2011
*Goodbye to All That*—February 7, 2011
*The View from Mount Olympus*—April 13, 2010
*The Perfect American Weapon*—June 24, 2010
*Whose Hands, Whose Blood?*—August 5, 2010
*One November's Dead*—December 7, 2010
*Obama's Af-Pak Flip-Flop*—May 16, 2010
*Clueless in Afghanistan—and Washington*—July 26, 2010 (also included in this section is part of *The Petraeus Syndrome*—July 11, 2010)
*Forever War*—September 30, 2010
*The Stimulus Package in Kabul*—November 14, 2010
*How to Schedule a War*—November 23, 2010
*Numbers to Die For*—April 6, 2010
*A Reluctance to Leave* (original title: *The Urge to Stay*)—April 24, 2010
*Will Our Generals Ever Shut Up?*—September 7, 2010
*Cutting $100 Billion—Easy, If Only Washington Had a Brain*—February 17, 2011
*Ballot Box Blues*—November 2, 2010
*The Nuclear Story That Refuses to Go Away* (original title: *Three Characters, No Dialogue*)—August 5, 2004
*Nine War Words That Define Our World*—June 23, 2011

*Living in the Fifty-First State (of Denial)*—June 1, 2010
*One and a Half Cheers for American Decline*—September 21, 2010
*Life in the Echo Chamber* (original title: *Washington's Echo Chamber*)—
    February 24, 2011
*Signs of the Great American Unraveling*—June 30, 2011
*Sleepingwalking into the Imperial Dark*—April 19, 2011
*All the World's a Stage (for Us)*—March 25, 2010

This book has no footnotes. The original posts at TomDispatch.com were, however, heavily footnoted in the style of the Internet—through links that led readers to my sources and also sometimes offered directions for further exploration. Linking is, in fact, the first democratic form of footnoting, making sources instantly accessible to normal readers who, unlike scholars, may not have ready access to a good library. URLs in a book, however, are both cumbersome and useless. So if you want to check my sources, you'll need to go to the originals online at TomDispatch.com. Fair warning, however: One of the debits of linking is that links regularly die, so the older the piece, the greater the chance that some of the links won't work.

# Acknowledgments

No man is an island. If that sentence applies to anything these days, it has to be to book writing in particular and to this book specifically. The lone (and lonely) author? Not me, at least. In fact, this book wouldn't exist without the ministrations of Anthony Arnove, my friend and editor at Haymarket Books. Among his many other talents he's a wizard on the page, and it was he who wove my TomDispatch essays of the past year into the book I now truly believe this is. I owe him thanks galore. He, in turn, is no island, being surrounded by the hardworking crowd from Haymarket Books, including eagle-eyed copy editor/proofreader J. Gabriel Boylan, and especially that key trio of Rachel Cohen, Julie Fain, and Dao X. Tran. They have my thanks as well.

When it comes to TomDispatch.com, it's land all the way to the horizon. I hardly know where to begin. How could I do it without my many friends who keep TomDispatch alive and kicking with their remarkable pieces, or the Nation Institute, which supports the site (special thanks to Taya Kitman), or Patrick Lannan and Lannan Foundation, who have made all the difference, or Joe Duax, Andy Kroll, Christopher Holmes, and Timothy MacBain, who ensure that the site remains always above the rising waters, or my pal Nick Turse, who hears from me far too often and keeps me sane in life and honest on the page. And speaking about a world of islands so close that they're just a raft's ride across any channel, I would never want to forget all the wonderful people at other websites—

too many to name—who repost TomDispatch pieces and whom I e-meet or even, on occasion, see face to face.

And then, of course, there are those who matter most of all: my wife, Nancy Garrity, and my children, Maggie and Will. They make life worth living.

And oh, yes, there's the world itself that has to be acknowledged somehow. But can I really thank it for offering up enough folly and misery to keep TomDispatch rolling along or for being, in TomDispatch terms, the gift that just keeps on giving? Perhaps not. So let me just stick to the people who matter most to me. A deep bow of thanks to all of you.

# Index

# About TomDispatch

Tom Engelhardt launched TomDispatch.com in October 2001 as an email publication offering commentary and collected articles from the world press. In December 2002, it gained its name, became a project of the Nation Institute, and went online as "a regular antidote to the mainstream media." The site now features three articles a week, all original. These include Engelhardt's regular commentaries as well as the work of authors ranging from Rebecca Solnit, Bill McKibben, Andrew Bacevich, Barbara Ehrenreich, and Mike Davis to Michael Klare, Adam Hochschild, Noam Chomsky, and Karen J. Greenberg. Nick Turse, who also writes for the site, is its associate editor and research director. Andy Kroll is an associate editor and its economic correspondent. Timothy MacBain produces regular TomCast audio interviews with the authors who write the site's weekly pieces. TomDispatch is intended to introduce readers to voices and perspectives from elsewhere (even when the elsewhere is here). Its mission is to connect some of the global dots regularly left unconnected by the mainstream media and to offer a clearer sense of how this imperial globe of ours actually works.

# About Tom Engelhardt

Don J. Usner

Tom Engelhardt created and runs the TomDispatch.com website, a project of the Nation Institute, where he is a fellow. He is the author of *The American Way of War: How Bush's Wars Became Obama's*, *The End of Victory Culture*, a highly praised history of American triumphalism in the Cold War, and *The Last Days of Publishing*, a novel. Many of his TomDispatch interviews were collected in *Mission Unaccomplished: TomDispatch Interviews with American Iconoclasts and Dissenters*. He also edited *The World According to TomDispatch: America in the New Age of Empire*, a collection of pieces from his site that functioned as an alternative history of the mad Bush years. TomDispatch is the sideline that ate his life. Before creating it he worked as an editor at Pacific News Service in the early 1970s, and, these last four decades, as an editor in book publishing. For fifteen years he was senior editor at Pantheon Books, where he edited and published award-winning works ranging from Art Spiegelman's *Maus* and John Dower's *War Without Mercy* to Eduardo Galeano's *Memory of Fire* trilogy. He is now consulting editor at Metropolitan Books, as well as the cofounder and coeditor of the American Empire Project (Metropolitan Books), where he has published best-selling works by Chalmers Johnson, Andrew Bacevich, and Noam Chomsky, among others. Many of the authors whose books he has edited and published over the years now write for TomDispatch.com. For a number of years, he was also a teaching fellow at the Graduate School of Journalism at the University of California, Berkeley. He is married to Nancy J. Garrity, a therapist, and has two children, Maggie and Will.

# About Haymarket Books

Haymarket Books is a nonprofit, progressive book distributor and publisher, a project of the Center for Economic Research and Social Change. We believe that activists need to take ideas, history, and politics into the many struggles for social justice today. Learning the lessons of past victories, as well as defeats, can arm a new generation of fighters for a better world. As Karl Marx said, "The philosophers have merely interpreted the world; the point, however, is to change it."

We take inspiration and courage from our namesakes, the Haymarket Martyrs, who gave their lives fighting for a better world. Their 1886 struggle for the eight-hour day reminds workers around the world that ordinary people can organize and struggle for their own liberation.

For more information and to shop our complete catalog of titles, visit us online at www.haymarketbooks.org.

# Also from Haymarket Books

*The American Way of War: How Bush's Wars Became Obama's*
Tom Engelhardt

*Breaking the Sound Barrier*
Amy Goodman

*Gaza in Crisis: Reflections on Israel's War on the Palestinians*
Noam Chomsky and Ilan Pappé

*War Without End: The Iraq War in Context*
Michael Schwartz

*Boycott, Divestment, Sanctions: The Global Struggle for Palestinian Rights*
Omar Barghouti

*Winter Soldier: Iraq and Afghanistan: Eyewitness Accounts of the Occupations*
Iraq Veterans Against the War and Aaron Glantz